THE
e-copyright handbook

THE
e-copyright
handbook

Paul Pedley

facet publishing

© Paul Pedley 2012

Published by Facet Publishing
7 Ridgmount Street, London WC1E 7AE
www.facetpublishing.co.uk

Facet Publishing is wholly owned by CILIP: the Chartered Institute of
Library and Information Professionals.

British Library Cataloguing in Publication Data
A catalogue record for this book is available from the British Library.

ISBN 978-1-85604-827-9

First published 2012

Text printed on FSC accredited material.

Mixed Sources
Product group from well-managed
forests and other controlled sources
www.fsc.org Cert no. SA-COC-1565
© 1996 Forest Stewardship Council
FSC

Typeset from author's files in 10/13 pt Aldine 401 and Humanist 521 by
Flagholme Publishing Services.
Printed and made in Great Britain by MPG Books Group, UK.

Disclaimer

Paul Pedley is not a lawyer and is not able to give legal advice. The contents of this book do not constitute legal advice and should not be relied upon in that way.

Contents

List of figures, tables and checklists

Enforcement

Table of cases

Table of legislation

European Regulations

COM DOCS

Statutes

Statutory instruments

Abbreviations

AC	Appeal Cases
ACAP	Automated Content Access Protocol
API	Application Programming Interface
ARL	Association of Research Libraries
ARROW	Accessible Registries of Rights Information and Orphan Works
BCSC	Supreme Court of British Columbia
BoB	Box of Broadcasts
BPI	British Phonographic Industry (now British Recorded Music Industry)
CD	Compact disk
CDPA	Copyright, Designs and Patents Act 1988
CJEU	Court of Justice of the European Union
CLA	Copyright Licensing Agency
CMO	Collective Management Organisation
COPIS	Common European IT system / Counterfeiting and Piracy System
DBIS	Department for Business, Innovation and Skills
DCMS	Department for Culture, Media and Sport
DEA	Digital Economy Act 2010
DMCA	Digital Millennium Copyright Act
DNS	Domain Name System
DPI	Deep Packet Inspection
DRM	Digital Rights Management
DTI	Department of Trade and Industry (now the Department for Business, Innovation and Skills)
DVD	Digital versatile disc
ECJ	European Court of Justice
ECR	European Court Reports
EIFL	Electronic Information For Libraries
ELSPA	Entertainment and Leisure Software Publishers Association
ERA	Educational Recording Agency
EU	European Union
EWCA	England and Wales Court of Appeal

EWHC	England and Wales High Court
FACT	Federation Against Copyright Theft
FOIA	Freedom of Information Act
FSR	Fleet Street Reports
GNU	GNU's not UNIX! (see www.gnu.org)
GSU	Georgia State University
GUI	Graphical User Interface
ICA	International Council on Archives
ICE	Immigration and Customs Enforcement
IEHC	High Court of Ireland
IFLA	International Federation of Library Associations
IFPI	International Federation of the Phonographic Industry
IPO	Intellectual Property Office
IPR	Intellectual property rights
ISP	Internet service provider
LOCKSS	Lots of copies keep stuff safe
LSG	Law Society Gazette
METS	Metadata Encoding and Transmission Standard
MLA	The Museums, Libraries and Archives Council
MPA	Music Publishers Association
MP3	Moving Picture Expert Group Layer-3 Audio (audio file format/extension)
ONIX	Online Information Exchange
OU	Open University
P2P	Peer-to-peer
PLO	Public Library Online
PLR	Public Lending Right
PLUS	Picture Licensing Universal System
POCA	Proceeds of Crime Act 2002
PPL	(Previously known as Phonographic Performance Limited)
PRS	Premium rate services
PRS (for Music)	Performing Right Society
QB	Queen's Bench
RDFA	Resource Description Framework in Attributes
RMI	Rights Management Information
RSS	Really Simple Syndication, Rich Site Summary
SABAM	Société belge des auteurs, compositeurs et éditeurs
SABIP	Strategic Advisory Board for Intellectual Property
SCC	Supreme Court of Canada
SOPA	US Stop Online Piracy Act bill
SRA	Solicitors Regulation Authority

TLIB	Proposed World Intellectual Property Organization (WIPO) treaty (for libraries) on copyright exceptions and limitations
TPM	Technical Protection Measures
TRIPS	Trade Related Aspects of Intellectual Property Rights
UGC	User-generated content
UKIE	Association for UK Interactive Entertainment
URL	Uniform Resource Locator
WLR	Weekly Law Reports
XML	Extensible Markup Language

Glossary of terms

BitTorrent – a peer-to-peer filesharing protocol used for distributing large amounts of data over the internet.

Blogs – a blog (short for weblog) is a form of website which is normally maintained by an individual with regular entries or posts/postings consisting of commentary. Some blogs take the form of an online diary or description of events.

Browse wrap agreements – where the terms and conditions are available on a website, but the website design doesn't force the user to go through them and indicate their acceptance of those terms.

Co-blogging – where a number of bloggers work together collaboratively. There are a number of different types of co-blogging arrangements, but co-blogging can be summed up as being where more than one person contributes content.

Content sharing sites – websites for sharing a whole range of content formats. This could, for example, be music, videos (e.g. YouTube), photographs (e.g. Photobucket, Flickr, Pinterest), or presentations (e.g. Slideshare).

Cyberlocker – Online services which enable users to share and store large files.

Database – The Copyright and Rights in Databases Regulations 1997: SI 1997/3032 define a database as 'a collection of independent works, data or other materials which are arranged in a systematic or methodical way and are individually accessible by electronic or other means'.

Deep links (as opposed to shallow links) – links to pages within a website, where those pages are at a lower level within the hierarchical structure of the site than the home page. Following a deep link means that the user doesn't have to navigate from the home page first.

Dooced – losing one's job as a result of something you wrote on your website or blog

Extraction – in the context of the Databases Regulations (SI 1997/3032) means the permanent or temporary transfer of any contents of a database to another medium by any means or in any form.

Filesharing – making files available for others to download over the internet. This can be achieved by a number of means, such as the use of peer-to-peer networks or the use of cyberlockers to distribute computer files among millions of users.

Graduated response – refers to a way of tackling online copyright infringement. It consists of a series of deterrent measures aimed at repeat infringers (an example would be the so-called 'three strikes law' in the Digital Economy Act 2010).

Hyperlink – A reference or pointer to an electronic document that the reader can directly follow. It would encompass both shallow and deep links. The hyperlink could be in the form of a word, phrase or image which when clicked on takes you to somewhere else within the same document or site, or to a completely different document or site.

Lending – defined in the Rental and Lending Directive (2006/115/EC) as making available for use, for a limited period of time and not for direct or indirect economic or commercial advantage when it is made through establishments which are accessible to the public.

Lifecasting – the continual broadcasting of events in a person's life through digital media, typically transmitted over the internet.

Mashups – Websites or applications which use content from more than one source in order to create a completely new service. These would often rely on APIs (application programming interfaces) in order to produce results which add value to the raw data sources upon which they rely.

Microblogging – A form of blogging which is distinguishable from traditional blogging by the way in which the content of the entries on microblogging sites is much smaller. For example, each microblog entry or 'Tweet' on Twitter can only be up to 140 characters long.

On-demand services – are services where the user determines when they listen to or watch them. This contrasts with broadcasts which are transmissions that are transmitted at a time determined solely by the person making the transmission for presentation to members of the public.

Orphan works – are works where the rights holder is either difficult or even impossible to identify or locate.

Out-of-commerce work – one which, in all its versions and manifestations, is no longer commercially available from customary channels, regardless of whether there are copies in libraries or second-hand bookshops.

Photostream – a link to a series of pictures, shown one after another at intervals.

Piggybacking – The use of someone else's internet access subscription. Normally refers to where this is undertaken without the subscriber's explicit permission or knowledge.

Podcasts – podcasting involves making media files (whether they be audio or video files) available via the internet for download at the instruction of the end-user.

Proxy site – A proxy server acts as an intermediary for requests from clients who want to access content from another server. With a proxy site you send your 'request' to a server, which sends a new request to the website's server, which sends that back to the proxy, and the proxy then sends the reply to your computer. It enables, but doesn't always consist of, anonymous surfing on the web.

Rental – defined in the Rental and Lending Directive (2006/115/EC) as making available for use for a limited period of time and for direct or indirect economic or commercial advantage.

Reutilization – in the context of the Databases Regulations (SI 1997/3032) means making the contents of a database available to the public by any means.

RSS feeds – the acronym 'RSS' can stand for a number of different possibilities, including really simple syndication, rich site summary, etc. RSS is an XML (extensible mark-up language) format which enables the syndication or sharing of content. People use web-based aggregation services (such as Google Reader) in order to read a wide range of RSS feeds from a single place.

Scraping – web scraping or harvesting is the technique whereby computer software is used in order to extract information from websites.

Second Life – a 3D virtual world where users are able to meet and socialize.

Shakedown scheme – in the context of copyright, a shakedown scheme involves coercing large numbers of people, who are alleged to have infringed copyright, to make a payment in order that any threat of legal action may be dropped.

Shallow links (as opposed to deep links) are hyperlinks to a home page, the top of the hierarchical structure of a website.

Social bookmarking – a means by which internet users are able to share, organize, search and manage a set of bookmarks to web resources. They are merely a set of references. Examples of social bookmarking sites include Del.icio.us and Digg.

Social networking – websites which facilitate the creation of online communities in which people are able to share common interests or activities. Examples would include Facebook or Bebo. There are also some which specialize in networking in a business context (such as LinkedIn).

Speculative invoicing – where law firms acting on behalf of rights owners demand payment from large numbers – often thousands – of people accused of filesharing.

Streaming – commonly seen in the forms of audio and video streaming, this is the transfer of data in real time over the internet in a continuous stream.

Torrent – a torrent file consists of metadata about a target file. The data relates only to the location of different pieces of the target file rather than providing details as to the contents of the file.

Webcasts – a webcast is in effect a broadcast over the internet. It can be distributed either live or on demand. This is significant because 'on-demand' services do not fall within the definition of a broadcast that appears in the Copyright, Designs and Patents Act 1988.

Weblogs – see the entry for 'blogs' above.

Wikis – a website that allows the easy creation and editing of any number of interlinked web pages via a web browser using a simplified mark-up language or a text editor. Examples of Wiki software: PeanutButter, TikiWiki. The term stands for 'What I know is'.

CHAPTER 1

Introduction

This book explores the copyright issues that arise in an era of information sharing and collaborative working. The internet has made it possible for everyone to be a publisher, without the content necessarily being subjected to the rigorous editorial checks that would routinely be undertaken by a professional publisher.

There are inherent legal risks in opening up the ability to publish to everyone. In the case of microblogging sites, for example, it is so tempting and so easy to quickly type a brief posting and press the ENTER key before thinking about the implications of what you have written – such as whether it is libellous, a contempt of court or an infringement of copyright.

Issues around jurisdiction arise in an era of global communications. The internet is no respecter of geographic boundaries. In Football Dataco Ltd v. Sportradar [2010] EWHC 2911 (Ch) the court ruled that a company is responsible for 'making available' internet-hosted material in the country where its host server is based, not in the country where the material is read or used. In the CJEU case (C-173/11), Advocate General Cruz Villalon said that where a party uploads data from a database protected by sui generis right under Directive 96/9/EC of the European Parliament and of the Council of 11 March 1996 on the legal protection of databases onto that party's web server located in Member State A and, in response to requests from a user in another Member State B, the web server sends such data to the user's computer so that the data is stored in the memory of that computer and displayed on its screen, the act of sending the information constitutes an act of 're-utilisation' by that party. He further concluded that the act of re-utilisation performed by that party takes place both in Member State A and in Member State B.

The book is intended to complement the other Facet Publishing titles for which I have been either the author or the editor – *Digital Copyright* (2nd edn, 2007), *Copyright Compliance: practical steps to stay within the law* (2008), *Managing Digital Rights: a practitioner's guide* (2005), and the copyright and licensing sections of *Essential Law for Information Professionals* (3rd edn, 2012).

The era of digital content, whether that be born digital material or content which has been digitized from hard copy, has brought about major changes to the way in which creative content is produced, distributed and consumed.

Cory Doctorow at a 2011 conference[1] said 'Here in the digital age we copy like we breathe, and so the stakes for getting the rules right on copyright have never been higher'.

In order to aid navigation the book uses symbols to identify four types of content. These are :

- Tip
- Useful resource
- Sample wording
- Case summary

(Tip) denotes short pieces of advice which, if followed, should help the reader to reduce the level of exposure to legal risks.

(Useful resource) denotes material which it is felt should be drawn to the attention of the reader as being of real practical value and as therefore being especially useful.

(Case summaries) denotes summaries of legal cases.

There are also a number of examples of ☰ **Sample wording** such as the wording for a warranty or indemnity clause, a copyright notice for an RSS feed, or a clause to prevent licences from being able to override the copyright exceptions or permitted acts.

The intention is to make the contents of the book as practical, helpful and accessible as possible. Throughout the book there are also a number of checklists covering topics such as deep linking, licence agreements, RSS feeds, blogging, measures to protect your content, or compliance with the Digital Economy Act 2010. The aim of the checklists is to suggest best practice and to minimize the legal risks associated with particular activities.

1.1   Background

The United Kingdom isn't able to set the legislative regime for copyright in isolation, but has to take into account the international treaties and conventions to which it is a signatory, as well as the *acquis communitaire* (the body of EU law that the UK is required to implement as a member state of the EU).

The main statute on copyright is the Copyright, Designs and Patents Act 1988, as amended by the many statutory instruments that have been published since the Act came into force.

Table 1.1 International, European and UK copyright legislation

International treaties and conventions
Berne Convention for the protection of literary and artistic works   1886
Universal Copyright Convention   1952
Trade Related Aspects of Intellectual Property Rights (the TRIPS agreement)   1994

WIPO Copyright Treaty 1996

Anti-Counterfeiting Trade Agreement   2011

European Directives

On the legal protection of computer programs
2009/24/EC (replaced 91/250/EEC)

On the rental and lending right and certain related rights
2006/115/EC (replaced 92/100/EEC)

On the coordination of certain rules concerning copyright and rights
related to copyright applicable to satellite broadcasting and cable
retransmission 93/83/EEC

Harmonizing the term of protection of copyright and certain related
rights 2006/116/EC (replaced 93/98/EEC)

On the legal protection of databases 96/9/EC

On the harmonization of certain aspects of copyright and related rights
in the information society 2001/29/EC

On the resale right for the benefit of the author of an original work of art
2001/84/EC

On the enforcement of intellectual property rights 2004/48/EC

Amending Directive 2006/116/EC on the term of protection of
copyright and certain related rights 2011/77/EC

UK Statutes

Copyright, Designs and Patents Act (CDPA)   1988

Copyright, etc. and Trade Marks (Offences and Enforcement) Act   2002

Copyright (Visually Impaired Persons) Act   2002

Legal Deposit Libraries Act 2003

Digital Economy Act   2010

1.2   Possible treaty on copyright exceptions for libraries and archives

The WIPO Copyright Treaty of 1996 has a provision for countries to extend exceptions and limitations in national law into the digital environment in the form of an agreed statement concerning Article 10 of the Treaty (see below), and to devise new exceptions and limitations appropriate for the digital environment. However, without an international mandate, this laudable gesture has had limited effect. The result is a copyright system that is not fit for purpose for libraries and archives today.

The agreed statement concerning Article 10 of the WIPO Copyright Treaty[2] says:

It is understood that the provisions of Article 10 permit Contracting Parties to carry forward and appropriately extend into the digital environment limitations and exceptions in their national laws which have been considered acceptable under the Berne Convention. Similarly, these provisions should be understood to permit Contracting Parties to devise new exceptions and limitations that are appropriate in the digital network environment.

It is also understood that Article 10(2) neither reduces nor extends the scope of applicability of the limitations and exceptions permitted by the Berne Convention.

A scientific study on exceptions and limitations for libraries and archives[3] by Kenneth Crews was published by WIPO in 2008. It identifies a number of major issues that need to be addressed at an international level. These include:

1 Exceptions to copyright which enabled libraries and archives to preserve and make available works in the print era have not been updated to the digital age, particularly with respect to digital archiving and virtual learning environments.
2 Imposed licences for the provision of digital information are often used to undermine exceptions and limitations to copyright designed to support education, learning and creativity.
3 Prohibitions to circumvent technological protection measures (TPM) to preserve, archive and enable permitted use of lawfully acquired digital content are hampering research, leading to an incomplete cultural, scientific and historical record.
4 The cross-border, multi-jurisdictional nature of the internet is not reflected in current copyright law. Restrictions on the legitimate flow of information and cultural content provided by libraries across international borders will constrain innovation and growth in under-developed and developing countries.

Library and archive users everywhere want digital access to information: for example, photocopying from printed books and journals and from other documents is being supplanted by scanning or downloading and libraries are switching their subscriptions from print to e-journals.

IFLA, EIFL, Innovarte (http://sitio.innovarte.cl) and the ICA have proposed a treaty on copyright exceptions and limitations for libraries and archives which is known by the abbreviation TLIB (see www.ifla.org/files/clm/publications/tlib.pdf). They believe that a treaty is needed because libraries and archives currently work under a patchwork of provisions that differ in scope and effect from country to country; and the existing framework increasingly fails to address the legal and policy challenges of the global digital environment. All the proposed exceptions and limitations in the draft treaty apply to non-commercial uses only. The treaty protects a number of activities including:

1 The preservation of materials for posterity, with the flexibility to access cultural works in copy-protected formats.
2 The circumvention of TPM for the purpose of permitting a non-infringing use of a work.
3 The limiting of the risk of liability to libraries and archives with respect to orphan works, in order to facilitate mass digitization projects.

TLIB also provides for:

1 An obligation to respect exceptions to copyright and related rights – voiding terms in contracts and licences for information goods that impede or remove statutory exceptions and limitations in national laws (Article 14).
2 Obligations concerning technological protection measures – permitting workarounds for libraries and archives to circumvent TPMs in specified circumstances (Article 15).
3 Limitation on liability for libraries and archives for actions performed in good faith (Article 16).

1.3   Is digital content treated differently?

A number of people and organizations argue that the CDPA 1988 should not treat digital content any differently than hard-copy content. In 2008, for example, the British Library published a set of five principles on copyright law.[4] These included:

Digital is not Different – Copyright law should enshrine the principles of creativity, access, recognition and remuneration as it always has done. Exceptions should apply to all formats including digital formats.

Technology Neutral – Copyright law must be informed by technological advances, but specific technologies should not be enshrined in law.

There are a number of provisions within the UK's copyright legislation which relate only to electronic content. The Copyright and Related Rights Regulations 2003 – which implemented the Copyright Directive 2001/29/EC – contain three such provisions, set out in Figure 1.1.

---

1) the right of communication to the public (see 1.3.1),
2) making circumvention of technical protection measures illegal (see 1.3.2), and
3) protecting electronic rights management information (see 1.3.3).

Figure 1.1 *Three things which only apply to digital content*

1.3.1   Communication to the public

The right of communication to the public relates only to communication by electronic means. It was implemented as Section 20 of the CDPA 1988, which specifies that communication to the public by electronic means is a restricted act. The author has the exclusive right to authorize or prohibit any communication to the public. It includes the electronic transmission of:

- literary, dramatic, musical or artistic works
- sound recordings or films
- broadcasts.

> **CDPA 1988 Section 20: Infringement by communication to the public**
>
> (1) The communication to the public of the work is an act restricted by the copyright in
>
> (a) a literary, dramatic, musical or artistic work,
>
> (b) a sound recording or film, or
>
> (c) a broadcast.
>
> (2) References in this Part to communication to the public are to communication to the public by electronic transmission, and in relation to a work include –
>
> (a) the broadcasting of the work;
>
> (b) the making available to the public of the work by electronic transmission in such a way that members of the public may access it from a place and at a time individually chosen by them.

As a result, any electronic act of transmission which results in communication to the public requires authorization. This includes display on a computer screen and it also specifically includes interactive on-demand acts of transmission, digital broadcasting and 'on-demand' services.

The concept of communication to the public was explored in the European Court of Justice case Sociedad General de Autores y Editores de Espana v. Rafael Hoteles CJEU C-306/05. In answering questions referred to it by a Spanish court, the European Court of Justice confirmed that the transmission by hotel owners of broadcasts through television sets in hotel rooms is a 'communication to the public', and could therefore constitute an infringement of copyright under Article 3(1) of the Copyright Directive (2001/29 EC). The court held that the private nature of hotel rooms did not preclude the communication of works in these rooms from being a 'communication to the public', since the test was whether a communication had been made to 'the public', not whether a communication occurred in a public or private place.

In another European Court of Justice case, however, SCF v. Marco del Corso, the court found that the playing of phonograms in dental surgeries does not trigger the remuneration right because it doesn't constitute a communication to the public.

⊕ SCF v. Marco del Corso (CJEU C-135/10)

The Societa Consortile Fonografici (SCF), an Italian collecting society, had pursued a Turin dentist, Marco del Corso, seeking a declaration by the court that the playing of background music in his surgery constituted a 'communication to the public' which would trigger the need for a licence to cover that use of the music. However, the European Court of Justice ruled that dental surgeries were not communicating the copyrighted works to the public.

The other two copyright provisions which only relate to electronic content cover the two components which together form a digital rights management system. So, before examining them in detail it is worth clarifying what is meant by a digital rights management system. This can be expressed using the sum:

$$DRM = TPM + RMI$$

In other words, a digital rights management system consists of both a technical protection measure as well as rights management information. To distinguish between the two, rights management information expresses the owner's intent whereas the technical protection measure ensures that this is honoured.

1.3.2 Technical protection measures

Technological protection measures are now backed up by the law, so that it is an offence to circumvent or break through them. In order to qualify for legal protection the copy-protection measure must be designed to protect the work and must be effective at doing so.

CDPA 1988 s. 296ZF Interpretation of ss 296ZA to 296ZE

(1) In sections 296ZA to 296ZE, "technological measures" are any technology, device or component which is designed, in the normal course of its operation, to protect a copyright work other than a computer program.
(2) Such measures are "effective" if the use of the work is controlled by the copyright owner through—
(a) an access control or protection process such as encryption, scrambling or other transformation of the work, or
(b) a copy control mechanism, which achieves the intended protection.

Most TPMs make copyright in effect perpetual, since they don't expire when the duration of copyright in the content they protect expires. So, even where the content is no longer protected by copyright, it could still be out of reach if it were behind a technical protection measure. If the manufacturer goes out of business it is quite plausible that in some instances the owner of the rights may be impossible to trace even after only a few years, thereby rendering the product orphaned. In such circumstances it is probable that no key would exist to unlock the DRM.

Section 296 of the Copyright, Designs and Patents Act 1988 deals with devices which are designed to circumvent copy-protection. Where someone applies a technical device to a computer program for the sole purpose of circumventing the copy-protection this is an offence. It is also an offence to publish details of how to circumvent the copy protection. In order to be convicted of such an offence, the person who does anything to circumvent the copy protection must have done so knowingly, or have reasonable grounds to know that he is pursuing that objective.

A number of people have gone to prison for offences relating to the circumvention of technical protection measures. They include:

1 Carl Morgan Davison and Mark Taylor, who were given 10-month and 5-month sentences respectively in 2008 for telling people how to bypass the security settings on set-top boxes (s296ZB).

2 Online trader Christopher Gilham was given a 12-month custodial sentence suspended for two years in January 2010 and ordered to carry out 300 hours of unpaid work after selling electronic 'chips' that enabled computer consoles to play counterfeit games. Worcestershire County Council Trading Standards, working with ELSPA (the Entertainment and Leisure Software Publishers Association), brought a prosecution against Mr Gilham. Evidence seized following test purchases established that the 'modchips', intended for most popular games consoles, would override the inbuilt security measures which would normally only permit the playing of genuine games. Following a seven-day trial Gilham was convicted on 15 counts under s. 296ZB of the CDPA 1988 at Worcester Crown Court in September 2008. Gilham lost his appeal against the decision when the case was heard at the Court of Appeal in October 2009 (R v. Gilham [2009] EWCA Crim 2293 www.bailii.org/ew/cases/EWCA/Crim/2009/2293.html).

3 Yuncan Meng was sentenced to a total of two years' imprisonment for trading in circumvention devices. On 15 January 2009 he pleaded guilty at Hull Crown Court to the possession and sale of circumvention devices under s. 296ZB of the Copyright, Designs and Patents Act 1988. These circumvention devices included R4, edge and DST as well as other game copier cards for the Nintendo DS Lite console. He was subsequently taken back to court under the Proceeds of Crime Act 2002 and warned that he faced a further four years in prison unless he paid back the £700,000 proceeds of the computer game scam.

4 Nintendo Company Ltd & Anor v. Playables Ltd & Anor [2010] EWHC 1932
   (Ch) (28 July 2010) www.bailii.org/ew/cases/EWHC/Ch/2010/1932.html –
   This High Court civil case, taken by Nintendo, established the illegality of
   circumvention device game copier cards for the Nintendo DS lite handheld
   games console. The evidence for this case was established when UKIE (the
   Association for UK Interactive Entertainment), HMRC (the UK tax and
   customs authorities) and trading standards officers from the London Borough
   of Camden co-ordinated an investigation into the sale and distribution of such
   devices from a number of websites operated by Mr Wai Dat Chan. Over
   165,000 devices were seized in the operation, highlighting the scale of the
   illegal activity. The defendants were found guilty of copyright infringement
   under ss 296ZD and 296 of the CDPA 1988. The court ruled in this case that
   the CDPA can be used to tackle pirated games as well as actual acts of piracy
   and circumvention.
5 On 9 December 2011 there was an article by Sonia Elks in Metro newspaper
   (www.metro.co.uk/news/884320-virgin-tv-con-worth-40m-run-from-a-back-
   bedroom-in-derby) entitled 'Virgin Media TV con run from a back bedroom
   in Derby' which reported that four men were facing jail after selling around
   44,000 set-top boxes which enable their owners to access Virgin's cable
   channels free of charge, thus depriving Virgin of around £1000 per box. A
   story in 'Thisisderbyshire.co.uk' dated 23rd February 2012
   (www.thisisderbyshire.co.uk/Derby-gang-jailed-massive-TV-box-
   swindle/story-15294742-detail/story.html) put the amount that Virgin would
   be defrauded of at £32 million. Anthony Ginnivan, 48, and Paul Hartrick, 51,
   pleaded guilty at Derby crown court to conspiring to defraud between
   February 2010 and February 2011. Melvyn Howard, 62, and Amber Ahmed,
   34, had already pleaded guilty. In February 2012 they received the following
   sentences:
   — Hartrick was jailed for 5 years
   — Howard was jailed for 2 years and 10 months
   — Ginnivan was jailed for 2 years and 1 month
   — Ahmed was sent to prison for a year.

Some commentators and lobbyists argue that librarians and archivists should be
given special status as 'trusted intermediaries' and that they should have a new
exception in order to allow them to:

• circumvent TPMs and/or
• require producers or publishers from the outset to give libraries and archives
  clean copies without a TPM controlling access to the content or else be given
  the key(s) to unlock access to the content, so that:

— they can make copies which are permitted under statutory exceptions and limitations to copyright or database right, including providing accessible copies to print disabled people;
— they can migrate content to different platforms and formats in order to continue to make it accessible and to preserve it in digital form and thereby avoid the problem of technological obsolescence.

The Gowers Review (a review of the UK's intellectual property laws led by Andrew Gowers, which looked at whether our IP laws were fit for the digital age) made two recommendations relating to DRM systems:

1 Recommendation 15 – Make it easier for users to file notice of complaints procedures relating to digital rights management tools by providing an accessible interface on the Patent Office website by 2008.
2 Recommendation 16 – DTI should investigate the possibility of providing consumer guidance on DRM systems through a labelling convention without imposing unnecessary regulatory burdens.

Neither of these recommendations has been implemented.

Consumers should be aware of the precise terms of the package of rights they are buying before they pay for digital goods and should be in a position to make an informed choice through the use of clear labelling.

In order to illustrate the difficulty of creating clear labels, the All Party Internet Group (now APComms, the All Party Communications Group) in its 2006 report on digital rights management systems cited the example of an e-book of *Alice in Wonderland*, a children's classic which has long been out of copyright, but which came in a protected form. The label on the product said 'this book may not be read aloud' because access to the e-book by speech synthesis devices had been blocked. Text-to-speech facilities are often used by visually impaired people. But by the use of clumsy and misleading labelling and saying 'this book may not be read aloud' they were risking the disappointment of parents looking for bedtime stories; whereas what they actually meant was that they had disabled the text-to-speech function.

In 2011 a new Consumer Rights Directive[5] was published which updates and consolidates parts of the European consumer law *acquis*, especially in the light of technological changes and the increasing importance of digital markets. Recital 19 to the Directive states explicitly that contracts for the supply of digital content such as the download of digital music, or the streaming of video, or the provision of online games, do fall within the scope of the Directive:

Digital content means data which are produced and supplied in digital form, such as computer programs, applications, games, music, videos or texts, irrespective of whether they are accessed through downloading or streaming, from a tangible medium or through any other means. Contracts for the supply of digital content should fall within the scope of this Directive.

Article 5 of the Directive sets out the information which must be provided before a consumer would be considered to be bound by any contract. The information should include details of any technical protection measure used as well as any relevant details regarding the interoperability of the digital content. It would also cover other restrictive or potentially invasive technologies such as regional coding or tracking and monitoring tools. The precise wording is:

> Before the consumer is bound by a contract other than a distance or an off-premises contract, or any corresponding offer, the trader shall provide the consumer with the following information in a clear and comprehensible manner, if that information is not already apparent from the context: . . .
> 1(g) where applicable, the functionality, including applicable technical protection measures, of digital content.
> 1(h) where applicable, any relevant interoperability of digital content with hardware and software that the trader is aware of or can reasonably be expected to have been aware of.

The Consumer Rights Directive also includes a right to withdraw from purchases of digital content before it is actually downloaded (as opposed to when it is made available for download, e.g. via a link in an e-mail).

1.3.3   Electronic rights management information

Electronic rights management information is any information provided by the copyright owner which identifies the work, the author or any other rightsholder, or information about the terms and conditions.

It is an offence to tamper with or to remove electronic rights management information associated with a copyright work. Indeed, it is an offence to knowingly and without authority distribute, import for distribution or communicate to the public copies of a copyright work from which electronic rights management information has been removed or altered without authority and where the offending party knows, or has reason to believe, that by so doing he is inducing, enabling, facilitating or concealing an infringement of copyright.

Notes and references

1   Doctorow, Cory (2011) *We Copy Like We Breathe*, SIGGraph 2011 Keynote Speaker, *NewsGrist*, 16 August,

http://newsgrist.typepad.com/underbelly/2011/08/art-revolution-and-ownership-cory-doctorow-siggraph.html.

2   www.wipo.int/treaties/en/ip/wct/trtdocs_wo033.html.

3   Crews, Kenneth (2008) *Study on Copyright Limitations and Exceptions for Libraries and Archives*, WIPO.

4   British Library (2008) *Digital is not Different – Maintaining Balance in Copyright*, http://pressandpolicy.bl.uk/imagelibrary/downloadMedia.ashx?MediaDetailsID=634.

5   Directive 2011/83/EC of the European Parliament and of the Council on Consumer Rights, amending Council Directive 93/13/EEC and Directive 1999/44/EC of the European Parliament and of the Council and repealing Council Directive 85/577/EEC and Directive 97/7/EC of the European Parliament and of the Council.

CHAPTER 2

Content types

This chapter considers the copyright implications of different types of electronic content, citing relevant legislation as well as case law and the lessons we can learn from the judgments in those cases.

The CDPA 1988 doesn't deal neatly with electronic content types by having sections of the Act cover e-journals, DVDs, podcasts, wikis and so on. In many ways that is a good thing, because otherwise we would find that our copyright legislation was always playing catch-up as new technologies emerge. Rather, it gives special protection to a number of categories or 'species'. These are:

- literary works
- dramatic works
- musical works
- artistic works
- sound recordings
- films
- broadcasts; and it also protects
- typographical layout.

So, in order to be protected by copyright, a work (or its constituent parts) would have to fall within one or more of these categories or 'species'. Software, for example, is protected as a literary work.

In the case of a website there wouldn't be special protection for the website as an entity in its own right; instead, each of the elements that goes to make up that website could potentially be protected by copyright – the string of text as a literary work, the metadata as a literary work, the pictures on the site as artistic works, the music that plays when the homepage loads as a musical work, etc; and then there is also the exclusive right of the copyright owner to communicate their work to the public by electronic means. In effect, we are talking about the content being protected by a bundle of rights.

Taking into account that the CDPA 1988 doesn't deal directly with content types such as weblogs, e-books, lifecasts, and so on, this chapter looks at a number of electronic content types and the copyright issues that they give rise to.

2.1   API (application programming interface)

⊕ 2.1.1 Oracle America Inc v. Google (10-03561, US District Court, Northern District of California (San Francisco))

In Oracle America Inc. v. Google Inc. (owners of Java and Android respectively), 10-03561, US District Court, Northern District of California (San Francisco), United States District Judge William Alsup found that the main subject matter of the motion, the APIs, was not sufficiently defined by Google to pass the copyright challenges presented in Oracle's original complaint, with the exception of names found within the APIs.

APIs, or application programming interfaces, are extremely brief pieces of code that wrap around either a program or a library (a grouping of smaller pieces of code that does not run by itself but provides functionality to other programs) and act as a local specification or standard for any connecting program to use.

Typically APIs are deliberately exposed to third parties in order to enable software to grow beyond its original design and use.

Google replaced the code within 12 files out of a total of several thousand code files, and Oracle objected to this. Google argued that the 12 code files were a small part of a larger monolithic Java copyright and thus too meagre to be considered copyright infringement and that the use of the Java APIs was 'fair use'. The judge ruled against Google and found that each individual file would have its own copyright protection. Google also asserted that the API specifications themselves were not subject to copyright protection due to the general nature of the specifications as names, the scènes à faire (an element of created work that is either obligated or expected within the work, and thus not copyrightable, as in http://en.wikipedia.org/wiki/Scenes_a_faire) nature of the technique.

- Justice Alsup found that the various names associated with the specifications (the names of the methods found within the API, the name of the API and any other class name) were not subject to copyright.
- The judge found that the use of APIs within software was not scènes à faire.
- The Court also disagreed with the argument that, as a 'method of operation' within software development, an API is not copyrightable (as defined by 17 U.S.C. 102(b)).
- The judge further rejected Google's arguments that in order to be deemed copyrighted work the material had to be virtually identifiable and not substantially similar (Android's versions of the APIs would be similar but not identical), and the Java API packages could not be deemed either fair use or not (as defined in 17 U.S.C. 107) due to existing disputed questions of material fact.

In May 2012 a California District Court jury said that Oracle had proven that Google infringed 'the overall structure, sequence and organisation' of a grouping of 37 'Java API packages' by implementing code in its Android platform. However, the court did not rule on whether Google were permitted to use the code under the US 'fair use' defence.

Oracle has estimated damages from the patent and copyright infringement at US$2.6 billion. However, in February 2012 several reports suggested that this had been revised downwards to around US$226 million. In June 2012 it was announced that Oracle and Google had met in court to decide on the amount of damages which Google should pay for copyright infringement, and that their lawyers had agreed a figure of $0.[1]

2.1.2 Peter Zabulis v. *The Independent*

Peter Zabulis took a picture of tyre tracks etched across a snow-covered field and posted it on Flickr. The picture was tagged as being 'all rights reserved'. Then in January 2010, on viewing the website of the London newspaper *The Independent*, he was surprised to find that his picture was being used in a section containing pictures of snowbound Britain.

Mr Zabulis contacted the newspaper to complain that the picture had been used without his consent. *The Independent* responded by stating that they had not copied the picture. It had instead taken a photostream from Flickr and incorporated this into its own website by means of an application programming interface. If the use of photostreaming does not involve copying the work, merely of transmitting it automatically to the user, the question arises as to whether or not that would constitute a communication to the public of the work by electronic means.

Mr Zabulis hadn't got the answer he wanted, and therefore put copies of all the correspondence between the newspaper and himself onto a Flickr page headed 'Breach of copyright – *The Independent*'. The matter was eventually resolved when the newspaper made a payment to Mr Zabulis.[2, 3]

2.2 Audiobooks

In 2006 *The Bookseller* (7 July, 5) reported that the Publishers Association had closed down nearly 1000 audiobook pirates who operate on online auction websites.

In 2008 Andrew Sloper was sentenced at Derby Crown Court to 21 months in prison for copying thousands of audiobooks with a total retail value of £1,175,000 and selling them on eBay for a fraction of their true value.[4]

2.2.1   Bonnier Audio AB and others v. Perfect Communication Sweden AB CJEU C-461/10

Bonnier Audio took legal action against Swedish ISP Perfect Communication because 27 of its audio books had been made available via a file sharing service. Bonnier Audio wanted a court order to force the ISP to disclose the identities of the alleged infringers, but Perfect Communication argued that the request wasn't in line with the data retention directive (2006/24/EC).

The European Court of Justice ruled that, provided the order of disclosure was based on proportionate and necessary evidence, there was nothing in the Data Retention Directive of the E-privacy Directive (2002/58/EC) which would preclude a member state from adopting such a rule.

2.3   Broadcasts

The *Consultation on Copyright* published in December 2011 (www.ipo.gov.uk/consult-2011-copyright.pdf) proposes extension of the archiving exception in s. 42 of the CDPA so that it would in future cover a wider range of material such as sound recordings, films and broadcasts.

The government is also proposing to simplify sections 61 (on recordings of folk songs) and 75 (recording for archival purposes [of broadcasts]) of the CDPA 1988 to make it easier to archive broadcasts and folk songs. This could be done by making it easier for an institution to become a designated body under the provisions by delegating authority to do this to the Comptroller General of the IPO; or alternatively by removing the need for formal designation altogether. Another option would be to merge these provisions with the more general preservation exception of Section 42.

The consultation paper also proposes extending the fair dealing exceptions for research and private study in s. 29 to enable students and researchers to copy sound recordings, films and broadcasts.

If you have signed a subscription contract to receive a broadcast signal via a set-top box or cable service, then you are bound by the terms of that agreement.

Broadcasts received in the UK unencrypted or free to air can be recorded by educational establishments under s. 35 of the CDPA 1988 unless or to the extent that there is a licensing scheme in place which has been certified under section 143 of the Act.

Where there is a licensing scheme in place, people wouldn't be able to rely on the section 35 exception, but would instead need to buy the relevant licence. There are two licences which currently operate under section 143 – The Educational Recording Agency licence[5] and the Open University transactional licence.[6]

2.3.1 Educational Recording Agency licence

An ERA licence permits educational establishments to record off-air, and make copies, for non-commercial educational purposes, of programmes broadcast by its members. It also permits electronic communication of licensed recordings within an educational establishment.

The licence does not cover on-demand and interactive services. However, broadcast programme services which are delivered via the internet at fixed viewing times are not on-demand services and may therefore be recorded.

There is an additional licence known as ERAplus, which enables licensees to access recordings even if they are not doing so on the premises of their school, college, or university, thereby facilitating distance learning.

Terms and conditions for access to online video on-demand services often limit licensed access to personal private use. In such cases access to such services is not authorized for educational establishments, even if the access is required for the educational purposes of the establishment. Following discussions with the BBC and Channel 4, changes have been made to the terms and conditions applicable to the access of some BBC and Channel 4 online services. These changes allow educational establishments holding a current ERA Licence to:

- record and access BBC Content in relevant BBC Online Services for educational purposes under the terms of an ERA Licence; and
- apply non-commercial educational use within the scope of the ERA Licence to access 4oD Content within Channel 4 Online Services on the conditions that would otherwise be limited to personal, non-commercial use.

Age of consent and viewer guidance terms continue to apply to any educational access. The changes have been confirmed independently of the ERA Licence and are reliant upon current published Terms of Use.

⇢ **Useful resource**

Terms of use of BBC Online Services

www.bbc.co.uk/terms/(Click on the Help and FAQ tab and refer to item 8 'How can educational establishments use BBC Online Services (including BBC iPlayer)'?)

⇢ **Useful resource**

Channel4.com terms and conditions

www.channel4.com/terms_and_conditions.html (see section 9)
The new terms clarify how ERA Licences support additional access to programmes and extracts for educational use,
www.era.org.uk/on_demand.html.

2.3.2   Open University licence

The Open University licence is a transactional rather than a blanket licence. Each year licensees are required to provide the Open University with a list of the recordings which have been made. The fee is based on the number of programmes you record and retain for use during the year, and it is charged on a sliding scale per programme, per year, depending upon the number you record. The main terms of the licence are:

- Recordings may be used for training and teaching purposes. The recording cannot be used in material subsequently made available for sale or hire.
- Additional copies of programmes may be made without further charge.
- Recordings must be made by a 'lecturer, instructor, teacher or other suitably qualified person appointed [. . .] by the Licensee'.
- Programmes may not be edited, cut or amended in any way, including digital manipulation, without prior permission from the OU.
- Complete and up-to-date records must be kept of any recordings made under the licence.
- All recordings must be clearly labelled with the title of the programme and the date on which it was recorded.
- All recordings must be deleted if the Licence expires or is terminated.
- The terms of the licence do not allow the public showing of material.

2.3.3   Box of Broadcasts

The British Universities Film and Video Council (http://bufvc.ac.uk) provides a service called 'Box of Broadcasts' (BoB) which enables people to record and view TV and radio online from over 50 free-to-air channels in the UK (www.bobnational.net).

Licensing arrangements do not permit Open University programmes to be recorded via BoB, as these have to be recorded under an OU licence. Nor can BoB be accessed outside the UK. For terms and conditions of using BoB see http://bobnational.net/content.php?view=term.

2.4   Databases

There is a provision in the CDPA 1988 relating to databases which cannot be overridden by contract:

50D Acts permitted in relation to databases

(1) It is not an infringement of copyright in a database for a person who has a right to use the database or any part of the database, (whether under a licence to do any of the acts restricted by the copyright in the database or otherwise)

to do, in the exercise of that right, anything which is necessary for the purposes of access to and use of the contents of the database or of that part of the database.

The Copyright and Rights in Databases Regulations 1997: SI 1997/3032 define a database as 'a collection of independent works, data or other materials which are arranged in a systematic or methodical way and are individually accessible by electronic or other means'. Databases could potentially be protected either by copyright or by database right, by both or by neither.

2.4.1 Database protection by copyright

In order to qualify for copyright protection, the selection or arrangement of the contents of the database must be original and it would only be original if that selection or arrangement constituted the author's own intellectual creation. Merely putting a list of names into alphabetical order would not qualify.

In Football Dataco and others v. Yahoo! UK Ltd and others CJEU C-604/10 it was held that a football fixture list cannot be protected by copyright when its compilation is dictated by rules or constraints which leave no room for creative freedom. In other words, the mere fact that significant labour and skill on the part of the creator was required in order for the list to be compiled does not of itself justify it being protected by copyright.

A distinction needs to be made here between the database and its individual component parts, because the component parts may or may not be protected in their own right completely independently of the question of whether there is copyright protection in the database as a whole as a compilation.

A database would fall within the category or species for literary works. Where a database does attract copyright protection this would last for 70 years from the end of the year in which the author dies.

2.4.2 Database protection by database right

To qualify for database right substantial investment must have taken place in the obtaining, verifying, and presenting of the contents of the database. Investment includes any investment, whether of financial, human or technical resources. Investment in the 'creation' of the data itself is to be disregarded.

⊕ **Football Dataco Limited v. Brittens Pools Limited, Yahoo et al. [2010] EWHC 841**

Mr Justice Floyd said that a four-step test should apply when someone tries to determine whether or not a database qualifies for protection:

It seems to me that the task for the court is as follows:

i) Identify the data which is collected and arranged in the database;
ii) Analyse the work which goes into the creation of the database by collecting and arranging the data so identified, to isolate that work which is properly regarded as selection and arrangement;
iii) Ask whether the work of selection and arrangement was the author's own intellectual creation and in particular whether it involved the author's judgment, taste or discretion;
iv) Finally one should ask whether the work is quantitatively sufficient to attract copyright protection.

Database right lasts for 15 years from the end of the year in which the database was completed. If there has been a further substantial investment, this could potentially trigger a further 15-year period of protection.

Database right exists to prevent the **extraction** or **reutilization** of substantial parts of the contents of a database. **Extraction** means the permanent or temporary transfer of any contents of a database to another medium by any means or in any form; while **reutilization** means making the contents of the database available to the public by any means.

There are a number of exceptions to database right, the main one being fair dealing. Regulation 20 of SI 1997/3032 sets out the fair dealing exception to database right which is available so long as:

- the person extracting part of the database is a lawful user of the database;
- that it is extracted for the purposes of illustration for teaching or research;
- that it is not for any commercial purpose;
- and that the source is indicated.

The Regulations do define the term 'lawful user', but the definition is not very enlightening. It says 'lawful user', in relation to a database, means any person who (whether under a licence to do any of the acts restricted by any database right in the database or otherwise) has a right to use the database.

In addition to the fair dealing exception, Schedule 1 to the Database Regulations (SI 1997/3032) sets out a number of public administration exceptions. These cover:

1 Parliamentary and judicial proceedings.
2 Royal Commissions and statutory inquiries.
3 Material open to public inspection or on official register.
4 Material communicated to the Crown in the course of public business.
5 Public records.
6 Acts done under statutory authority.

Creative Commons Licences can be used to license data or databases. Where a database is covered by the sui generis database right, Creative Commons adopted a policy that CC version 3.0 licences must waive those licence requirements and prohibitions (attribution, share-alike, etc) for uses triggering database rights – so that if the use of a database published under a CC licence implicated only database rights, but not copyright, the CC licence requirements and prohibitions would not apply to that use. However, the licence requirements and prohibitions do continue to apply to all uses triggering copyright. For further information see: Creative Commons (2007) *On the Treatment of the Sui Generis Database Rights in Version 3.0 of the Creative Commons licenses*, http://wiki.creativecommons.org/images/f/f6/ V3_Database_Rights.pdf.

Meanwhile the Open Government Licence (www.nationalarchives.gov.uk/doc/ open-government-licence) which is compatible with Creative Commons licences covers both copyright and database right. The same is true of the open parliament licence (www.parliament.uk/site-information/copyright/open-parliament-licence).

2.5 DVDs
2.5.1 Filmbank

Filmbank Distributors Limited is a joint venture company owned by Warner Bros Entertainment UK and Sony Pictures Releasing and it represents many leading Hollywood, Bollywood and independent film studios in the field of film usage outside the cinema and home. In 2009 Filmbank introduced a DVD Concierge licence (www.filmbank.co.uk/dvdconcierge) to enable guesthouses, B&Bs and hotels to legally offer DVDs to their guests for in-room use. Licence holders pay an annual fee in return for being able to offer their guests unlimited movies from the participating studios during their stay.

2.5.2 MPLC

MPLC (the Motion Picture Licensing Corporation) offer a licence for the viewing or showing of DVDs in public (www.themplc.co.uk).

Section 34 of the CDPA 1988 deals with performing, playing or showing work in the course of activities of an educational establishment. Section 34(2) allows the playing or showing of a film to an audience of teachers and pupils, and other relevant people, at an educational establishment but only for the purposes of instruction.

JISC Legal in a note entitled 'Are FE and HE institutions required to purchase the MPLC umbrella licence to view pre-recorded films in public?' (www.jisclegal.ac.uk/ManageContent/ViewDetail/ID/1910/Are-FE-and-HE-institutions-required-to-purchase-the-MPLC-Umbrella-Licence-to-view-pre-recorded-films-in-public.aspx) says that FE and HE institutions are not required to take out the MPLC licence when showing DVDs or pre-recorded films for educational purposes.

2.5.3   Enforcement action

In 2009 Steven Healey was convicted of 14 trademark and copyright offences and was given a 16-month prison sentence. He ran a counterfeit films, music and games enterprise from a rented house in which thousands of counterfeit disks, two computers and 20 DVD burners were found.

In 2009 a gang providing a one-stop shop supply service for other criminal gangs producing and selling counterfeit DVDs in London and the south-east with international links were sentenced:

* Sami Asgar-Sheikh – 6 years (3 custodial and 3 on prison licence)
* Rafi Asgar-Sheikh – 6 years (3 custodial and 3 on prison licence)
* Khalid Asgar-Sheikh – 4 years (2 custodial and 2 on prison licence).

In 2010 David Martin was given a five-year prison sentence for counterfeiting of DVDs and handling of stolen goods

In 2010 Jalal Mansoor was given a 1-year, 4-month prison sentence and Ahmed Zeeshan an 8-month prison sentence (suspended for 12 months) for conspiracy to make and sell counterfeit DVDs.

2.6   E-books

The business models between the print and the electronic world can and do differ. When a physical copy of a book is purchased, the purchaser owns the physical object, but they don't own the intellectual property rights in the content within the book. In the electronic world, the purchaser is paying for access to the content, governed by a licence agreement.

Rights owners are still experimenting with a variety of different business models and they are monitoring closely the impact on their bottom line. In 2010 the UK Publishers Association advised that e-book lending licences should prevent public library users from downloading e-books from their libraries remotely and only allow them to do so in person at the library premises.

Meanwhile HarperCollins chose to introduce a checkout limit of 26 checkouts for each e-book licensed, after which the licence would expire unless libraries paid an additional fee.

➜ Useful resource

Ebook model licence: www.licensingmodels.org/E-bookLicense.html

E-book piracy is growing. Publishers wishing to prevent piracy of e-books often deploy digital rights management technology which will control access to and use of the e-book. For example, a DRM system can be used to limit which devices can display the e-book, or to restrict the copying and pasting of extracts.

⊕ John Wiley & Sons, Inc. v. John Does Nos. 1-43

In 2011 the publishing company John Wiley filed a lawsuit in Manhattan federal court against people who downloaded illicit copies of its popular 'For Dummies' series. The lawsuit included a list of anonymous users and the titles they had downloaded.

The most popular title was *Photoshop for Dummies*. John Wiley claims that its Photoshop book, which retails for around US$20, had been downloaded more than 74,000 times since the summer of 2010 and that lost revenue from filesharing may harm its ability to publish and pay authors.

The case suggests that unauthorized filesharing, which has long plagued the music and movie industries, is now beginning to have a significant impact on traditional book publishers as well. Book files are easier to swap because they are much smaller than music or movie files, and new technologies have made it easier to scan and upload a book.

In this case, John Wiley sued 27 'John Doe' defendants residing in New York on the basis of their IP address. The John Does in the case traded the books on a Montenegro and Ukraine-based site called demonoid.me.

The 'For Dummies' series began in 1991 with the publication of *DOS for Dummies*. The 'For Dummies' franchise has sold more than 200 million copies since it was launched and John Wiley has published more than 1800 titles in the series in 30 languages.

In 2009 Amazon recalled two Kindle e-books which had been posted onto Amazon Marketplace because the publisher concerned didn't have the rights to the books.[7] The books were *Animal Farm* and *1984* by George Orwell and these had been added to Amazon's catalogue by a third party using their self-service platform. The recall of the books caused an outcry. In one instance Justin Gawronski was reading *1984* on his Kindle for a summer assignment and when the book was recalled he lost all of his annotations and notes.

It may have come as a shock to customers to realize that when they purchase an e-book, they do not necessarily own it for life. It is important to distinguish between an e-book which is governed by a set of terms and conditions (i.e. a contract) and a physical book which is governed by copyright law.

A number of providers of e-book readers such as Nook, Kobo and Sony have lending programmes which enable readers to borrow e-books from libraries.

In April 2011, for example, Amazon and Overdrive announced the launch of the Kindle Library Lending program which at the time was only available for libraries, schools, and colleges in the United States.

Library supplier Overdrive reported in the summer of 2011 that a growing list of suppliers had agreed to provide simultaneous access to e-books to libraries, on annual subscription. These publishers will enable libraries to provide 'always available' e-books without waiting lists or holds, in addition to offering the publishers' titles under the one-copy one-user model, the most common model used. The e-books can be transferred to compatible devices, and will expire at the end of the lending period.

Bloomsbury Publishing has an online access subscription service called 'Public Library Online' (PLO) which offers themed digital bookshelves containing both fiction and non-fiction content for both adults and children. In 2012 Google sponsored two virtual shelves through PLO, one on the environment and one on Shakespeare through the Arden Shakespeare series; the Shakespeare virtual shelf will make ten plays that are on the GCSE national curriculum available to all users. This sponsorship arrangement made the works available to public libraries throughout the UK. The Public Library Online is sold on an annual subscription to library authorities after a free trial period. It provides concurrent access for users in and out of libraries and can be accessed through library terminals, library Wi-Fi or through the library's website.

In July 2009 the DCMS undertook a *Consultation on the Extension of Public Lending Right to Rights Holders of Books in Non-print Formats* (www.dcms.gov.uk/ reference_library/consultations/6283.aspx). The consultation paper sought views on policy proposals to:

- extend eligibility for Public Lending Right (PLR) to non-print books, in particular audiobooks and e-books;
- extend PLR to the lending rights holders in respect of these non-print works where they are not currently eligible under the PLR Scheme.

Expanding the PLR Scheme to include new types of works and new types of rights holders would require a consequential expansion to the 'infringement exemption' under the CDPA 1988 and would therefore remove the possibility of enforcement of lending rights by rights holders against lending libraries for newly eligible works. Or in other words, it would remove the need for libraries to obtain consent for lending of the newly eligible works. In exchange for this expanded 'exemption', the Scheme would be required to remunerate the rights holders of newly eligible works where such rights holders were eligible and registered with the Scheme.

Under the proposals set out in the 2009 consultation, the categories of publications eligible for PLR would be extended to include non-print books –

whether experienced aurally or visually. The government had in mind a number of specific formats:

- hard-copy audiobooks – primarily CDs;
- soft-copy audiobooks – digital audio files (e.g. MP3) provided to library users either as a download, for licensed short-term access or loaded on appropriate hardware (e.g. MP3 player); and
- e-books – digital files as above, but to be read rather than heard. This may include image-based, as well as text-based, books, such as graphic novels.

The consultation ran from 24 July 2009 through to 16 October 2009. In due course, the Digital Economy Act 2010 included a provision in Section 43 of the Act to extend PLR to electronic content. At the time of writing (July 2012), this provision has not been implemented, and it was an early casualty of the government cuts.[8]

2.6.1   Privacy concerns

Librarians have expressed concerns relating to e-books. These cover a wide range of issues, including privacy policies, device incompatibilities and the use of proprietary systems.

⇢ Useful resource

In 2010 The Electronic Frontier Foundation published an e-book buyer's guide to e-book privacy[9] which compared the privacy policies of a number of the main e-book suppliers. For each supplier they ask the following questions:

- Can they monitor what you're reading?
- Can they keep track of book searches?
- Can they keep track of book purchases?
- With whom can they share the information collected?
- Do customers have any control over the information?
- Can customers access, correct or delete the information?

2.7   E-journals

There is a need to clearly differentiate between **ownership** and **leasing**, because in the electronic world people are usually paying for the right to **access** information for a limited period of time. If someone takes out a subscription to an electronic journal, unless the contract under which the information is governed says otherwise, they won't have access to any of the information once the subscription to the product has been terminated. Indeed, the licence terms might even stipulate that anything which has been downloaded during the subscription period must be deleted once that subscription has expired.

The International Association of Scientific Technical and Medical Publishers (STM) proposes that e-journal licences should only allow libraries to provide printed copies, not digital copies, of documents to users (see the STM statement on document delivery, www.stm-assoc.org/industry-news/stm-statement-on-document-delivery).

⚫ Useful resource

The model NESLi2 licence for journals:
www.jisc-collections.ac.uk/nesli2/NESLi2-Model-Licence-/.

2.8   E-learning materials

The creation of e-learning materials raises issues around copyright in software, learning platforms, text, images and sound recordings, which can all form part of e-learning material. Particular care needs to be taken when considering the use of third-party materials in order to create new resources, especially where these are subsequently stored in digital libraries and institutional repositories. In order to ensure legal compliance it is essential to collect and store the associated rights information, so that it is absolutely clear who owns the rights in the e-learning material, who can access it and use it, and on what basis the resource has been made available.

2.9   E-mails

The case of Cembrit Blunn Ltd & anor v. Apex Roofing Services LLP & anor [2007] EWHC 111 (Ch) makes clear that business correspondence such as letters or e-mails can be protected by copyright and that forwarding them to other people can be an infringement. In order to qualify for copyright protection they must involve original skill and labour and not copy the work of another person. There must be originality in the expression of the inventive thought.

In the US case Stern v. Does 09-cv-01986 (C.D.Cal.; Feb 10, 2011) a lawyer tried to bring a copyright infringement claim against someone who forwarded a 23-word e-mail of his. In that particular case the court held that the e-mail lacked sufficient creativity.

2.10 E-reserves

The phrase 'electronic reserves' is taken from the American term for short-loan collections. Traditional paper 'reserves' were either books or copies of articles kept in the library to facilitate teaching. Electronic reserves are either scanned or digital copies of copyright works which are made available to students through the library.

Georgia State University faced legal action (Cambridge University Press, Oxford University Press & Sage Publications v. Mark P. Becker Case 1:08-cv-01425-ODE USDC Atlanta, originally Cambridge University Press et al. v. Patton et al.) as a result of their practice of putting class readings on electronic reserve and on faculty websites. See also Section 7.10 of this book.

➻ Useful resource

The Association of American Publishers has a set of frequently asked questions on e-reserves on its website at:
www.publishers.org/GSU/ereservesqanda.

➻ Useful resource

There is also a document entitled 'Questions & answers on copyright for the campus community', 7th edn, AAP et al., 2006,
www.elac.edu/collegeservices/doc/PC-029-08-06-CopyrightQA_v3.pdf.

2.11 Films

Copyright can subsist in a number of the component parts of a film such as the original screenplay, the musical score and so on.

Films are protected for 70 years from the end of the year in which the death occurs of the last of the principal directors, the author of the screenplay, the author of the dialogue, or the composer of music specially created for and used in the film; or if the identity of these people is unknown 70 years from the end of the calendar year in which the film was made; or if it was made available to the public in that time, 70 years from the end of the year in which the film was first made available.

In the case of film clips and 'captured stills', the restricted acts are:

- copying a substantial part (a clip or an image)
- storage in any medium by electronic means
- making a photograph of the whole or any substantial part of any image (a still) forming part of the film
- publication/distribution
- rental/lending

- public showing/playing
- communication to the public (such as over the internet).

There is currently no exception in CDPA 1988 for fair dealing with films for a non-commercial research purpose or private study, although there are exceptions for:

- fair dealing with a publicly available film for criticism or review or news reporting (section 30);
- acts for non-commercial instruction where they are accompanied by a sufficient acknowledgement (section 32(2));
- playing or showing a film before an audience at an educational establishment for the purposes of instruction (section 34(2)).

The Motion Picture Licensing Corporation (MPLC) and Filmbank (www.filmbank. co.uk) license the use of films for entertainment purposes on behalf of film producers and distributors.

There is also a moral right of privacy (section 85) where a person commissions the making of a film for private and domestic purposes. It means that the person commissioned cannot issue the film to the public, exhibit or show it in public, or communicate the film to the public without permission.

2.11.1 Convictions for film copyright offences

1 On 14 November 2007 a 38-year old woman from Penrith, Cumbria, was given a six-month jail sentence at Penrith Magistrates Court, having pleaded guilty to 18 charges of breaching trade mark and copyright law, in a case brought by Cumbria Trading Standards. The court heard that the woman was copying films and selling them to order over the internet, initially using eBay to advertise but then also using direct e-mail selling to her existing client base. The matter came to light as a consequence of enquiries undertaken by the Federation Against Copyright Theft (FACT) Internet Investigations Team.

2 In 2010 Emmanuel Nimley was given a six-month prison sentence for recording films in a cinema using a Smartphone and then uploading them to the internet, from where other people would be able to watch them or burn them onto illegal DVDs. He was charged under ss 6 and 7 of the Fraud Act 2006 and s 107(1) of the CDPA 1988. It was the third conviction under the Fraud Act 2006 in the UK for illegally recording in a cinema and the first to receive a prison sentence.

3 In 2011 three founders of NinjaVideo.net pleaded guilty to criminal copyright conspiracy. The website provided millions of users with the ability to illegally download infringing copies of copyright-protected films and TV programmes

in high-quality formats. Website users were able to download a lot of the infringing content free of charge, but those visitors who 'donated' US$25+ were able to gain access to private forum boards containing a wider range of infringing content. The website generated US$500,000+ additional income from internet advertising during the two and a half years that it was operational. In January 2012 Ms Hana Beshara, founder of Ninjavideo, was sentenced to 22 months in prison for conspiracy and criminal copyright infringement.

4 Christopher Clarke became the first person in Scotland to be convicted of illegally recording in a cinema and uploading films for profit. In June 2011 he was sentenced at Glasgow Sheriff's Court to 160 hours of community service.[10]

5 In October 2011 a man was convicted of 781 separate copyright violations and given a one-year suspended sentence by a German court. The copyright violations were in connection with the operation of a BitTorrent film-sharing network. The accused did make a full confession and also showed remorse. [11]

2.11.2 Case study on counterfeit films

Intelligence was received by The Federation Against Copyright Theft (FACT) which suggested that a college teacher had placed counterfeit copies of films onto the college computer network. This network was accessible by all staff and students. FACT contacted the college headmaster who investigated the allegation. As a result, a teacher was given an official warning and the illegal content was immediately withdrawn. College staff were subsequently warned against this kind of activity, and informed of the consequences, including the possibility of formal disciplinary proceedings. Formal disciplinary might constitute gross misconduct and lead to their dismissal. All staff are now fully conversant with college policy and the appropriate legislation.[12]

2.12   Games

People who play illegal copies of video games on chipped or modified consoles cost at least £1.45 billion in lost sales in 2010, according to the Association of UK Interactive Entertainment (UKIE). Some games can take several years to make, at a cost of millions of pounds.[13]

The Cambridge (UK)-based anti-piracy firm Envisional, which offers services that help to detect and guard against the threat of internet copyright infringement, claims that the number of 'illegally' pirated video games by broadband ISP customers in the UK has risen by almost 20% over the past five years. The firm warned that the top five video games of 2010 were downloaded nearly one million times.

➕ R v. Gilham [2009] EWCA Crim 2293

The Court of Appeal upheld a conviction of a man who sold modification chips allowing gamers to play pirate or counterfeit games. The CDPA 1988 makes it a criminal offence to sell or distribute 'any device, product or component which is primarily designed or produced . . . for the purpose of enabling or facilitating the circumvention of effective technological measures'. Broadly speaking, effective technological measures means any technology designed to protect a copyright work other than a computer program.

Christopher Paul Gilham ran a business importing and selling devices known as modchips for use in conjunction with a variety of games consoles. They are so-called because they modify a games console so as to enable people to use them to play unlicensed copies of video games. Gilham was convicted by the High Court but appealed to the Court of Appeal that his modchips did not enable copying of a 'substantial part' of the copyright in the games. To secure a conviction, the use of the device, product or component in question must have involved 'substantial copying' of a copyright work.

The Court of Appeal dismissed the appeal and upheld his conviction. The Court emphasized that there are a variety of copyrights which protect a computer game. Amongst other things, there is artistic copyright in the various drawings making up the display on the TV screen, and these were reproduced in full while playing the game.

Gilham argued that only a small portion of a game is copied from a disc into a games console's memory at any one time, and that the amount copied at any given moment was far less than a 'substantial part'. Lord Justice Stanley Burton said that the case did not have to be decided on the question of whether a substantial part of the whole game was copied or not. He said that constituent parts of it were copyrighted, and when substantial parts of those constituent parts were displayed, infringement occurred. He went on to say:

> In the present case, if the only copyright work that is copied is the game as a whole, the 'little and often' would be material. But the game as a whole is not the sole subject of copyright. The various drawings that result in the images shown on the television screen or monitor are themselves artistic works protected by copyright.

Even if the contents of the RAM of a game console at any one time is not a substantial copy, the image displayed on screen is such.

In 2009 BBC News Online reported that thousands of gamers may have been cut off from Microsoft's online gaming service Xbox Live for modifying their consoles in order to play pirated games.[14] Microsoft confirmed that it had banned a 'small percentage' of the 20 million Xbox Live users worldwide (perhaps as many as 600,000 gamers). Microsoft said that modifying an Xbox 360 console 'violates' the service's 'terms of use', that it would void their warranty and result in a ban from Xbox Live. The Xbox 360 is equipped with DRM technologies to detect pirated software. But many gamers modify their consoles by installing new chips or software that allows them to run unofficial programs and games, with some chips having been specifically designed to play pirated games. Microsoft didn't say how it was able to determine which gamers to disconnect, but did confirm that all of the consoles affected had been verified as having violated the terms of use.

In 2008 it was reported that a woman who had put a copy of Dream Pinball 3D on a filesharing network would have to pay £16,000 to the games maker and its lawyers.[15] The games maker Topware Interactive had been awarded £6086.56 in damages and £10,000 in lawyers' fees by the Patents County Court in London. At the time the lawyers Davenport Lyons said that they had identified thousands of filesharers and that there were more cases to come. The Swiss firm Logistep had been used in order to identify suspected filesharers. Davenport Lyons subsequently wrote to some 500 people it reckoned were sharing Topware's Pinball game, demanding payments of £300 to settle.

In 2009 ELSPA, the Entertainment and Leisure Software Publishers Association, announced that trading standards had conducted the largest-ever seizure of counterfeit gaming devices in the UK. ELSPA's anti-piracy team worked with Surrey Trading Standards in a case which led to a raid at a detached house in Surrey where they discovered thousands of game-copying devices which allegedly infringed both the Trade Marks Act 1994 and the Copyright, Designs and Patents Act 1988. The items were seized and sent for forensic examination. Records found at the property revealed evidence of trading worth hundreds of thousands of pounds. A web-based business was alleged to be importing and selling Nintendo DS™ copying devices worldwide via the internet. HMRC knew something was wrong when large consignments of the illegal game copying devices started showing up at airports across the UK. These were seized and HMRC alerted IP investigators from ELSPA.

2.13 Graphical user interfaces

In a case arising in the Czech Republic, the CJEU ruled that a GUI is not a form of expression of a computer program.

⊕ **Bezpe nostní softwarová asociace (Security software association) v. Ministerstvo kultury (Ministry of Culture of the Czech Republic) CJEU C-393/09**

Following a reference from the Czech Regional Court, the CJEU ruled that a GUI is not a form of expression of a computer program and cannot therefore be protected by copyright as a computer program under Directive 91/250/EEC. However, they did emphasize that a GUI can be protected by copyright, as a work, under Directive 2001/29/EC, if that interface is its author's own intellectual creation. Indeed, a GUI can be considered as a literary or artistic work in the traditional sense, and its original elements should therefore benefit from copyright protection.

The CJEU also held that a television broadcast of a GUI does not constitute communication to the public of a work protected by copyright within the meaning of Article 3(1) of Directive 2001/29/EC because the television viewers receive a communication of that GUI in a passive manner, without having the possibility to interact with the program. According to the CJEU, as the individuals do not have access to the essential element characterizing the interface, namely interaction with the user, 'there is no communication to the public of the graphic user interface within the meaning of Article 3(1) of Directive 2001/29'.

2.14   Lifecasting

Lifecasting is the continual broadcasting of events in a person's life through digital media, typically transmitted over the internet. It captures personal experiences, daily routines as well as interactive communication with viewers.

An article by Mike Masnick[16] mentions that the Premier League were suing Justin.tv, the online service which enabled users to broadcast a live streaming video (or 'lifecast') from their computer camera. The Premier League had noted how a number of lifecasters had a Premier League game playing on television which they considered to be an infringement of copyright. So, by its very nature, lifecasting could lead to the accidental or inadvertent inclusion of copyright protected material if a television is switched on in the background of the person who is lifecasting.

2.15   Multimedia

Webopedia defines 'multimedia' as 'The use of computers to present text, graphics, video, animation, and sound in an integrated way.' As such, multimedia content types could include: still images (such as photographs or drawings), moving images (such as animations or video), audio items (such as sound recordings or music) or indeed any combination of these.

Where copyright restrictions limit the use that can be made of multimedia content one option would be to look for copyright-cleared content such as that which is governed by a Creative Commons Licence.

In the Google advanced search at www.google.co.uk/advanced_search?hl=en there is an option for Date, usage rights, region and more; and within the option for usage rights there is a drop-down from which it is possible to search for Creative Commons licensed content. Similarly, in Google Images the advanced search facility www.google.co.uk/advanced_image_search?hl=en lets you search for images labelled for reuse, and to limit further to ones available for commercial use and/or ones available for modification.

Within Flickr's advanced search facility www.flickr.com/search/advanced/? it is possible to search by media type for photos and videos and also to search for Creative Commons licensed content.

The JISC Media Hub http://jiscmediahub.ac.uk is a multimedia platform offering a wealth of digital image, video and audio collections.

➡ Useful resource

Sources of royalty-free pictures:
1 Public Domain Pictures: www.publicdomainpictures.net
2 Public Domain Photos: www.public-domain-photos.com
3 Stock.XCHNG: www.sxc.hu
4 Flickr: www.flickr.com
5 Image After: www.imageafter.com
6 Wikimedia Commons: http://commons.wikimedia.org/wiki/Main_Page.

2.16   Music

Copyright is a 'bundle' of rights, and therefore there are often a number of rights within a single item. Copyright applies to the composition, the musical score, the lyrics, as well as any artwork or cover designs. So, when you want to get copyright clearance for an item, it can involve having to seek out the permission of a number of different rights holders. For example, where each of these applies, you would need to get clearance:

- in the music and words – with the publisher
- in the performance – with the artist
- in the recording – with the recording company.

Copyright in a musical work expires at the end of 70 years after the author's (composer's) death.

Recorded musical performances are currently protected for a maximum of 50 years, although this will be extended to 70 years once Directive 2011/77/EC[17] comes into force. The extended term will enable performers to earn money for a longer period of time and in any event throughout their lifetime. It will also benefit record producers who will generate additional revenue from the sale of records in shops and on the internet. This should allow producers to adapt to the rapidly changing business environment and help them maintain their investment levels in new talent.

The Directive also contains accompanying measures which aim specifically to help performers.

1 If music companies don't make material publicly available after the 50-year term has passed, the artist can apply to terminate the original contract completely and take over the control of copyright themselves. The 'use it or lose it' clauses which will now have to be included in the contracts linking performers to their record companies will allow performers to get their rights back if the record producer does not market the sound recording during the extended period. In this way the performer will be able to either find another record producer willing to sell his music or do it himself, something that is possible easily via the internet.

2 Finally, record companies will have to set up a fund into which they will have to pay 20% of their revenues earned during the extended period. The money from this fund will be destined to help session musicians.

At the moment, unpublished works – including unpublished musical works – are protected until at least 2039. The government's *Consultation on Copyright* of 2011 asks what are the pros and cons of changing this to the life of the author plus 70 years.

➡ Useful resource

Museums, Libraries and Archives Council (2010) *Public Performance Licences – An Information Guide: music and film activities in public libraries*, www.iaml.info/iaml-uk-irl/resources/pub_perf_licenses.pdf.

➡ Useful resource

Collecting societies:
PRS: www.prsformusic.com
PPL: www.ppluk.com
Music Publishers Association: www.mpaonline.org.uk
NB: CLA licences do not cover printed music (including the words).

➡ Useful resource

PRS for Music has a code of practice which relates to its public performance licensing activities. The code sets out the level of service that people can expect from them; and what to do if things go wrong:
www.prsformusic.com/users/businessesandliveevents/codeofpractice/Documents/CodeofPractice.pdf.

2.17   News aggregators

In an article entitled 'Who's afraid of the news aggregators?' (Citizens Media Law Project, 30 August 2010), and the accompanying White Paper 'The rise of the news aggregator: legal implications and best practices', Kimberley Isbell distinguished between four different types of news aggregators:

1 Feed aggregators – websites containing material from a number of sites organized into various 'feeds', typically arranged by source, topic or story.
2 Specialty aggregators – websites which collect information from a number of sources on a particular topic or location.
3 User-curated aggregators – websites which feature user-submitted links and portions of text taken from a variety of websites.
4 Blog aggregators – websites that use third-party content to create a blog about a given topic (and the White Paper gives the Gawker media sites http://gawker.com as an example of blog aggregators).

In March 2012 it was reported that the German coalition government has decided to create a new neighbouring right for newspaper publishers which will mean that in future commercial ISPs, search engine providers and news aggregators will be required to pay an equitable remuneration to publishers for the use of media products such as newspaper articles.[18]

 Where you subscribe to an online database from a news aggregator it is important to check that the licence agreement contains a clause on warranties and indemnities. The key thing to check is whether they have the legal right to license the content to you.

☰ Sample warranty and indemnity clause

The publisher warrants to the library that it has full rights and authority to grant the licence to the library and that the use by the library of the licensed material in accordance with this agreement will not infringe the rights of any third party. The publisher undertakes to indemnify the library against all loss, damage, costs, claims and expenses arising out of any such actual or alleged infringement. This indemnity shall survive the termination of this licence however terminated. The indemnity shall not apply if the library has modified the licensed material in any way not permitted by this licence.

There are a number of examples of legal cases where people got a licence from the wrong person. These include:

- Retail Systems Technology v. Mcguire [2007] IEHC 13, 2nd February 2007.
- Lady Anne Tennant v. Associated Newspapers [1979] FSR 298 (involving the UK *Daily Mail*'s use of photographs of Princess Margaret, though the judge said that the *Mail* should have doubted the source of the licence).
- Mansell v. Valley Printing [1908] 2 Ch 441 (in which a publisher relied on permission from a person who owned no rights, and was found to have infringed).

2.17.1 Google News

Launched in 2002, Google News is a free news aggregator provided by Google Inc. It aggregates and provides access to recent content from thousands of publications.

Since it was launched there have been a number of legal cases against Google by newspaper publishers. In March 2005, for example, Agence France Presse sued Google for US$17.5 million, alleging that Google News infringed on its copyright by including photos, stories and news headlines on Google News without permission. The case was eventually settled out of court in 2007 when Google signed a licensing agreement with AFP giving them the right to post AFP content on Google News and other Google services.

Google has also entered into licensing deals with other publishers such as Associated Press. The deal with AP in 2006 settled a dispute between the two companies in which Google agreed to pay AP for use of its news stories and pictures, although financial terms of the agreement were not disclosed.

Copiepresse began legal action against Google over its Google News service back in 2006. Copiepresse manages copyright for Belgian newspapers and they claimed that Google had no right to use the online newspaper information in Google News without the explicit permission of the rights owners. In May 2011 the Belgian Court of Appeals ruled that Google infringed the copyrights of Belgian newspapers by placing links to articles and portions of articles on Google News.[19]

The newspaper publishers have for many years been able to determine whether or not their content is indexed on Google using the robots exclusion protocol (REP). This refers to a file called robots.txt which is placed in the root of a domain in which websites can put instructions to restrict access to their site by search engine robots that crawl the web.

Google's has a program called 'first click free' (see http://support. google.com/webmasters/bin/answer.py?hl=en&answer=74536) which enables publishers to block access to their content after the first click and to require users to sign in or register in order to read further. First click free enables content to be indexed for which users need a subscription.

Only a small proportion of web traffic to newspapers comes from Google News. A much bigger proportion comes via Google's main search index.

Newspaper publishers developed ACAP (the Automated Content Access Protocol) which allows publishers to describe how their online content can be used in a way that the news aggregators' automated indexing crawlers can read. The intention behind ACAP is for rights holders to have more effective control over the ways in which their content can be used online. However, the major search engines and content aggregators have so far declined to adopt ACAP.

2.18 Podcasts

Unlike a webcast, which involves an internet streaming of a live or online simulcast of a broadcast signal, a podcast involves the downloading of an audio program at a time of the choosing of the person accessing the podcast. As such it would be viewed as an 'on-demand' service. This is significant as far as UK copyright law is concerned, because it means that a podcast does not fall within the definition of a broadcast. CDPA 1988 Section 6 – Broadcasts states:

(1) In this Part a "broadcast" means an electronic transmission of visual images, sounds or other information which -
(a) is transmitted for simultaneous reception by members of the public and is capable of being lawfully received by them, or
(b) is transmitted at a time determined solely by the person making the transmission for presentation to members of the public, and which is not excepted by subsection (1A); and references to broadcasting shall be construed accordingly.
(1A) Excepted from the definition of "broadcast" is any internet transmission unless it is -
(a) a transmission taking place simultaneously on the internet and by other means,
(b) a concurrent transmission of a live event, or
(c) a transmission of recorded moving images or sounds forming part of a programme service offered by the person responsible for making the transmission, being a service in which programmes are transmitted at scheduled times determined by that person.

Instead, the component parts of a podcast would be protected individually (such as a sound recording, or a musical work). A podcast would also be protected by the exclusive right of the owner to communicate the work to the public by electronic means.

 There are a number of organizations offering licences for the use of pod-casts. They include:

AIM – the UK Association of Independent Music:
www.musicindie.com/home

ASCAP: www.ascap.com

PRS for Music: www.prsformusic.com/SiteCollectionDocuments/
Online%20and%20Mobile/Podcasting%20Licence%202010.pdf.

➻ Useful resource

Further information:

Out-law.com (2008) *Podcasting – the Legal Issues*, www.out-law.com/
page-7845.

Sutter, Gavin and Gibson, Dr Johanna (2008) Podcasts and the Law, *JISC
Legal*, 2008, www.jisclegal.ac.uk/Portals/12/Documents/PDFs/podcasts.pdf.

Vogele, Colette and Garlick, Mia (2006) *Podcasting Legal Guide – Rules for the
Revolution*, The Berkman Center Clinical Program in Cyberlaw, 7 May,
http://cyber.law.harvard.edu/publications/2006/podcasting_legal_guide.

2.19 Ringtones

Pink Floyd won a high court case (Pink Floyd Music Limited v. EMI Records
Limited (2010) 107(12) LSG 25, [2010] EWHC 533 (Ch)) in which EMI were told
that they couldn't sell single tracks as downloads. The band had a contract in which
there was a clause which prevented the unbundling of their records, in order to
preserve artistic integrity. The judge ruled that EMI can no longer sell the songs
from any Pink Floyd albums as single downloads or as mobile phone ringtones.[20]

2.20 RSS feeds

RSS is an XML format which enables the syndication or sharing of content.

The acronym RSS can stand for a number of different things, such as really
simple syndication or rich site summary. People use web-based aggregation
services to read a collection of RSS feeds from a single web page through an RSS
reader such as Google Reader.

Some websites will have a set of terms and conditions setting out what can and
what can't be done with their content. Where this is the case, it will be a question
of whether this establishes a contract between you and the information provider.
If it does, then it will be governed by contract law rather than by copyright law.
Look out for any legal notices on the site in question. They could, for example, say
something along the lines of the sample wording shown here.

≡ This RSS feed is limited to personal use only. Publishing of this feed in its entirety
for commercial use is strictly forbidden.

I think that the best approach would always be, if in doubt, to ask for permission
to use the feed, and in such a situation to ensure that the permission is given in

writing. Keep a copy of the written permission just in case of a problem arising later on.

It is possible that a website doesn't provide an 'official' RSS feed, but that someone has taken it upon themselves to scrape the site in question in order to create an unofficial RSS feed. I would certainly advise against using a feed of that kind (see Section 3.3 below on scraping). See Checklist 2.1.

The use of RSS feeds on a website also raises a number of other legal issues, such as defamation law. A French court punished web publishers because of snippets of text that appeared on their sites via an RSS reader. The case is believed to be the first time that a website operator has been held responsible for content delivered by a third party's RSS feed.[21]

But in another case covering a similar set of issues – this time a Canadian case – the court took the opposite point of view. The Canadian court said that liability could only exist if the link publisher made any statement relating to the defamatory material itself.[22, 23]

Checklist 2.1 *RSS checklist*

I   Check to see if there is a set of terms and conditions covering use of the RSS feeds.

2   Don't use an 'unofficial' RSS feed which has been generated by scraping someone else's site.

3   If in doubt, ask for permission to use an RSS feed.

4   If you do ask for permission, make sure that you get it in writing and that it is kept safely.

The New York Times Co submitted a DMCA notice which at the time caused the removal of the Pulse RSS reader produced by Alphonso Labs Inc. from the Apple Apps Store.[24] The notice said that the Pulse News Reader app made commercial use of the NYTimes.com and Boston.com RSS feeds, in violation of their terms of use. However, at the time of writing (July 2012), the Pulse RSS reader app was available for purchase on the iTunes App Store at http://itunes.apple.com/us/app/pulse-news-reader/id371088673?mt=8.

2.21   Second Life

Second Life is a 3D virtual world or online virtual universe where people are able to meet and socialize. Even though it is a virtual world, it nevertheless raises a number of real-life intellectual property issues.

Linden Lab are the company behind Second Life. Second Life's terms of use make clear that players retain any and all intellectual property rights in the content they submit to the service. But by submitting content to the service, the terms of service also state, users automatically grant Linden Lab a non-exclusive, worldwide, royalty-free, sublicenseable and transferable licence to use, reproduce, prepare derivative works of, display and perform the content solely for the purposes of providing and promoting the service. Linden Research Inc. has a web page which covers the filing of DMCA notifications and counter-notifications (see http://secondlife.com/corporate/dmca.php). Meanwhile, Second Life's policy on third-party viewers says that developers of third-party viewers must not use or design third-party viewers to infringe intellectual property rights or to promote their infringement; and that they shouldn't encourage, instruct or assist others in using third-party viewers to infringe intellectual property rights (http://secondlife.com/corporate/tpv.php).

In 2006 it was reported that businesses in Second Life were upset about a software program called Copybot which duplicates 'in world' items. The value of goods in Second Life is related to their scarcity; so copying or duplication impacts upon their intrinsic value. Filing a DMCA notice may lead to Linden Lab having to delete copied items, but if an out-of-court financial settlement can't be reached, then a rights owner would be left with the dilemma of whether to file a lawsuit seeking financial compensation for the infringement. It begs the question as to how many people would find it worthwhile suing.

In 2007 there was a Second Life copyright dispute over a sex bed.[25] Kevin Alderman founded a company called Eros to make and sell digital goods in Second Life and one of these products was a SexGen bed, a software application that allows two characters to have sex in the game.

Alderman became aware of similar beds being sold by someone else for less than the US$46 cost of his software, thereby undercutting him and taking his sales. The copies were being passed off as though they were made by his company, using his mark, the SexGen mark. In 2007 Alderman successfully sued some Second Life residents for infringing his online sex wares. Then in 2009 lawyers for Eros LLC filed a federal copyright- and trademark-infringement lawsuit against Linden Lab (www.wired.com/images_blogs/threatlevel/2009/09/linden.pdf).

A library or information service might conceivably buy an island in Second Life which could be used for a number of different reasons, such as to provide reference services, perform user surveys or host public discussions. The virtual objects created by users in Second Life are protected by copyright. If a user copies someone else's content and then displays it on other islands this would raise a number of copyright infringement issues such as copying, or communicating content to the public. If the content is adapted this could also raise moral rights issues where, for example, the copied content involves derogatory treatment of an avatar.

2.22   Social networking sites

Social networks such as Facebook, LinkedIn, and Twitter have become an integral part of many people's personal and professional lives; and they are often the means through which information is shared.

What matters with social networking sites are the site's terms and conditions, because it is these which will govern the use of the site. See for example:

- Twitter: https://twitter.com/tos
- Facebook: www.facebook.com/legal/terms
- LinkedIn: www.linkedin.com/static?key=user_agreement.

People want to share ideas and more and more they are using social networking sites as the means through which to share content.

Links posted to social networking sites such as Facebook could potentially infringe copyright. In 2009, for example, Facebook blocked users of The Pirate Bay website from being able to share links via the social networking site.[26]

There is a real dilemma for people who create content. Imagine that the website you want to post content to has terms and conditions which say that when you post your content to the website you agree to give them the right to use the content in any way that they want to. Imagine, further, that the site is one of the most popular sites on the web. The dilemma is whether to refrain from publishing your content to that site and keep your rights, or else to give up your rights in order to get the exposure that you desperately want.

2.23 Software

Copyright protects an author's original expression in a computer program as a 'literary work' and reformulating a program in a different language as a translation. Source code can thus be viewed as a human-readable literary work, which expresses the ideas of the software engineers who authored it. Not only the human-readable instructions (source code) but also binary machine-readable instructions (object code) are considered to be literary works or 'written expressions,' and, therefore, are also protected by copyright.

It is common commercial practice to keep source code of computer programs as a trade secret in addition to copyright protection. (Trade secrets would come under the law of breach of confidence).

Beyond legal protection, another facet in protecting software is provided by technology itself, such as the use of lockout programs or encryption methods. Thus, technology allows clever producers to craft their own extra-legal protection. For example, a games manufacturer might rely on lockout technology and/or copyright law to protect its object code.

Fair dealing and software
CDPA s. 29(4(a)) It is not fair dealing to observe, study or test the functioning

of a computer program in order to determine the ideas and principles which underlie any element of the program (these acts being permitted if done in accordance with section 50BA (observing, studying and testing)).

50C Other acts permitted to lawful users

(1)   It is not an infringement of copyright for a lawful user of a copy of a computer program to copy or adapt it, provided that the copying or adapting—

(a) is necessary for his lawful use; and

(b) is not prohibited under any term or condition of an agreement regulating the circumstances in which his use is lawful.

(2)   It may, in particular, be necessary for the lawful use of a computer program to copy it or adapt it for the purpose of correcting errors in it.

(3)   This section does not apply to any copying or adapting permitted under section 50A, 50B or 50BA.

There are only a few places in UK copyright law where copyright law cannot be overridden by contract law. The main ones are each the result of EU directives (the Database Directive and the Software Directive). There is a further instance in the CDPA 1988 where contract cannot override copyright. Section 36 entitles educational establishments to undertake reprographic copying of passages from published works up to 1% per quarter, although this is not authorized if, or to the extent that, licences are available authorizing the copying in question.

Section 36(4) prevents people from being able to contract their way out of this provision because it says that 'The terms of a licence granted to an educational establishment authorizing the reprographic copying for the purposes of instruction of passages from published works are of no effect so far as they purport to restrict the proportion of a work which may be copied (whether on payment or free of charge) to less than that which would be permitted under this section'.

As far as software is concerned, the acts which cannot be overridden by contract relate to:

s. 50A   Back-up copies

s. 50B   Decompilation

s. 50BA Observing, studying and testing of computer programs.

CDPA s. 50A Back-up copies

s. 50A

(1)   It is not an infringement of copyright for a lawful user of a copy of a

computer program to make any back up copy of it which it is necessary for him to have for the purposes of his lawful use.

(2) For the purposes of this section and sections 50B and 50C a person is a lawful user of a computer program if (whether under a licence to do any acts restricted by the copyright in the program or otherwise), he has a right to use the program.

(3) Where an act is permitted under this section, it is irrelevant whether or not there exists any term or condition in an agreement which purports to prohibit or restrict the act (such terms being, by virtue of section 296A, void).

(This section was inserted into the CDPA as a result of Statutory Instrument 1992 No. 3233 – The Copyright (Computer Programs) Regulations 1992.)

So in other words, even if someone tries to contract their way out of this obligation, any such provision within a contract would be deemed to be void by a court. It isn't clear the extent to which the making of a back-up copy would be permitted under this section. It all revolves around what is meant by the word 'necessary'. One scenario where I think it would allow a back-up copy to be made is where this is used to restore the software if the original version of the software gets corrupted; because only by making a back-up copy would the person who is legally entitled to use the software be in a position to restore the software so that it continues to work as it should.

50B Decompilation

(1) It is not an infringement of copyright for a lawful user of a copy of a computer program expressed in a low level language –
(a) to convert it into a version expressed in a higher level language, or
(b) incidentally in the course of so converting the program, to copy it, (that is, to 'decompile it'), provided that the conditions in subsection (2) are met.

(2) The conditions are that -
(a) it is necessary to decompile the program to obtain the information necessary to create an independent program which can be operated with the program decompiled or with another program ('the permitted objective'); and
(b) the information so obtained is not used for any purpose other than the permitted objective.

50BA Observing, studying and testing of computer programs

(1) It is not an infringement of copyright for a lawful user of a copy of a computer program to observe, study or test the functioning of the

program in order to determine the ideas and principles which underlie any element of the program if he does so while performing any of the acts of loading, displaying, running, transmitting or storing the program which he is entitled to do.

⊕ SAS Institute Inc. v. World Programming Ltd [2010] EWHC 1829 (and CJEU C-406/10)

SAS is a developer of software which is used to carry out a wide range of data processing and statistical analysis tasks. World Programming Ltd created the World Programming System to meet the demand for an alternative software which could execute programs written in the SAS language. In doing so they emulated the functionality found in the SAS components. The case considered whether functionalities found in a computer program are protected by the software directive. It established that:

1 The protection of a computer program protects the source code and the object code and any other element expressing the creativity of the author.
2 The functionalities of a computer program aren't eligible as such for copyright protection. To conclude otherwise would lead to the monopolization of ideas.
3 It is legitimate to copy a program's functionality and/or a programming language, provided that in reproducing the functionality, the alleged infringer has not reproduced a substantial part of the elements of the original program which are the expression of the author's own intellectual creation.
4 A programming language cannot be protected as such because it is the means which permits the expression to be given (as with the language used by the author of a novel) rather than being the expression itself.

The UK court referred a number of points to the CJEU for clarification. The Advocate General's opinion, published in November 2011, concluded that, subject to two conditions, the holder of a licence to use a computer program may, without the author's authorization, reproduce the program code or translate the form of the code of a data format in that program so as to write, in his own computer program, a source code which reads and writes that data format. First, that operation must be absolutely indispensable for the purposes of obtaining the information necessary to achieve interoperability between the elements of the various programs. Second, that operation must not have the effect of enabling the licensee to recopy the code of the computer program in his own program, a question which it will be for the national court to determine.

In May 2012 the Grand Chamber of the CJEU gave its ruling. It ruled that:

- neither the functionality of a computer program nor the programming language and the format of the data files used in the computer program are protected by copyright.
- a person who has obtained a copy of a computer program under a licence is entitled, without the authorisation of the owner of the copyright, to observe, study or test the functioning of that program so as to determine the ideas and principles which underlie any element of the program, in the case where that person carries out acts covered by that licence and acts of loading and running necessary for the use of the computer program, and on condition that that person does not infringe the exclusive rights of the owner of the copyright in that program.
- the reproduction, in a computer program or a user manual for that program, of certain elements described in the user manual for another computer program protected by copyright is capable of constituting an infringement of the copyright in the latter manual if – this being a matter for the national court to ascertain – that reproduction constitutes the expression of the intellectual creation of the author of the user manual for the computer program protected by copyright.

➕ Microsoft v. Comet

In January 2012 it was reported that the UK electrical retailer Comet was being sued by Microsoft for allegedly creating and selling over 94,000 counterfeit Windows Vista and Windows XP recovery disks. These were sold for £14.99 to customers who had purchased Windows loaded PCs and laptops, netting some £1.4 million gross. ('Microsoft takes legal action against UK retailer Comet', press release 12 January 2012, www.microsoft.com/Presspass/press/2012/jan12/01-04CometPR.mspx.)

2.24 Streaming

Does the live streaming of broadcasts without permission constitute an infringement of copyright?

ITV Broadcasting Ltd & Ors v. TV Catch Up Ltd [2011] EWHC 1874 (Pat)

In July 2011 in the High Court Mr Justice Floyd took the view that TV Catch Up's interception of broadcasts and the making of them available via the internet did constitute a communication to the public and that they were therefore subject to copyright laws. The judge referred to the European Court of Justice the question of whether TV Catch Up's streaming service was indeed a communication to the public.

There is an exception in s73 of the CDPA (on the reception and re-transmission of wireless broadcast by cable) which allows a service such as TV Catch Up to retransmit broadcasts over cable, but not over mobile devices; although s73 would only be a valid defence if the transmission is:

- simultaneous,
- unaltered,
- unabridged,
- to a closed user group,
- through a cable infrastructure, and
- within the territory of the original terrestrial broadcast.

The sports industry has been telling the government of an increasing threat from the unlawful streaming of sports fixtures.

In 2011 UCLA won a court case over DVD streaming. Judge Marshall threw out the case because UCLA, as a state institution, benefits from a doctrine called 'sovereign immunity'. A group (the Association for Information Media and Equipment) representing the copyright owners had initiated the lawsuit, but the judge held that they didn't have standing to sue because they weren't the actual owners of the copyrights in question.[27]

➡ Useful resource

Library Copyright Alliance, *Streaming of Films for Educational Purposes*, 2010, www.librarycopyrightalliance.org/bm~doc/ibstreamingfilms_021810.pdf.

➡ Useful resource

JISC Legal, *Can a College or University Stream Feature Films Through its VLE?*, 2011, www.jisclegal.ac.uk/ManageContent/ViewDetail/ID/2262/Can-a-college-or-university-stream-feature-films-through-its-VLE.aspx.

2.25   Webcasts

A webcast is in effect a broadcast over the internet. They can be distributed either live or on demand. This is significant, because 'on-demand' services do not fall within the definition of a broadcast that appears in the Copyright, Designs and Patents Act 1988.

PRS For Music offers a 'limited online music licence for small online services' which covers organizations or services offering music online to the UK public through downloads, on demand, webcasts (internet radio), and podcasts. There are a number of specific licences[28] within the limited online music licence including:

- limited download/on-demand streaming service
- pure webcasting service
- premium and interactive webcasting service.

There is an interactive webcast (subscription) licence[29] which covers performing and mechanical rights in musical works in interactive webcasting services funded by subscription, as well as another licence for interactive webcasts which aren't funded by subscription.

PRS for Music also have a Limited Manufacture Licence which covers the copyright in the musical work (MCPS) and the copyright in the sound recording (PPL) where these are used in DVDs of voluntary or non-registered charities and community projects, CDs of choirs or orchestras, weddings, funerals, etc.

The European Commission has acknowledged[30] that currently 'Online music services need to duplicate complex clearing processes in order to be available across several territories'. In 2012 the EU are planning to introduce a proposal for a directive on collective rights management which will tackle barriers to cross-border online music licensing.

In the United States of America webcasters pay SoundExchange (for performance rights) and either ASCAP (www.ascap.com, the American Society of Composers, Authors and Publishers), BMI or SESAC (www.sesac.com) for the rights to play musical compositions or musical works (the words and music of the song); although in May 2011 EMI announced that it was withdrawing the licensing of new media from ASCAP and BMI and would instead license these works directly.

In a 2006 American case (SFX Motor Sports v. Robert Davis) US district judge Sam Lindsay in the Northern District of Texas ruled that it was unlawful to provide a hyperlink to a webcast if the copyright owner objects to it.[31]

2.26   Weblogs

According to Blogpulse (which no longer exists, but which used to be located at www.blogpulse.com), there were 181 million blogs on the internet as at December 2011. Technically, it would be easy to copy and paste content from another website onto a blog. However, bloggers do need to be mindful of copyright law when they post content to the web.

A blogger who publishes copyright-infringing content via a blog may be directly liable for that infringement. Where a copyright infringement has taken place the rights owner might file a notice of alleged infringement with the blog hosting site. Rights owners should, however, take care when submitting such a notice. They should consider the copyright exceptions or permitted acts before sending a notice; the notice should be easy to understand and easy to verify; and above all the rights owner should ensure that they are indeed the owner of the rights in the content whose copyrights have allegedly been infringed.

In Lenz v. Universal Music Corp., 572 F. Supp. 2d 2008, UMC had to pay over US$100,000 in costs and attorneys' fees after claiming copyright infringement in content which was protected by the US copyright law doctrine of fair use. The court held that fair use of a copyrighted work is not an infringement, and that for a copyright owner to proceed with a DMCA notice they must first evaluate whether or not the material makes fair use of the copyright.

The reason for saying that rights owners should check that they are indeed the copyright owner is because this can't be automatically assumed to be the case.[32]

Checklist 2.2 *Checklist for bloggers*
Text
- Don't copy the whole, or virtually the whole, of an article from someone else on your blog without permission.
- If you do reproduce someone else's text, make sure that it is an insubstantial part.
- Make sure that you properly acknowledge the source.
- If you are quoting someone else's work in order to be able to comment on that work, ensure that your usage is short on quotation and long on comment and analysis.

Images
- Make sure that you have permission to use an image before copying it to your blog.
- One option would be to use Creative Commons licensed images.
- Another option would be to use royalty-free pictures (see the list of sources for royalty-free pictures in Section 2.15 above).

General advice
- Respect web copyright notices and any copyright statements attached to works.
- Don't just copy the layout of someone else's website.
- If in doubt, ask permission before using someone else's content.
- Bear in mind that information supplied in response to an FOI request may contain third-party content, that the public authority you got the response from may not be the owner of all of the copyrights and cannot therefore give you permission to publish the item on your blog.

In 2008 the Associated Press filed six DMCA takedown notices against the Drudge Retort. These related to quotes of no more than 80 words from Associated Press articles. Company executives at AP decided to suspend the challenge, and were planning instead to create a clear set of guidelines.[33]

At the beginning of 2012 an organization called Newsright (www.newsright.

com) was established, with Associated Press as one of its founding members, to collect fees for the use of their content by bloggers and news aggregators.

In January 2012 the Copyright Clearance Center announced that *The Economist* had chosen Rightslink to handle online copyright permissions on its 20+ blogs. Rightslink is CCC's point-of-content licensing solution.[34]

In February 2011 it was announced that the copyright troll Righthaven were pursuing a blogger, Brian Hill, for copyright infringement for using a picture taken from the *Denver Post*. However, Righthaven dropped the lawsuit against Mr Hill when they were unable to answer his dismissal petition.[35, 36]

Another copyright-related issue that bloggers should be aware of relates to information that they might receive in response to a freedom of information request. Public authorities subject to the Freedom of Information Act 2000 are required to respond to requests based on the information that they hold, regardless of whether or not they are the copyright owner. They could, for example, be in possession of third-party content. As a result, if a public authority provides a response to an FOI request in an electronic format it would be easy to republish it on a blog. But if it contains third-party content, the blogger should first contact the third party in order to get permission to publish the material on his or her weblog.

There are occasions where employees use their personal blogs in a way which brings their employers into disrepute and for which they could face disciplinary sanctions up to and including dismissal. Joe Gordon, an employee of Waterstones, was sacked in 2005 after making critical comments about his boss and the company that he worked for on his personal blog. However, he successfully appealed against the dismissal and was offered reinstatement (www.out-law.com/page-5518). There is even a word for losing one's job as a result of something that you wrote on your blog or website. The word in question is 'dooced'.

2.27 Wikis

Wikis aim to facilitate creativity, collaboration and sharing between users. Where a work is the result of contributions from multiple contributors, the end result may not reflect any specific or identifiable individuals at all. It may be more like a large, accessible wall upon which each of a lengthy procession of passers-by has written a few words, a sort of literary coral reef that has come into being through the gradual accumulation of a myriad of words whose shape and character is determined at any given moment by the nature of the most recent addition of words. Indeed, by the very nature of a wiki it is likely that the individual contribution of each of the multiple authors cannot be detected, or certainly not easily. If the contributions of the respective authors could be separately identified in the final work, then they would be treated as separate works in each of which a separate copyright exists.

The Database Directive defines a 'database' as a 'collection of independent works, data or other materials arranged in a systematic or methodical way and individually accessible by electronic or other means'. This definition may apply to a wiki.

In the case of Wikipedia the text is available under the Creative Commons Attribution-Share Alike License (CC BY-SA). But the legal notice on the site says that additional terms may apply and refers visitors to the site to their terms of use for details (http://wikimediafoundation.org/wiki/Terms_of_use).

➨ Useful resource

When using content from a wiki, it is important to acknowledge or attribute the source. In the case of Creative Commons licensed content, the Open Attribute (http://openattribute.com) plug-in can help to achieve this in the correct manner.

In 2009 the Wikimedia Foundation undertook a survey[37] on attribution.

They asked: 'As an author, which of the following models for giving credit to article authors do you consider appropriate for Wikipedia text, including third party use of Wikipedia content?'

The question asked respondents to rank the answers. The list below shows the first choice for the survey respondents:

Link to the article must be given	32.42%
Collective credit (e.g. Wikipedia community)	24.77%
Link to the version history must be given	11.62%
For online use: link. For other uses: full list of authors	10.19%
No credit is needed	10.40%
Full list of authors must always be copied	6.52%

⊕   G and G v. Wikimedia Foundation Inc. [2009] EWHC 3148 (QB)

(www.bailii.org/ew/cases/EWHC/QB/2009/3148.html)

The case of G and G v. Wikimedia concerned an application to the High Court for a Norwich Pharmacal order against Wikimedia Foundation Inc., the organization responsible for Wikipedia. The purpose of a Norwich Pharmacal order is to compel a third party who is not the alleged wrongdoer but who is in a position to help identify the wrongdoer (see Section 7.5 of this book).

In this case, a mother sought an order to require Wikimedia to disclose the IP address of a person in order to identify them as she was seeking legal remedies to prevent any further breach of privacy or disclosure of confidential information. The person in question had amended an article on Wikipedia and inserted private and sensitive information in relation to her and her child. The applicant suspected that the person who had amended the website was the same individual who had sent her an anonymous communication about the relevant information in an attempt to blackmail her. She also suspected that the person was an employee who was engaged in a dispute with a company with which she was associated. At the end of the hearing Mr Justice Tugendhat made the order that the Respondent disclose the IP information.

➕ National Portrait Gallery v. Derrick Coetzee

In 2009 lawyers acting on behalf of the National Portrait Gallery sent a cease and desist letter to Derrick Coetzee, an American citizen, complaining about him posting several thousand high-resolution images onto the Wikimedia Commons website. The images were of portraits within the Gallery's collections.

The National Portrait Gallery charges people a licence fee in order to make use of the high resolution images, and raises hundreds of thousands of pounds a year from those licences, which is then ploughed back into the project of digitizing their collections. The NPG were concerned that Mr Coetzee's actions would affect the monies raised through this revenue stream.

NPG's lawyers said:

> Clearly visible on every page of our client's website where an image can be seen there is a 'Use this Portrait' menu on which two links are clearly visible:
> 'License this image' and
> 'Use this image on your website'
> If you click on either of these links the first thing that you are told is that you need permission to reproduce our client's images. Your downloading of our client's images and subsequent uploading of those images to the Wikipedia website has therefore been carried out in direct contravention of the clear rules and this amounts to a breach of contract.

Notes and references

1 Oracle accepts a nice round number in damages from Google, The Register, www.theregister.co.uk/2012/06/21/oracle_nothing_in_damages.
2 http://tech.blorge.com/Structure:%20/2010/01/17/flickr-user-gets-in-a-copyright-fight-with-uk-newspaper.
3 www.guardian.co.uk/technology/2010/jan/26/copyright-cory-doctorow.
4 Pirated Audiobook Seller Jailed, *BBC News Online*, 20 November 2008, http://news.bbc.co.uk/1/hi/england/derbyshire/7740412.stm.
5 SI 2011/159 and SI 2007/266.
6 The Copyright (Certification of Licensing Scheme for Educational Recording of Broadcasts) (Open University) Order 2003, SI 2003/187.
7 Amazon Erases Orwell Books from Kindle Devices, *New York Times*, 17 July 2009, www.nytimes.com/2009/07/18/technology/companies/18amazon.html.

8   Department for Media, Culture and Sport (2010) *DCMS Savings Announced,* DCMS news release 066/10, 17 June.

9   Electronic Frontier Foundation (2010) *E-Book Buyer's Guide to E-Book Privacy,* https://www.eff.org/deeplinks/2010/12/2010-e-book-buyers-guide-e-book-privacy.

10 Man Guilty of Illegally Recording in Scottish Cinema, *BBC News Online,* 30 June 2011, www.bbc.co.uk/news/uk-scotland-glasgow-west-13980091.

11 Roxborough, Scott (2011) German Internet Pirate Gets One-Year Suspended Sentence, *Hollywood Reporter,* 21 October, www.hollywoodreporter.com/news/german-internet-pirate-sentenced-251958.

12 Source: IPO website, www.ipo.gov.uk/ipenforce/ipenforce-crime/ipenforce-role/ipenforce-group/ipenforce-workplace/ipenforce-workplace-activity/ipenforce-workplace-activity-staff.htm.

13 Whitworth, Dan (2011) *Gaming Industry lose 'Billions' to Chipped Consoles,* 21 January, www.bbc.co.uk/newsbeat/12248010 BBC Newsbeat.

14 Fildes, Jonathan (2009) Microsoft Disconnects Xbox Gamers, *BBC News Online,* 11 November, http://news.bbc.co.uk/1/hi/8354166.stm.

15 Oates, John (2008) Game Sharer Gets £16K Fine, *The Register,* 19 August, www.theregister.co.uk/2008/08/19/file_sharing_gamer_fined.

16 Masnick, Mike (2008) Who Will be the First Person Sued for Copyright Infringement over Lifecasting, *TechDirect,* 4 November, www.techdirt.com/articles/20081103/1047072724.shtml.

17 Directive 2011/77/EC amending Directive 2006/116/EC on the term of protection of copyright and certain related rights.

18 New Neighbouring Right to be Introduced in Germany, *The 1709 blog,* 6 March 2012, http://the1709blog.blogspot.co.uk/2012/03/new-neighbouring-right-to-be-introduced.html.

19 Google Infringes Copyright When Its Services Link to Newspaper Sites, Belgian Court Rules, *Out-law News,* 10 May 2011, www.out-law.com/page-11911.

20 Pink Floyd Score Victory for the Concept Album in Court Battle over Ringtones, *The Guardian,* 11 March 2010.

21 French Websites Liable for Story in RSS Reader, *Out-Law News,* 18 April 2008, www.out-law.com/page-9058.

22 Linking to Defamatory Material is Not the Same as Publishing It, Says Canadian Court, *Out-Law News,* 28 October 2008, www.out-law.com/page-9538.

23 RSS's Copyright Debate, www.feedforall.com/rss-copyright-debate.htm.

24 Is The New York Times Really Claiming that All Paid RSS Readers Infringe its Copyright?, *Citizen Media Law Project,* 21 June 2010,

www.citmedialaw.org/blog/2010/new-york-times-really-claiming-all-paid-rss-readers-infringe-its-copyright.

25 Second Life Gets its First Copyright Law Suit: sex bed tussle leads to court, *Out-law.com*, 18 July 2007.

26 Facebook Blocks all Pirate Bay Links, *Torrent Freak*, 8 April 2009, http://torrentfreak.com/facebook-blocks-all-pirate-bay-links-090408.

27 http://newsroom.ucla.edu/portal/ucla/document/UCLA_Streaming_Video_Ruling.pdf.

28 www.prsformusic.com/SiteCollectionDocuments/Online%20and%20Mobile/Webcast%20licence%20-%20Scheme%20Summary-BJ200509.pdf.

29 www.prsformusic.com/SiteCollectionDocuments/Online%20and%20Mobile/Interactive%20Webcast%20_SUBS_%20licence%20-%20Scheme%20Summary-BJ200509.pdf.

30 European Union (2011) *A Single Market for Intellectual Property Rights: boosting creativity and innovation to provide economic growth, high quality jobs and first class products and services in Europe*, COM (2011) 287 final.

31 McCullagh, Declan (2006) Can't Link to Webcast if Copyright Owner Objects, *CNET News*, 21 December, http://news.cnet.com/2100-1030_3-6145744.html.

32 See, for example: Lee, Timothy B. (2011) Warner Bros: We Issued Takedowns for Files We Never Saw, Didn't Own Copyright To, *Ars Technica*, November, http://arstechnica.com/tech-policy/news/2011/11/warner-admits-it-issues-takedowns-for-files-it-hasnt-looked-at.ars.

33 Hansell, Saul (2008) The Associated Press to set guidelines for using its articles in blogs, *New York Times*, 16 June, www.nytimes.com/2008/06/16/business/media/16ap.html.

34 *The Economist Chooses Rightslink for Copyright Permissions on its Blogs*, CCC press release, 17 January 2012.

35 Local Blogger Facing Copyright Infringement Lawsuit, *Winston Salem News*, 22 February 2011, www.wxii12.com/news/26956369/detail.html.

36 Righthaven Drops Suit Against Brian Hill, *Righthaven Victims Blog*, 11 April 2011, http://righthavenvictims.blogspot.com/2011/04/righthaven-drops-suit-against-brian.html.

37 Moeller, Erik (2009) *Wikimedia Attribution Survey Results*, for the Wikimedia Community, 6 March, http://upload.wikimedia.org/wikipedia/foundation/9/93/Attribution_Survey_Results.pdf.

CHAPTER 3

Activities

This chapter considers a range of activities undertaken in connection with digital content. These include deep linking; the 'lending' of digital content such as e-books; projects which involve the mass digitization of published works; filesharing; the use of proxy sites; digital preservation; mashups – website applications which use content from more than one source in order to create a completely new service; and scraping or web harvesting – the technique whereby computer software is used in order to extract information from websites. The chapter explores the copyright implications of these activities, and illustrates them with examples of relevant legal cases.

3.1   Deep linking

Hyperlinks are references or pointers that the reader can immediately follow to an electronic document or web page. It could be a link to another place within the same document or site, or to an entirely different document or site.

There are several different types of hyperlinks. 'Shallow links' are links to the home page of a website, whereas 'deep links' are links to a lower level within the website's hierarchy of pages.

What does a deep link consist of, and in what way does copyright law apply? A deep link consists of several elements. For example, the HTML code:

<a href="www.bbc.co.uk/news/uk-16326370"> Christmas shopping sees millions take to streets</a>

consists of:

- the source code of the URL (<a href=www.bbc.co.uk/news/uk-16326370>)
- the pointer text/image (Christmas shopping sees millions take to streets).

Thinking of how copyright applies to deep links, one might argue that the source code of the URL could be protected as a computer program; and that the pointer text or image could be protected as an original literary work. Deep linking could potentially result in legal action being taken on the grounds of copyright infringement, database right infringement, or possibly an action for defamation, trade mark dilution, or passing off.

Hyperlinks don't reproduce the content, they merely facilitate access to it. Nevertheless, it would be prudent for anyone creating deep links to think about the nature of the content that they are linking to; not just in terms of the copyright implications, but the whole range of legal issues that web publishers need to be aware of. And I would recommend that people don't link to content which:

- infringes copyright
- is defamatory/libellous
- is blasphemous
- is obscene
- is an incitement to racial hatred
- encourages terrorist activity.

TorrentSpy was at one time the most popular BitTorrent tracker. It acted as a search engine with links to content rather than as a content host. The MPAA (Motion Picture Association of America) took legal action against TorrentSpy, which faced allegations of contributory copyright infringement or vicarious liability for the allegedly infringing actions of its users. The site subsequently applied a filter known as FileRights which automatically removed offending search links using a database of copyrighted works. It also decided to block access to users in the USA. However, this didn't appease the MPAA, which pursued the matter. The court ruled against Torrentspy, and in 2008 the company was ordered to pay damages of over US$110 million – or US$30,000 x the 3699 infringements listed in the proceedings – to the MPAA for copyright infringement.[1]

In 2008 a French court held sites responsible for linking to material that illegally invaded the privacy of Olivier Martinez, Kylie Minogue's ex-boyfriend. The Paris Tribunal held that by sending the reader to a website (as a result of a hyperlink) the defendant Eric Dupin had in effect made an editorial decision which had contributed to the spread of illicit information and that as editor of the information he was responsible for it. Mr Dupin was fined 1000 euros and ordered to pay a further 1500 euros in costs.[2]

There are a number of points to bear in mind if you create deep links:

1 Be transparent. In other words, make sure that it is clear what you are doing and that you aren't doing anything to mislead other people.
2 Where possible avoid the use of frames technology. If you create deep links to external websites from within a set of 'frames' you could be accused of passing off the external content as though it were your own.
3 Make use of disclaimers. Where deep links on your site point to external websites, it would be advisable to make clear to visitors to your site that the deep links will take people to content on external websites; and also to make

clear that you are not responsible for the content on those sites. On the BBC News website, for example, hyperlinks are grouped under a heading for 'Related internet links' and are accompanied by a note to the effect that 'The BBC is not responsible for the content of external Internet sites'.

Checklist 3.1 *Checklist of things to bear in mind when deep linking*
- Check to see if the site you are linking to has a set of terms and conditions which forbids deep linking
- Be transparent
- Avoid using frames technology
- Include a disclaimer
- Have a robust notice and takedown procedure in place
- Where a website objects to your links remove them promptly.

A compilation of links could be protected as a database. Deep links could potentially infringe the sui generis database right. In Stepstone v. OFIR, Stepstone argued successfully that the job advertisements on its site constituted a database and that OFIR was infringing the rights in the database.

⊕ Newspaper Licensing Agency v. Meltwater and PRCA [2011] EWHA Civ 890

In January 2009 the UK's Newspaper Licensing Agency (NLA) announced it was planning to introduce licences to cover the supply of paid-for online media monitoring services. There are two licences: the web database licence, intended for media monitoring organizations, which would cost an organization like Meltwater an annual fee of £10,000, and the web end-user licence, for the end-users of those monitoring services. Meltwater monitors media websites with a 'spider' computer programme so as to 'scrape' or read the contents of those sites (for the law relating to scraping, see Section 3.3.6 later in this chapter). News aggregators and PR industry reps said that the NLA's attempts to charge them for redistributing news article hyperlinks were 'legally baseless'. A statement signed by Meltwater, NewsNow, the PR Consultants Association (PRCA) and Updatum said: 'The NLA has absolutely no legal basis for demanding that people sign up to this Licence [which] is nothing more than a blatant and unjustified attempt to tax the internet.' Meltwater referred the NLA to the Copyright Tribunal. The reference to the tribunal was made because of the need for clarity as to how copyright laws define and cover online aggregation services. Meanwhile the NLA launched a High Court action in order to get legal clarity on aggregator and end-user licences.

In the High Court[3] the judge was asked to rule on the following issues:

1 *Is a newspaper headline capable of being a free-standing original literary work?*
Mrs Justice Proudman said: 'In my opinion headlines are capable of being literary works, whether independently or as part of the articles to which they relate'.

2 *Does the text extract constitute a 'substantial part' of the article as a literary work?*
'On the basis of Infopaq, the text extract and indeed the text extract excluding the headline . . . are capable of being substantial enough for the purposes of s. 16 (3).'

3 *Do the PRCA and its members need a web end-user licence from the NLA or its members in order to lawfully use and receive Meltwater's service?*
The conclusion reached was that, without a licence, end-users are infringing the publishers' copyright.

Mrs Justice Proudman said 'When an End User clicks on a Link (to) a copy of the article on the Publisher's website which appears on the website accessible via that Link (a copy) is made on the End User's computer.... it seems to me that in principle copying by an End User without a licence through a direct Link is more likely than not to infringe copyright'; and the High Court judgment was upheld in a July 2011 ruling by the Court of Appeal ([2011] EWCA Civ 890).

It is worth bearing in mind:

1 The scale of the use that is being made of the work, because a single end user could well receive (and copy) text extracts from around 50,000 articles in a year.

2 The Publishers have devoted very substantial resources in developing those websites and to the selection, arrangement and presentation of the material on them. Meltwater is making millions of pounds from its own activities, which include 'scraping' the Publishers' websites for information for its own commercial gain.

Source: paragraph 19 of NLA v. Meltwater and PRCA [2010] EWHC 3099 (Ch)

In 2011 the UK Court of Appeal ruled that the material on newspaper websites was protected and that users of clippings services must have a licence from newspaper publishers to click on links taking them to articles on the papers' websites, otherwise they would be infringing the publishers' copyrights.

Meanwhile, the Copyright Tribunal looked at the reasonableness of the terms of the licence (CT114/09).

The Tribunal said:

We believe the [NLA's licence] scheme should have a fixed rate tariff available within it but it should be one which recognises the reality of the paid for [online media monitoring] market. Some licensees under the [NLA's scheme] charge their clients a flat fee regardless of the number of snippets provided. The service provided is not like the hand picked service of a PCA, it is a service in which not every link will be selected and clicked through to the newspaper's website. Many links sent will be irrelevant and so the newspaper is not really losing a customer in such cases.

In May 2012 the Copyright Tribunal issued its final judgment in the case. The decision sees publishers rewarded for the use of their content by third party business-to-business web monitoring companies. The Tribunal also set the 2012 starting price for the web end user licence fixed fee tariff at £100 per annum for new licencees, or £67 per annum for existing licensees. The average fee works out at around £450 per year, although the NLA anticipate that this figure will fall as more small companies take out a licence.

The Tribunal rejected Meltwater's claims that if it operated a 'headline only' service then its customers would not need a licence from the NLA, saying that it was trying to argue a point which it had previously lost – the Court of Appeal had said that headlines were copyrightable.

Meltwater and the PRCA are taking the case to the Supreme Court because they believe that the NLA licence is unfair and unreasonable and that the issue of temporary copies has far wider ramifications than the Court of Appeal appreciated (www.prca.org.uk/PRCA_and_Meltwater_take_NLA_to_Supreme_Court).

In a separate development, Associated Press (AP) announced their intention of suing Meltwater for using its content without permission. In February 2012 AP requested that a New York court force Meltwater to both cease its infringing actions and award damages to AP. Tom Curley, the CEO of Associated Press, has gone on record as referring to Meltwater as a 'parasitic distribution service'.

AP has licensing deals with companies such as Google, Yahoo and AOL. In addition, in January 2012 AP launched NewsRight, a registry aiming to ensure that people pay for use of their content, with AP, the *New York Times*, *Washington Post* and others as founding members; and in March 2012 it was announced that NewsRight has secured its first licensing agreement. Moreover it has entered into a multi-year agreement which gives the right to use content from NewsRight's repertoire of hundreds of newspaper websites.

3.1.1 The 'safe harbour' provisions of the E-Commerce Directive

In the UK, a site called TV Links (tv-links.co.uk) linked to videos found on YouTube, Veoh, DailyMotion and other sites. FACT, the Federation Against Copyright Theft, took legal action against the site. The crown court ruled that the site had not infringed on the copyrights of movie studios, and that it didn't directly infringe on anyone's copyrights.[4]

His Honour Judge Ticehurst took the view that the TV Links site could not be subject to criminal sanctions because of the legislation enshrined in the E-commerce Directive (2000/31/EC) that allows a website to not be liable where it is a mere conduit:

Article 12 "Mere conduit"

1. Where an information society service is provided that consists of the transmission in a communication network of information provided by a recipient of the service, or the provision of access to a communication network, Member States shall ensure that the service provider is not liable for the information transmitted, on condition that the provider:

(a) does not initiate the transmission;
(b) does not select the receiver of the transmission; and
(c) does not select or modify the information contained in the transmission.

2. The acts of transmission and of provision of access referred to in paragraph 1 include the automatic, intermediate and transient storage of the information transmitted in so far as this takes place for the sole purpose of carrying out the transmission in the communication network, and provided that the information is not stored for any period longer than is reasonably necessary for the transmission.

3. This Article shall not affect the possibility for a court or administrative authority, in accordance with Member States' legal systems, of requiring the service provider to terminate or prevent an infringement.

The Directive was implemented in the UK through The Electronic Commerce (EC Directive) Regulations 2002: SI 2002/2013.

The problem is that no matter how strong your case is, if representatives of the entertainment industry pursue you for copyright infringement you are likely to face a huge, costly and time-consuming legal battle. You would be well advised to seek permission to deep link if any of the following circumstances apply to the would-be deep-linked site:

- the website's home page contains a disclaimer, a copyright notice, or a set of terms and conditions with an 'I agree' button and where these are not present on the deep-linked page
- the home page has advertisements that do not appear on the deep-linked page
- the home page makes explicit reference to registered trade marks belonging to the owner of the page.

It boils down to a question of risk management. In order to assess the risk of action being taken against you, imagine that you are the owner of the website you want to deep link to. Ask yourself whether in all honesty you would have any reason to object to the proposed deep link(s).

3.1.2   Does hyperlinking in and of itself constitute publication?

A hyperlink doesn't reproduce the work. Nevertheless, some people are concerned that the mere act of publishing a link to copyright-infringing material on a website could be considered to be an act of copyright infringement.

In the case of Crookes v. Newton 2011 SCC 47 (http://scc.lexum.org/en/2011/2011scc47/2011scc47.html) the Supreme Court of Canada said that authors can't be sued for linking to libellous material.[5] The court ruled that hyperlinking does not constitute publication unless a number of circumstances are satisfied. Only when a hyperlinker presents content from the hyperlinked material in a way that actually repeats the defamatory content should that content be considered to be 'published' by the hyperlinker.

In the UK people often refer back to the 19th-century case Hird v. Wood (1894), 38 S.J. 234 (CA) for guidance on liability for linking to defamatory material. In that case a man pointed to a placard bearing defamatory material and this was held to be sufficient evidence of publication.

The US Bankruptcy Court for the Southern District of Texas said that a man committed defamation by forwarding an e-mail which contained links to defamatory material, that he had 'published' the content under defamation law.[6]

In Government of the United States of America v. Richard O'Dwyer, a student at Sheffield Hallam University, faces the prospect of extradition for maintaining a website containing links to infringing content (see a detailed summary of the case in Section 7.7 below). 'Linking' websites of the kind operated by Mr O'Dwyer catalogue links to files on third-party websites which contain illegal copies of copyrighted content such as movies, TV programmes and music. The website contained a list of the 'Most popular movies today', which were all available for downloading or streaming via links from TVShack.net. The links directed users to a cyberlocker from which the movie or TV programme could be downloaded or streamed. In March 2012 the Home Secretary Theresa May approved the extradition, and gave Mr O' Dwyer two weeks within which to lodge an appeal if he intended to do so. Lawyers acting for Mr O'Dwyer did subsequently lodge an appeal.[7] Mr O'Dwyer could not claim the innocent disseminator or 'mere conduit' defence available in the Electronic Commerce (EC Directive) Regulations 2002 because within a day of receiving a US seizure warrant which seized the domain name 'TVShack.net' he had switched to a new identity 'TVShack.cc' and carried on as before.

3.1.3   Can a deep link infringe copyright?

Twitter regularly receives DMCA takedown notices. At first glance one wonders how it is possible to infringe copyright in no more than 140 characters. Many of these takedown notices consist of copyright holders objecting to tweets which link to their material hosted elsewhere. And sites such as Twitter wishing to benefit from the DMCA's safe harbour provisions are likely to remove the tweets in order to avoid any potential liability for copyright infringement.

In Capitol Records Inc. et al. v. MP3Tunes LLC et al. No. 07 Civ. 9931 (S.D.N.Y. Aug. 24, 2011) the New York district court ruling found that the music website company wasn't responsible for copyright infringement by users of the service posting hyperlinks to infringing content which was hosted elsewhere.

3.2   Mashups

A mashup is a website or application which uses content from more than one source in order to create a completely new service. They often rely on APIs (application programming interfaces) in order to produce results which add value to the raw data sources upon which they rely.

When creating a mashup it is important to be especially careful about taking material from a third-party source without permission because that could well constitute either an infringement of copyright or database right or indeed both.

Database right prevents others from extracting or reutilizing the whole or a substantial part of the contents of a database; and it also prevents other people from being able to systematically and repeatedly extract or reutilize insubstantial parts of the database if the content copied would collectively amount to a substantial part and in doing so that it had prejudiced the substantial investment made by the database owner in the selection and arrangement of the contents of the database.

Mashups wouldn't qualify as fair dealing for the purposes of research or private study if they were accessible to multiple users, because that would be the equivalent of multiple copying. Another problem to bear in mind is that copyright owners have the exclusive right to communicate their work to the public by electronic means.

Library catalogue records can be mashed with other 'mashable' resources such as encyclopedia articles, book covers or book reviews. A JISC Information Paper entitled *Transfer and use of bibliographic records: legal constraints on activities* (JISC, 2009) explores what librarians are legally entitled to do with the bibliographic records which they hold within their institutional library catalogues: www.jisclegal.ac.uk/ Projects/TransferandUseofBibliographicRecords.aspx.

Technological advances have opened up new potential ways for the transfer and aggregation of bibliographic records. The records may be protected by both copyright and by database right. Where bibliographic records are received from other parties they may be covered by a licence agreement or contract. If one asks what the legal constraints are on using the catalogue records, the answer will differ depending upon the nature of the licence agreement in place with the provider of the catalogue records.

There are examples of mashups of library and publisher metadata which involve a data enrichment process. OCLC, for example, offers a metadata service for publishers:

- The publisher or vendor provides title metadata to OCLC in ONIX format.
- Title metadata is automatically added to WorldCat.
- WorldCat data is mined to enrich the publisher or vendor title metadata.
- Enriched ONIX metadata is then delivered back to the publisher or vendor.

The UK government's response[8] to the European Commission's green paper *Copyright in the Knowledge Economy*[9] argued against an exception for mashups:

> The suggestion for an exemption for user-created content seems to create a distinction between those who use and those who create works, which in many cases is not justified . . . Another significant concern is the extent to which such an exemption might allow others to use the works in a way that the existing rights holders do not approve of and the impact that exemptions in this area might have on remuneration.

3.3   Scraping

Scraping, web harvesting or web data extraction takes place when automated software applications known as spiders or bots access websites and scrape content from those sites. It can be used to retrieve the contents of entire back-end databases from other websites. There are companies who offer web scraping or data extraction services or who have produced software which is designed to scrape websites.

There have been a number of legal disputes where scraping has occurred without permission because this activity is potentially illegal on several grounds:

- copyright infringement
- an infringement of database right
- a breach of the website's terms and conditions
- an offence under the Computer Misuse Act 1990
- passing off.

3.3.1   Copyright infringement

In order for website scraping to infringe copyright, it would have to involve the copying of either the whole or a substantial part of a copyright work. Scraping is in effect copying. If the content that is being scraped qualifies for copyright protection, then the scraping of that content will amount to an infringement of copyright.

3.3.2   Database right infringement

Database right gives special protection to databases. A 'database' is defined in The Copyright and Rights in Databases Regulations 1997 (SI 1997/3032) as being 'a collection of independent works, data or other materials which – (a) are arranged in a systematic or methodical way, and (b) are individually accessible by electronic or other means'. Many websites would qualify as being databases under that definition.

In order for database right to be infringed, it would be necessary to show that someone had extracted or reutilized either the whole or a substantial part of the database without the consent of the database owner. (In the Database Directive (96/9/EC) *extraction* means the transfer of the contents of the database to another medium; while *reutilization* means making available to the public the contents of a database.)

3.3.3   Breach of contract

In order for a court to acknowledge that a breach of a website's terms and conditions has taken place, it would be necessary to establish that they created an enforceable contract. The Electronic Frontier Foundation has published (November 2009) a white paper, entitled *The Clicks that Bind: ways users 'agree' to online terms of service* by Ed Bayley, who remarks that:

A clearly presented clickwrap agreement represents the 'best practice' mechanism for creating a contractual relationship between an online service and a user. Such a mechanism should:

1. conspicuously present the TOS [terms of service] to the user prior to any payment (or other commitment by the user) or installation of software (or other changes to a user's machine or browser, like cookies, plug-ins, etc.);
2. allow the user to easily read and navigate all of the terms (i.e. be in a normal, readable typeface with no scroll box);
3. provide an opportunity to print, and/or save a copy of, the terms;
4. offer the user the option to decline as prominently and by the same method as the option to agree;
5. ensure the TOS is easy to locate online after the user agrees.

3.3.4 Computer misuse

If the terms and conditions of the website expressly forbid data mining, it could potentially be an offence under the Computer Misuse Act 1990. The Computer Misuse Act provides for a specific offence in the case of unauthorized access to a computer:

(1) A person is guilty of an offence if– (a) he causes a computer to perform any function with intent to secure access to any program or data held in any computer; (b) the access he intends to secure is unauthorised; and (c) he knows at the time when he causes the computer to perform the function that that is the case.

(2) The intent a person has to have to commit an offence under this section need not be directed at– (a) any particular program or data; (b) a program or data of any particular kind; or (c) a program or data held in any particular computer.

(3) A person guilty of an offence under this section shall be liable on summary conviction to imprisonment for a term not exceeding twelve months or to a fine not exceeding the statutory maximum or to both.

3.3.5 Passing off

The common law tort of passing off is intended to protect the goodwill of a business. Where an individual scrapes someone else's website and proceeds to present the contents as though they were their own, especially if they re-branded it with their own branding, it could result in an action for passing off. Or if the contents of the site which had been scraped were used in a way that falsely implied that there was some sort of association or connection with the person who had scraped the site, this could also be problematic. Scraping could lead to accusations of passing off in cases involving the unauthorized use of a trade mark, or where a website trades on the goodwill associated with another site.

3.3.6 Scraping disputes

Shopping comparison websites facilitate price comparisons between products and services advertised online. They show side by side the prices from a whole range of different merchants for particular products, thereby enabling users of these sites to see at a glance who has the cheapest prices.

Over the years there have been a number of different business models. These include charging for advertising or for sponsored links; charging an inclusion rate to the companies they feature; or getting commission from the service providers each time one of their products or services is sold via the price comparison website. Price comparison websites are popular in the personal finance (e.g. car insurance, home insurance, credit cards or personal loans) and travel industries. They also cover other areas such as gas and electricity suppliers and their various tariffs.

There are a number of different ways in which the price comparison websites can gather the pricing data. They can collect the data directly from merchants; they can collect it through a data feed file which is then imported by the price comparison website; or they can crawl the web for prices. By scanning and 'scraping' online shopping and e-commerce sites for pricing data a price comparison website wouldn't need to rely on the retailers to provide them with the pricing information.

There have been a number of instances where companies have been unhappy at the way in which their sites were being scraped without their direct permission, and in some cases this has led to action through the courts.

In August 2008 Ryanair introduced a new policy which involved the cancellation of any passenger bookings which had been made through sites which had relied on people scraping the Ryanair website. Ryanair's website terms of use (www.ryanair.com/en/terms-of-use) specifically forbid the use of its information for commercial purposes. The terms prohibit screenscraping, except where a third party enters into a written licence agreement directly with Ryanair. The company has taken legal action against firms which have scraped the Ryanair website without permission:

- **Ryanair Ltd v. Bravofly and anor [2009] IEHC 41**, in which Ryanair took the Dutch airline website Bravofly to court over its scraping of the Ryanair website, and they did so on the grounds that this was both an infringement of copyright and also a breach of Ryanair's website terms and conditions. They also alleged 'passing off'. The company sought an injunction to prevent Bravofly continuing to scrape the website.
- **Ryanair Ltd v. Lastminute.com**: in 2008 Ryanair complained to the Advertising Standards Authority over Lastminute.com's scraping and reselling of its flights on the grounds that this was a breach of its website terms and conditions.
- **Ryanair Ltd v. Vtours**: in a German case the Hamburg Regional Court awarded Ryanair an injunction against Vtours preventing Vtours from using information from Ryanair's website to sell flights to Vtours customers.
- **Ryanair Ltd v. Billigfluege.de Gmbh [2010] IEHC 47**, in which the court found that the terms of use on the Ryanair website were legally binding.

⊕ **United States of America v. Aaron Swartz No. 11-cr-01260 (D. Mass. Filed, July 14, 2011)**

In July 2011 Aaron Swartz was charged with computer fraud after downloading the contents of the JSTOR subscription service, consisting of over 4 million articles and reviews. The contents come from some of the most prestigious and indeed expensive scientific and literary journals. Mr Swartz was arrested on a number of felony counts including wire fraud, computer fraud, unlawfully obtaining information from a protected computer and recklessly damaging a protected computer. Potentially he could face up to 35 years in prison and US$1 million in fines. The federal case against Mr Swartz was still continuing at the time of writing (July 2012). [10]

➕ Century 21 Canada Limited Partnership v. Rogers Communications Inc. 2011 BCSC 1196

Century 21 Canada sought an injunction and damages against the defendants for their conduct in accessing Century 21's website and copying photographs and real estate listings data from that website without consent for display on a competitor website.

The court held that browse wrap agreements (where the website user is not forced to indicate their acceptance of the terms and conditions displayed) can be valid enforceable contracts, and that the defendants breached the terms of use by scraping content contrary to those terms. The judgment explains that 'a browse wrap agreement does not require that the purchaser indicate their agreement by clicking on an "I Agree" button. All that is required is that they use the product after being made aware of the product's Terms of Use'.

The Supreme Court of British Colombia granted nominal damages for breach of the website's terms of use and awarded statutory damages in favour of the individual plaintiffs for copyright infringement; but the court dismissed the claim for trespass to chattels.

In January 2012 the news registry NewsRight was launched by 29 US news organizations, led by Associated Press. The organization licenses digital content and it has been set up in order to help its member organizations to track the use of their content by bloggers and news aggregators. NewsRight has technology in place to track the use of its members' content by bloggers and web scrapers.

The case of Newspaper Licensing Agency v. Meltwater has already been described in Section 3.1 of this book.

There is a product called ASSASSIN (Automated Assessment Anti Scraping Surveillance Network) which was specially built for Yell.com by IT security specialist Sentor, who also have a product called Scrapesentry (www.scrapesentry.com) and maintain a website which deals with data scraping issues (http://blockscraping.com).

One way of trying to deal with data scraping is the use of data seeding. This involves seeding the data with easily identifiable records in order to be able to trace where the data ends up, and also to help prove that it was your data that has been copied. Especially helpful is the use of a telephone number or an address over which you have control, because if these are used it will alert you to when someone has been using your data without permission.

3.4 Rental and lending

There is a European directive on rental and lending: Council Directive 2006/115/EC on rental right and lending right and on certain rights related to copyright in the field of intellectual property. Article 2 of the Directive defines 'rental' and 'lending':

- 'Rental' means making available for use, for a limited period of time and for direct or indirect economic or commercial advantage.
- 'Lending' means making available for use, for a limited period of time and not for direct or indirect economic or commercial advantage, when it is made through establishments which are accessible to the public.

The Directive (which was previously numbered 92/100/EEC) was implemented in the UK through the Copyright and Related Rights Regulations 1996 (SI 1996/2967).

The owner of the copyright in a work has the exclusive right to rent or lend the work to the public. It is listed in s. 16(1) of the CDPA 1988 as being one of the copyright owner's economic rights and this is set out in more detail in s. 18A of the Act:

18A Infringement by rental or lending of work to the public
'(1)   The rental or lending of copies of the work to the public is an act restricted by the copyright in -
(a) a literary, dramatic or musical work,
(b) an artistic work, other than -
(i) a work of architecture in the form of a building or a model for a building, or
(ii) a work of applied art, or
(c) a film or a sound recording'.

In Vereniging van Educatieve en Wetenschappelijke Auteurs (VEWA) v. Belgische Staat (CJEU C-271/10) the European Court of Justice said that organizations that loan or rent copyrighted material available to the public should have to pay compensation based upon the harm that it does to the rights holders. This calculation should be based upon the number of copyright-protected works that organizations make available and the number of people who are able to access them.

There are a couple of UK copyright exceptions relating to the lending of material. Section 40A of the CDPA says that copyright in a work of any description is not infringed by the lending of a book by a public library if the book is within the public lending right scheme; while s. 36A says that copyright in a work is not infringed by the lending of copies of the work by an educational establishment. The exception for educational libraries doesn't specify that the material to be loaned is hard-copy only, and as such does extend to digital content, although a lot of digital material will have been made available under a licence agreement and where that is the case it will be a matter of checking what the licence says about lending of the content. The exception for public libraries specifies that the material can be lent if it is covered by the public lending right scheme. The problem is that the public lending right scheme doesn't currently cover any digital content.

3.4.1   Public lending right scheme

Public libraries are entitled to loan out **books** because they are covered by public lending right (PLR), which was established in the United Kingdom through the Public Lending Right Act 1979. Authors who register with the public lending right scheme are able to receive payments which are based on the numbers of loans in sample libraries. In order to qualify for payment, applicants are required to apply to register their books with the Public Lending Right Office. Registration is currently restricted to books which are 'printed and bound'. It doesn't currently cover electronic content such as e-books or audiobooks.

The Public Bodies Act 2011 gives government ministers the power to abolish the PLR organization and to transfer the management of the scheme to another public body. The government does intend to abolish the Public Lending Right Office as a quango and for its functions to be taken over by another public body. In May 2012 DCMS published a consultation on proposals to transfer PLR funding and functions (www.culture.gov.uk/consultations/9019.aspx). The options considered included: transferring the function of distributing public lending right funds to the Authors Licensing and Collecting Society; to Arts Council England; to the British Library; to administer the distribution from within DCMS; or to continue with the arrangements in their current form.

PLR payments are made annually on the basis of loans data collected from a sample of public libraries in the UK.

Public libraries are covered by the Music Publishers Association *Code of Fair Practice*, which accepts that lending of **printed music** happens (see www.iaml.info/en/activities/copyright/survey/uk_and_ireland).

The problem is that the public lending right scheme doesn't currently cover **digital content**, which means that if public libraries wanted to lend out digital content they would normally need to enter into licence agreements with the rights owners.

Sound recordings are not covered by public lending right. As a result public libraries entered into an agreement which was signed on 7 January 1994 between the British Phonographic Industry (now British Recorded Music Industry) and the Library Association (now CILIP). Under the BPI/LA Agreement libraries are entitled to hold no more than three copies of a recording per branch; and no lending is permitted until three months after the release date.

In July 2009 DCMS published a *Consultation on the Extension of Public Lending Right to Rights Holders of Books in Non-print Formats*, which sought views on policy proposals to:

- extend eligibility for PLR to non-print books, in particular audiobooks and e-books
- extend PLR to the lending rights holders in respect of these non-print works where they are not currently eligible under the PLR Scheme.

Expanding the PLR Scheme to include new types of works and new types of rights holders would require a consequential expansion to the 'infringement exemption' under the CDPA 1988 and would thus remove the possibility of enforcement of lending rights by rights holders against lending libraries for newly eligible works; i.e. it would remove the need for libraries to obtain consent for lending of the newly eligible works. In exchange for this expanded 'exemption', the Scheme would be required to remunerate the rights holders of newly eligible works where such rights holders were eligible and registered with the Scheme.

Under the proposals set out in the consultation, the categories of publications eligible for PLR would have been extended to include non-print books – i.e. works which are primarily based on an authored text – whether experienced aurally or visually. The consultation was undertaken with specific formats in mind:

- Hard copy audiobooks – primarily CDs;
- Soft copy audiobooks – digital audio files (e.g. MP3) provided to library-users either as a download, for licensed short-term access or loaded on appropriate hardware (e.g. MP3 player); and
- E-books – digital files as above, but to be read rather than heard. This may include image-based, as well as text-based books such as graphic novels.

In their response to the consultation paper,[11] the government made clear that it believed it was important to extend PLR to non-print formats:

- to keep libraries relevant to users in the digital age
- to reward authors and creators.

In 2009 the government's proposals were to extend PLR to digital files, although remote downloads (files downloaded outside library premises) would not have been eligible for PLR payment; and to extend PLR to all rights holders. In 2010 the Digital Economy Act was passed, and in view of the government's intentions regarding PLR, s. 43 of the DEA does make provision for public lending of electronic publications. However, while we do now have primary legislation which would permit the extension of PLR to e-books and audio books, the problem is that there has been no secondary legislation to bring s. 43 into force.

Indeed, in June 2010 the DCMS announced that the extension of the public lending right to non-print format books was being suspended as part of the government cutbacks. It had been estimated that this would have involved an additional £300,000 per year in costs.

3.4.2 Lending of e-books

Librarians have been frustrated by a number of issues connected to e-books, such as:

- lending restrictions
- device incompatibilities
- proprietary systems
- interface issues
- privacy concerns.

Nook, Kobo and Sony Reader users can borrow e-books from libraries, while Amazon has also launched an e-book lending service for the Kindle e-reader, enabling Kindle users to check out and read e-books from over 11,000 American libraries.[12] Meanwhile Afictionado has a UK subscription 'lending' (i.e. rental) service[13] and Bilbary (http://uk.bilbary.com) are planning to charge 20% of a book's retail price for a 30-day loan.

OverDrive, a leading player in the library e-book market, has over 15,000 partner libraries sharing thousands of e-books and audiobooks everyday. In 2011 NewsCorp subsidiary HarperCollins set a checkout limit of 26 for each e-book that was licensed through OverDrive, after which the e-book would expire unless libraries paid additional fees to relicense the title. This move proved to be highly controversial and led a number of US librarians to boycott HarperCollins titles.

In October 2010 at the CILIP PLA conference in Leeds Stephen Page, chief executive of Faber, speaking on behalf of the Publishers Association, set out a baseline position on e-books which had been agreed amongst major publishing houses. It included a ban on remote downloading, requiring instead the library user to go to the library premises in order to download the e-book.

In August 2011 Nottinghamshire Public Libraries became the first UK library service to charge for e-book loans (www.thebookseller.com/news/notts-libraries-to-charge-e-book-loans.html). Adults can borrow five e-books from Nottinghamshire libraries for loan for periods of between 1 and 21 days at a cost of £1 per book.

3.4.3 Textbook rental services

A number of companies such as Chegg, Bookrenter, Barnes & Noble and Bookswim have been providing textbook rental services in America for some time now. The market for textbook rental is still evolving, as are the business models. Services offered include rental of a hard-copy edition of the textbook which is posted back to the rental company at the end of the rental period. However, in 2011 Amazon introduced a service for US students to be able to rent textbooks for use on their Kindle e-readers.

There are a number of companies in the UK offering textbook rental services, such as Acadreamia and Blackwells. In April 2011 the Publishers Association announced that having sought preliminary legal opinion they were advising providers of textbook rental services that they should first ensure that they have gained the explicit permission of the relevant rights holders before they rent out works. The PA advised that rental schemes be put on hold until the requisite permissions have been confirmed. The PA had become increasingly concerned by textbook rental schemes which hire out textbooks to students, but which may not have secured permission from the original rights holder or publisher to do so. Where textbook rental schemes hire out textbooks to students for which they haven't secured the permission of the rights owner or publisher to do so, their actions are open to challenge under the CDPA 1988, ss 16 (The acts restricted by copyright in a work) and 18A (Infringement by rental or lending of work to the public).

⊕ GEMA v. RapidShare AG Higher Regional Court of Hamburg 14 March 2012

In this case, textbook publishers won a court ruling against a filesharing website. A German court ruled that RapidShare, a filehosting or cyberlocker site, must do more to stop the unauthorized swapping of some copyrighted books on its service. The Landgericht in Hamburg, a district court, issued a preliminary ruling against RapidShare in February 2010 prohibiting the company from making available certain copyrighted books on its site.

Six major publishers (Bedford, Freeman & Worth; Cengage Learning; Elsevier; the McGraw-Hill Companies; Pearson; and John Wiley & Sons) brought the legal action against RapidShare, and they specified a list of 148 titles that are frequently pirated on the site. The list of works covered under the court order includes a number of textbooks. Rapidshare say that they quickly remove any copyrighted material that users post to the service once officials become aware of it; but to install filters that check each work for copyright infringement would violate strict German privacy laws.

The court ruling said the company must go further: 'It is not only necessary to promptly block access to the specific file, but rather to also take precautions going beyond this in order to prevent to the largest possible extent the occurrence of further similar infringements.' The court said it would issue fines of up to 250,000 euros (about US$340,000) or jail sentences for company executives of up to two years per instance that a specified book is present on the filesharing site.

In February 2012 it was reported that RapidShare has deliberately slowed its download speed for non-registered users. This was done in order to make the service unattractive to pirates who have turned to it in the wake of the high-profile closure of Megaupload.

3.5 Mass digitization

Copyright or other IPR restrictions are one of the reasons why people don't digitize content. Indeed a 2006 survey[14] found that copyright was the most frequent hindrance to public access.

In order to digitize content which is still within copyright it is important to ensure that you have the necessary permission to digitize. To obtain permission for thousands of works as part of a mass digitization project, which involves locating many different copyright owners, can be both time-consuming and expensive. Digitization can be incredibly costly. The costs involved include:

- the costs of preservation of the orphan work
- the costs of conducting a diligent search
- the copyright clearance fee.

In the context of mass usage of rights, transaction costs can be high for users who need to seek multiple permissions.

Barabara Stratton, in her research in 2011,[15] found that it took an average of four hours per book to undertake a 'diligent search', and that this time covered clarifying the copyright status of the work, identifying the rights holder and requesting permissions. This was by way of contrast with the period of less than five minutes per title required when using the ARROW system to upload the catalogue records and check the results.

Copyright is automatic. It doesn't require the owner of the rights to go through a formal registration process. As soon as a work is created, it will automatically qualify for copyright protection provided that it is original and that it is in a fixed format. That is true across the board, regardless of whether or not there is an intention to sell the work commercially and whether it is the manuscript for a book, a letter, an e-mail, a Powerpoint presentation, and so on, provided that it is original and fixed, and fits into one of the categories of works that the law protects (a literary work, an artistic work, a dramatic work, or a musical work, a sound recording, film or broadcast). The corollary of copyright being an automatic right is that there isn't a comprehensive central register of copyright owners. Indeed, if there were a compulsory register, it would contravene the Berne Convention.

If libraries make the digitized content widely available, then by definition the content becomes highly visible not only to potential users of that material, but also to the rights owners, and, as such, the digitization of content without permission which is subsequently made available for anyone to access on the internet is high-risk.

There have been a number of high-profile legal cases relating to the unauthorized digitization of content on a large scale. These include the Google Book Search project (see Section 7.10 of this book), which Georgia Harper[16] says is 'arguably the grandest of the grand mass digitization projects', and the HathiTrust case (see Section 7.10).

3.5.1   Europeana

The European Digital Library, known as Europeana, aims to give access to all of Europe's digitized cultural heritage by 2025.[17] One of the biggest barriers to this goal's being achieved is the intellectual property barrier to digitization. To ensure that access to 20th- and 21st-century material is achieved, more concerted efforts are needed at a European level to deal with orphan works and rights harmonization.

> **➡ Useful resource**
> The European Digital Library, known as Europeana:
> www.theeuropeanlibrary.org.
> The Comité des Sages of the European Commission engaged the help of
> The Collections Trust in order to assess the overall financial cost of digitizing
> Europe's cultural heritage.[18] The report concluded that the estimated cost
> of digitizing the total collections of Europe's museums, archives and libraries,
> including the audiovisual material they hold, is approximately 100 billion euros.
> The figure includes the digitization of 77 million books, 24 million hours of
> audiovisual programmes, 358 million photographs, 75.43 million works of art
> and 10.45 billion pages of archives. However, the Comité says that it does
> not have the ability, competencies or means to assess the accuracy of the
> numbers.

The European Commission brokered an agreement which was published in September 2011 as a *Memorandum of Understanding on Key Principles on the Digitisation and Making Available of Out-of-Commerce Works* in which libraries, publishers, authors, and their collecting societies agreed to a set of principles that will give European libraries and similar cultural institutions the possibility of digitizing and making available on line out-of-commerce books and learned journals which are part of their collections. This Memorandum is an essential part of the efforts of stakeholders and of the Commission to address the needs of mass digitization by European cultural institutions

Out-of-commerce works are works that are still protected by copyright but are no longer available in customary channels of commerce. The MoU deals specifically with books and learned journals. The Key Principles contained in the MoU will encourage and underpin voluntary licensing agreements to allow cultural institutions to digitize and make available online these type of works while fully respecting copyright.

➻ Useful resource

The Memorandum of Understanding on Key Principles on the Digitisation and Making Available of Out-of-Commerce Works,
http://ec.europa.eu/internal_market/copyright/docs/copyright-infso/20110920-mou_en.pdf.
and the accompanying set of FAQs:
MEMO/11/619 of 20 September 2011 *Memorandum of Understanding on Key Principles on the Digitisation and Making Available of Out-of-Commerce Works – frequently asked questions*,
http://europa.eu/rapid/pressReleasesAction.do?reference=MEMO/11/619.

3.5.2   British Library digitization project

In June 2011 the British Library announced[19] a major project to digitize 250,000 books, pamphlets and periodicals, representing up to 40 million pages, in order to make them available for all. But on further examination the project specifically relates to out-of-copyright books from the Library's collections covering the period 1700–1870, from the French Revolution to the end of slavery. Once digitized these items will be available for full-text search, download, and reading through the British Library website and through Google Books.

In May 2010 the British Library announced a partnership between the Library and online publisher brightsolid, owner of online brands including findmypast. co.uk and Friends Reunited. The ten-year agreement involves the mass digitization of up to 40 million historic pages from the BL's national newspaper collection, with a minimum of 4 million pages digitized over the first two years. In the case of in-copyright content, this is scanned following negotiation with rights holders.

3.5.3   Wellcome Library

The Wellcome Library has embarked on a major programme to create a new digital library, starting with a collection of approximately 1700 books on the history of modern genetics, many of which are in copyright and often out of print. Identifying rights holders to enquire whether their works can be digitized and made available is a problem which besets any mass digitization project. To help overcome the problem of identifying rights holders and enquiring whether their works can be digitized, ALCS and PLS have entered into a collaborative arrangement with the Wellcome Library to provide an innovative rights owner identification service using the ARROW (Accessible Registries of Rights Information and Orphan Works) system.

➨ Useful resource

Hirtle, Peter, Hudson, Emily and Kenyon, Andrew (2009) *Copyright and Cultural Institutions : guidelines for digitization for US libraries, archives and museums,* Cornell University Library.

3.6   Sharing of passwords

In 2009 the London *Financial Times* sued private equity firm Blackstone Group for sharing an FT.com login between multiple users.

In 2010 data provider Ipreo sued Goldman Sachs for alleged copyright infringement. Ipreo alleged that at least two Goldman Sachs employees illegally accessed its Bigdough contacts and profiles database more than 200 times.

In 2011 one survey respondent of a FreePint copyright survey[20] said 'When there are massive downloads by single users the vendors get in touch with us.' I wouldn't recommend waiting until a vendor got in touch with you to alert you to high levels of usage. It would be better to be proactive and to monitor usage data for key products. Otherwise you could find that a supplier decides to cut off your access to content on the grounds that your organization has breached the terms of the contract.

Checklist 3.2 *Checklist for complying with licence terms regarding the use of passwords*
- Make clear when giving out passwords that they must not be shared.
- Remember that rights owners may well monitor usage of the service in order to detect where userIDs have been shared.
- If there is a 'Remember me' log in facility enabling you to be logged in automatically to the service, don't enable this feature if the computer may be used by anyone other than you.
- Ensure that for each online product you have access to usage data.
- Monitor the usage data regularly.
- If the usage by a particular individual seems unusually high, arrange for their password to be changed and remind the person concerned that the licence agreement doesn't allow the password to be shared.

3.7 Proxy sites

A proxy server acts as an intermediary for requests from clients who want to access content from another server. Associated Newspapers, the owners of the London *Daily Mail*, issued a cease and desist order against IstyOsty, a proxy site which didn't link back to the *Mail*, and threatened to demand payments of US$150,000 for each cached story in the event that the proxy site didn't comply.[21]

3.8 Filesharing

There are a number of ways in which people access infringing content. These include peer-to-peer (P2P) filesharing, illegal MP3 sites, MP3 search engines, or links to content held in cyberlockers.

3.8.1 Penalties for illegal filesharing

Two cases summarized here illustrate the penalties that may be incurred for infringement of copyright by filesharing.

⊕ **The Pirate Bay case**

The founders of The Pirate Bay website were found guilty of copyright violations and they were given jail sentences as well as being ordered to pay 30 million Swedish kronor (£2.4 million) damages. When the founders appealed both the damages and the jail sentences a Swedish appeals court did reduce their jail terms but increased the fines to around the equivalent of £4.1 million. They then filed for a hearing of their case at the Supreme Court which upheld the prison sentences of the four founders: Peter Sunde (8 months), Fredrik Neij (10 months), Carl Lundstrom (4 months) and Gottfrid Svartholm (1 year).

Both the operators of The Pirate Bay website and its users were held to be guilty of infringing the copyright of music industry rights owners by the UK High Court (Dramatico Entertainment Ltd & Ors v. British Sky Broadcasting Ltd & Ors [2012] EWHC 268 (Ch) 20 February 2012). In his ruling Mr Justice Arnold said 'The matters I have considered in relation to authorisation lead to the conclusion that the operators of TPB induce, incite or persuade its users to commit infringements of copyright, and that they and the users act pursuant to a common design to infringe'.

On 30 April 2012 the High Court issued orders requiring five ISPs (Sky, Everything Everywhere, TalkTalk, O2 and Virgin Media) to block access to The Pirate Bay filesharing website. BT had been included in the application by the BPI but had asked for more time to consider its response and wasn't therefore included in the original blocking order, although they did subsequently block access to the Pirate Bay website.[22]

➕ Anne Muir case

In 2011 a woman from Ayr became the first person in Scotland to be convicted of illegally sharing music online. Anne Muir admitted distributing £54,000 worth of copyright-protected music files via a peer-to-peer file sharing application. Strathclyde Police searched Muir's home address and seized her computer equipment. They discovered 7493 digital music files and 24,243 karaoke files. Muir was found guilty of contravening s. 107(1)(e) of the Copyright, Designs and Patents Act 1988 and sentenced to three years' probation.

The website YouHaveDownloaded (www.youhavedownloaded.com) shows what people behind an IP address have downloaded using torrent networks. It has details of such information for over 50 million users.

3.8.2 Tactics of lawyers acting in filesharing cases

In August 2011 the Solicitors Regulation Authority announced that two solicitors, Mr Miller and Mr Gore, had been fined £20,000 each and suspended for three months by the Solicitors Disciplinary Tribunal for sending intimidating letters to people about illegal filesharing. The solicitors were also ordered to pay interim costs to the SRA of £150,000. The breaches related to conduct between 2006 and 2009, when, on behalf of various clients, over 6000 letters were sent to individuals claimed to have been involved in unlawful filesharing in breach of the CDPA 1988. The letters demanded compensation and costs and warned that recipients faced further action and increased costs if the matter was not settled as a matter of urgency. An investigation by the Solicitors Regulation Authority (SRA) found that the concerns of those who had received letters and protested their innocence were disregarded. The Solicitors Disciplinary Tribunal found, in effect, that Mr Miller and Mr Gore became too concerned about making the scheme profitable for themselves and their firm. Their judgment became distorted and they pursued the scheme regardless of the impact on the people receiving the letters and even of their own clients.

In January 2012 the Solicitors Disciplinary Tribunal suspended Andrew Crossley (of the defunct law firm ACS:now) from acting as a lawyer for two years and ordered him to pay over £76,000 in costs. He had used 'speculative invoicing' to receive cash settlements from alleged file sharers.

What with speculative invoicing and shakedown schemes, a number of companies seem to work on the basis that people will pay up just to get rid of the threat of legal action, even though in a number of cases people swear that they are innocent.

Enforcement action against filesharers has become a technological arms race where copyright infringers or 'pirates' swiftly move on to using other technologies in order to circumvent any bans on access to content which in turn require internet service providers to find other technologies to combat those used by the pirates.

➕ Imperial Enterprises, Inc. v. Does 1-3,545

Lawsuits were filed against thousands of alleged infringers, many of whom were accused of downloading and sharing adult films. This case, in which anti-piracy lawyers accused a blind man of downloading porn, demonstrates the problem of identifying copyright infringers purely on the basis of an IP address: it doesn't automatically follow that the infringer will be one and the same person in whose name the account is held.

In May 2011 Doe number 2057 received a letter from Comcast informing him that Imperial Enterprises had filed a lawsuit against him for illegally downloading and sharing one of their adult titles and that they were demanding a few thousand dollars as settlement. But Doe 2057 is legally blind. He isn't able to watch movies; and as his children are only four and six years old, they aren't likely to watch porn either. According to Doe 2057, one of his neighbours must have used his open Wi-Fi connection to grab the file. Like many other defendants, Doe 2057 chose to pay the money demanded by Imperial Enterprises simply to get them off his back. There is absolutely no guarantee that a judge would have held him liable for the alleged infringement, but he took into account the fact that paying for a lawyer would have incurred costs whether or not a court might find him to be guilty, whereas by paying the plaintiff the matter would be settled.

➕ Danish filesharing case

In 2008 two Danish women were taken to court by Antipiratgruppen for music filesharing. Initially they were sent letters demanding around 21–23,000 euros compensation each. But when they claimed that they had not been the authors of the infringements, the anti-piracy group took them to court because they were of the view that an internet subscriber is responsible for what is done on their internet connection. The women did not deny that unauthorized filesharing had taken place on their internet connections, but they stated clearly that they were not the ones who had carried it out. Instead, they claimed that their Wi-Fi connections must have been piggybacked by someone without their knowledge. Being unaware of the alleged infringements, they believed they shouldn't pay any damages. The court agreed and acquitted the women on all charges. Both the First City Court and then the Eastern Regional High Court ruled that the plaintiff has the burden of proof, rather than the women being expected to prove that they had not shared music with others.[23]

3.8.3   Cyberlockers

Cyberlockers are online services which allow users to store and share large files. Examples include Rapidshare, Scribd, Hotfile, Mediafile, and Megaupload. Cyberlocker sites generate many billions of visits or hits each year. In order to stay on the right side of the law these sites need to respond promptly to takedown notices from rights holders. The Publishers Association's Copyright Infringement Portal lists the companies or organizations which have responded best and those which have responded worst to takedown notices. As at January 2012, Rapidshare, Hotfile and several other cyberlocker sites were amongst the best respondents to takedown notices.

In a court filing in November 2011 Warner Brothers admitted that they had issued takedown notices for files on the cyberlocker site Hotfile without looking at them first.[24]

3.8.4   Inadvertent filesharing

According to Thomas D. Sydnor II,[25] there are a number of features in filesharing programs which cause users to share files inadvertently:

- redistribution features, causing users to upload all files that they download;
- share folder and search-wizard features, which can cause users to share infringing files as well as sensitive personal files (such as tax returns or financial records);
- partial uninstall features that leave behind a file which causes any subsequent installation of any version of the same program to share all folders shared by the 'uninstall' copy of the program;
- coerced sharing features, which make it difficult for users to disable sharing of the folder used to store downloaded files.

The way in which some filesharing software packages work makes it difficult for users to control the software settings in a way that reflects their wishes, and as such they can end up sharing files inadvertently, where the sharing takes place without their knowledge or active consent.

3.9   Selling digital content second-hand

In January 2012 an American start-up called Redigi found itself in trouble for selling digital music tracks second-hand. The digital music tracks had been downloaded legally.

There is a principle in copyright law known as the 'exhaustion of rights' which does allow an *original* copy of something to be resold. However, this legal principle, which is enshrined in US copyright law as the 'first sale doctrine', wouldn't cover the scenario involved in the Redigi case, because in order to transmit the digital files from one person to another it would involve the making of a *copy*, and it is this that breaches the rights holder's copyright. In any case, the copyright issues are academic if the lawfully downloaded music was obtained under a set of terms and conditions, because to sell a copy second-hand could well breach the terms of the contract. The iTunes T&Cs, for example, clearly state that music is licensed to users on a purely personal and non-commercial basis.[26]

In the last few years there have been a number of articles about people leaving details of their passwords in their wills, so that when they die the digital assets that they have built up are not lost.[27]

There are even digital legacy companies which will look after your online assets in the event of your death. They work on the basis that you nominate a person to whom your passwords will be given when you die.

My question would be whether the terms and conditions of the social networking, music downloading, or photosharing sites, or sites that offer cloud computing services allow the ownership of your digital assets to be transferred.

Think about the digital assets with a financial value that you have, and who would you like to leave them to when you die, including:

- bank account
- ISA
- digital music collection
- paid for 'apps'
- online subscriptions.

3.10 Preservation and digital curation

In 2011 the Association of Research Libraries published *Digital Preservation: SPEC Kit 325*,[28] which was based on a survey of ARL member libraries. The survey found that all of the libraries preserved some digital content. That included licensed materials such as e-journals and databases as well as still images, electronic theses, moving images and audio materials. Some of the libraries preserved research datasets and geospatial data or managed web-harvested material. All of the institutions responding to the ARL survey collected administrative metadata covering areas such as access privileges, rights and ownership of the material; and almost all made use of multiple schemas such as Dublin Core, Qualified Dublin Core or METS[29] to describe their digital collections.

In the UK, academic researchers, funders and institutions support a number of data centres.[30] These organizations take on responsibility for supplying research data to the academic community, as well as collecting and storing that data. Data centres also have a role in the curation and preservation of datasets, ensuring long-term access to research data.

Criteria used to select which content to concentrate efforts on include local scholarly use (research needs, user needs, etc.), investment level (purchased content, digitization projects, etc.), and risk factors (uniqueness, rarity, condition, etc.). A number of institutions use digital surrogates for fragile materials that preclude handling of the originals.

In terms of preservation strategies, institutions are migrating to archival quality formats such as XML. They are concentrating on a small number of formats in which they can have confidence that the content won't become a victim of technological obsolescence.

➻ Useful resource

LOCKSS (Lots of Copies, Keep Stuff Safe), www.lockss.org, provides libraries with digital preservation tools and support so that they are able to easily and inexpensively collect and preserve their own copies of authorized e-content.

➻ Useful resource

CLOCKSS (Controlled LOCKSS): www.clockss.org/clockss/Home. Content which is no longer available from any publisher is available for free. CLOCKSS uniquely assigns this abandoned and orphaned content with a Creative Commons Licence in order to ensure that it remains available permanently.

3.11   Common myths

Table 3.1 sets out some commonly held beliefs about copyright in electronic data and contrasts them with the reality.

Table 3.1 *Common myths about copyright in electronic data*

Myth	Reality
Everything on the world wide web is in the public domain.	'Publicly accessible' is not the same thing as being in the 'public domain'. The term 'public domain' refers to material which is not protected by copyright.
It's on the internet, so I have an implied licence to copy.	In some instances there may be an argument to be made that you have an implied licence to copy (such as where the site includes buttons to print, e-mail to a friend, etc.); but it would be very dangerous to work on the basis that there is always an implied licence to copy. Every case of copyright infringement has to be looked at on the basis of the specific facts involved in that particular instance.

Table 3.1 *Continued*

Myth	Reality
It's okay because I acknowledged the source.	It is important to give credit for your use of someone else's work by properly attributing them as the source. But attribution doesn't automatically mean that you won't have infringed copyright. All it guarantees is that you aren't a plagiarist, because you have admitted where you obtained/'nicked' it from.
If no copyright symbol appears on the work, then it's not in copyright.	Copyright protection is automatic, as soon as a work has been created it will be protected and no formalities are required. So copyright owners don't have to register their rights, nor do they have to put a copyright symbol onto the work; although it might be sensible to do so in order to remind everyone that the work is protected by copyright. It is true that the Universal Copyright Convention requires the © symbol to be present in order for people to benefit from the rights set out in that Convention, but it is irrelevant because every country signed up to the UCC is also signed up to the Berne Convention (apart from Cambodia, and Cambodia are required to abide by the Berne Convention by virtue of their membership of the World Trade Organization).
It's alright to copy because the database is on the web and it only consists of names and addresses.	A collection of names and addresses could potentially be protected by database right.
It's okay because I am not charging people.	If you were charging people, a court could require you to provide an account of the profits made as a result of the copyright infringement. But the mere fact that you aren't charging people doesn't mean you aren't infringing copyright.
Changing a work by 10% avoids liability for infringement.	There isn't a foolproof rule along these lines. Every instance of copying has to be considered based on the facts relevant to that particular instance of copying. It doesn't necessarily have to be a direct replication of the original work in order to qualify as a copyright infringement.

Notes and references

1   TorrentSpy Ordered to Pay US$110m, *BBC News Online*, 8 May 2008, http://news.bbc.co.uk/1/hi/7389485.stm.

2   French Sites Fined for Linking to Privacy-Invading Content, *Out-law News*, 10 April 2008, www.out-law.com/page-9038.

3   The High Court case was Newspaper Licensing Agency v. Meltwater & PRCA [2010] EWHC 3099. The subsequent Court of Appeal case was [2011] EWCA Civ 890.

4   Masnick, Mike (2010) UK Court Finds that Simply Linking to Infringing Videos is not Infringing, *Techdirt*, 15 February, www.techdirt.com/articles/20100212/1549298157.shtml.

5   Authors Can't Be Sued for Linking to Libellous Material, *PaidContent*, 19 October 2011, http://paidcontent.org/article/419-court-authors-cant-be-sued-for-linking-to-libelous-material.

6   Links to Defamatory Content in Email Made Sender Liable, Says US Court, *Out-law.com*, 9 June 2010, www.out-law.com/page-11092.

7   'Richard O'Dwyer case: lawyers lodge extradition appeal', BBC News Online, 22 March 2012, www.bbc.co.uk/news/uk-england-south-yorkshire-17472142.

8   www.ipo.gov.uk/c-eupaper.pdf.

9   European Commission (2008) *Copyright in the Knowledge Economy,* Green Paper, COM(2008) 466/3.

10 State Drops Charges Against Swartz; Federal Charges Remain, *The Tech*, 16 March 2012, http://tech.mit.edu/V132/N12/swartz.html.

11 Department for Media, Culture and Sport (2009) *Government Response to the Consultation on the Extension of Public Lending Right to Rights Holders of Books in Non-Print Formats*, November.

12 Kindle Connects to Library e-Books, *New York Times*, 22 September 2011, www.nytimes.com/2011/09/22/books/amazons-kindle-to-make-library-e-books-available.html?_r=1.

13 Page, Benedicte (2011) Afictionado Plans Subscription Lending Service, *The Bookseller*, 14 September, www.thebookseller.com/news/afictionado-plans-subscription-lending-service.html.

14 Bultmann, Barbara et al. (2006) Digitized Content in the UK Research Library and Archives Sector, *Journal of Librarianship and Information Science,* **38** (2), June.

15 Stratton, Barbara (2011) *Seeking New Landscapes: a rights clearance study in the context of mass digitization of 140 books published between 1870 and 2010*, British Library Board.

16 Harper, Georgia K. (2008) *Mass Digitization and Copyright Law, Policy and Practice*.

17 European Commission (2011)*The New Renaissance: report of the Comité des Sages,* http://ec.europa.eu/information_society/activities/digital_libraries/doc/refgroup/final_report_cds.pdf.

18 Poole, Nick (2010) *The Cost of Digitising Europe's Cultural Heritage: a report for the Comité des Sages of the European Commission*, The Collections Trust, November 2010, http://ec.europa.eu/information_society/activities/digital_libraries/doc/refgroup/annexes/digiti_report.pdf.

19 http://pressandpolicy.bl.uk/Press-Releases/The-British-Library-and-Google-to-make-250-000-books-available-to-all-4fc.aspx.

20 FreePint (2011) *Copyright Policies and Practices 2011,* FreePint Research Report, http://web.freepint.com/go/shop/report/1796.

21 Lunden, Ingrid (2011) Daily Mail Proxy Site IstyOsty Goes Down after Cease and Desist Order, *PaidContent*, 16 August, http://paidcontent.co.uk/article/419-daily-mail-proxy-site-istyosty-goes-down-after-cease-and-desist-order.

22 See www.bbc.co.uk/news/technology-17894176; and The Pirate Bay says BT block already breached', BBC News Online, 20 June 2012.

23 Danish File-Sharers Not Responsible for Wi-Fi Theft, TorrentFreak, 6 September 2008, http://torrentfreak.com/danish-file-sharers-not-responsible-for-wi-fi-theft-080906.
A Huge Legal System Defeat for IFPI, Denmark, Could Create a Precedent in Europe, Aom3, 9 June 2008, www.aom3.org/forum/f5/huge-legal-system-defeat-ifpi-denmark-could-2698.html.
Victims of WiFi Theft Not Responsible for Illegal Uploads, TorrentFreak, 9 July 2008, http://torrentfreak.com/victims-of-wifi-theft-not-responsible-for-illegal-uploads-080709.

24 Lee, Timothy B. (2011) Warner Bros: *We Issued Takedowns for Files We Never Saw, Didn't Own Copyright To*, Ars Technica, November, http://arstechnica.com/tech-policy/news/2011/11/warner-admits-it-issues-takedowns-for-files-it-hasnt-looked-at.ars.

25 Sydnor, Thomas D. II, Knight, John and Hollaar, Lee A. (2006) Filesharing Programs and 'Technological Features to Induce Users to Share', US Patent and Trademark Office, www.uspto.gov/ip/global/copyrights/cpright_filesharing_v1012.pdf.

26 Law Will Not Permit Sale of Second-Hand MP3's, Says Expert, *Out-law.com*, 13 January 2012.

27 'Digital Legacies' Lost as People Omit Passwords from Wills, *Daily Telegraph*, 30 March 2011, www.telegraph.co.uk/technology/internet/8415771/Digital-legacies-lost-as-people-omit-passwords-from-wills.html.
McGuinness, Ross (2012) What Happens to Your Online Life After You

Die? *The Metro*, 11 March,
www.metro.co.uk/news/newsfocus/892795-what-happens-to-your-online-
life-after-you-die.

28 McMillan, Gail et al. (2011) *Digital Preservation: SPEC Kit 325*, Association of
Research Libraries.

29 *Metadata Encoding and Transmission Standard*, www.loc.gov/standards/mets.

30 Research Information Network (2011) Data Centres: their use, value and
impact, JISC, September 2011, www.rin.ac.uk/data-centres.

CHAPTER 4

The copyright exceptions

4.1   Introduction

The owner of the copyright in a work has a number of exclusive rights. These are set out in s. 16 of the CDPA 1988. They are the right:

- to copy the work (see CDPA s. 17);
- to issue copies of the work to the public (see s. 18);
- to rent or lend the work to the public (see s. 18A);
- to perform, show or play the work in public (see s. 19);
- to communicate the work to the public (see s. 20);
- to make an adaptation of the work or do any of the above in relation to an adaptation (see s. 21).

To do any of these things without permission would constitute a primary infringement of copyright. That 'permission' could be gained by approaching the copyright owner directly, but it could also be in the form of one of the copyright exceptions or permitted acts which are set out in the CDPA 1988.

There are around 50 exceptions in the legislation (see Table 4.1, which is a list I have manually put together covering most of the exceptions contained within the CDPA 1988; it is not comprehensive). They include four fair dealing exceptions (fair dealing for non-commercial research, fair dealing for private study, fair dealing for news reporting, and fair dealing for criticism or review); two exceptions for visual impairment; seven educational exceptions; and a series of exceptions covering public administration.

Table 4.1 *Copyright exceptions or permitted acts in the CDPA 1988*

Section	Exception or permitted act
28A	Making of temporary copies
29(1)	Fair dealing for the purposes of research for a non-commercial purpose
29(1C)	Fair dealing for the purposes of private study
30(1)	Fair dealing with a work for the purpose of criticism or review

Continued on next page

Table 4.1 *Continued*

Section	Exception or permitted act
30(2)	Fair dealing for the purpose of reporting current events
31(1)	Incidental inclusion in an artistic work, sound recording, film or broadcast
31A	Making a single accessible copy for personal use
31B	Multiple copies for visually impaired persons
31C	Intermediate copies (for the purposes of the production of further accessible copies)
32(1)	Things done in the course of instruction or preparation for instruction
32(3)	Things done for the purposes of an examination
33	Anthologies for educational use
34	Performing, playing or showing work in course of activities of educational establishment
35	Recording by educational establishment of broadcasts
36	Reprographic copying by educational establishments of passages from published works
36A	Lending of copies by educational establishments
38	Copying by librarians: articles in periodicals
39	Copying by librarians: part of published works
40A	Lending of copies by libraries and archives
41	Copying by librarians: supply of copies to other libraries
42	Copying by librarians or archivists: replacement copies of works
43	Copying by librarians or archivists: certain unpublished works
44	Copy of work required to be made as condition of export
45	Parliamentary and judicial proceedings
46	Royal Commissions and statutory inquiries
47	Material open to public inspection or on official register
48	Material communicated to the Crown in course of public business
49	Public records
50	Acts done under statutory authority
50A	Back-up copy of a computer program
50B	Decompilation of computer programs
50BA	Observing, studying and testing of computer programs
50C	Making a copy or adapting a computer program
50D	Acts permitted in relation to databases
51	Design documents and models

Table 4.1 *Continued*

Section	Exception or permitted act
57	Anonymous or pseudonymous works – acts permitted on assumption as to expiry of copyright or death of the author
59	Public reading or recitation
60	Abstracts of scientific or technical articles
61	Recordings of folksongs
62	Representation of certain artistic works on public display
63	Advertisement of sale of artistic work
64	Making of subsequent works by same artist
65	Reconstruction of buildings
66	Lending to public of copies of certain works
66A	Films – acts permitted on assumptions as to expiry of copyright
68	Permitting incidental recording for the purposes of making a broadcast
70	Recording for purposes of time-shifting
72	Free public showing or playing of broadcast
73	Reception and re-transmission of wireless broadcast by cable
75	Permitting recording of broadcasts for the purposes of placing them in an archive
171 (3)	The public interest – 'Nothing in this part affects any rule of law preventing or restricting the enforcement of copyright, on grounds of public interest or otherwise'.

The UK's copyright legislation doesn't contain a clear and unequivocal statement that the exceptions or permitted acts apply in both a print and a digital context and the current copyright legislation doesn't adequately reflect the digital environment. Both the Gowers Review[1] of 2006 and the Hargreaves Review[2] of 2011 put forward a series of recommendations to try to address this issue that would, if implemented, introduce a number of new exceptions and changes to existing exceptions in order to make copyright law more fit for purpose in the digital age (Chapter 8 is devoted to the Hargreaves Review).

In the light of the Hargreaves Review's recommendations, the government in 2011 published a *Consultation on Copyright*,[3] which argues that there should be a significant opening up of the copyright exceptions. If the recommendations in the 2011 consultation paper are implemented, it would result in the copyright exceptions being opened up to the maximum degree permitted within EU law. The proposals include allowing limited private copying, widening the exception for non-commercial research, widening the exception for library archiving and introducing an exception for parody and pastiche.

The Copyright Directive (2001/29/EC) tried to harmonize copyright law across the EU. It singularly failed to do so, not least because of the way in which it dealt with the copyright exceptions, treating them as though they were 'pick and mix'. In the Directive there is only one mandatory exception that all member states are required to implement, and that relates to the making of copies which are temporary or transient (see Section 4.3 below).

Article 5 of the Copyright Directive sets out a series of exceptions and limitations to the reproduction right and the right of communication to the public that are available to member states. It works on the basis that each country can look through the list of available exceptions and decide which ones they would like to implement. When the Directive came into force, member states were required to ensure that the exceptions that they already had in place could be fitted within that list. Any that didn't fit would either have to be amended so that they could be slotted into the options available, or else would have to be removed. So, in effect, member states were presented with an exhaustive pick-list from which they could select which exceptions they wanted; but they couldn't add to the list of available exceptions.

Digital content is often governed by a licence agreement or a set of terms and conditions. As such, rights owners are currently able to use contract law to override the copyright exceptions. This point was certainly something that Ian Hargreaves had in mind when putting together his recommendations for changing the copyright exceptions, because it is clear from the Hargreaves report that he didn't want new exceptions to be introduced only to find that they were rendered worthless by copyright owners using licences to determine what an information user could do with the content.

One measure proposed in the 2011 *Consultation on Copyright* relates to how the government is planning to introduce a clause applying to every exception provided by the Copyright Act which would make clear that any contract term purporting to prohibit or restrict the use of an exception is unenforceable.

Some exceptions, including those for education and disabled people, explicitly permit licensing of the acts covered by them. In such instances the government is planning to consider separately the merits of these licensed exceptions and, to the extent to which they are preserved, any licensing scheme explicitly authorized by an exception will not be affected by the contract override clause (see Table 4.1).

4.2   Berne three-step test

The Berne Convention of 1886 is the main international instrument governing copyright throughout the majority of the world. At the time of writing (July 2012), 165 countries were signed up to the Convention. Article 9(2) of the Berne Convention contains a 'three-step test', which mandates that copyright exceptions or limitations shall:

- be confined to certain special cases;
- not conflict with a normal exploitation of the work; and
- not unreasonably prejudice the legitimate interests of the right holder.

The precise form of words to be found in the Convention is: 'It shall be a matter for legislation in the countries of the Union to permit the reproduction of such works in certain special cases, provided that such reproduction does not conflict with a normal exploitation of the work and does not unreasonably prejudice the legitimate interests of the author.' Substantially the same form of words can be found in Article 5 of the Copyright Directive (2001/29/EC). The significance of this is that UK copyright law can only contain exceptions or permitted acts which meet those three tests.

4.3   Temporary or transient copies

In the Copyright Directive (2001/29/EC) there is only one mandatory exception which all member states are required to implement. It relates to the making of temporary copies. This was implemented in the UK through s. 28A of the CDPA 1988.

> **28A Making of temporary copies**
> Copyright in a literary work, other than a computer program or a database, or in a dramatic, musical or artistic work, the typographical arrangement of a published edition, a sound recording or a film, is not infringed by the making of a temporary copy which is transient or incidental, which is an integral and essential part of a technological process and the sole purpose of which is to enable –
> (a)   a transmission of the work in a network between third parties by an intermediary; or
> (b)   a lawful use of the work;
> and which has no independent economic significance.

The following cases illustrate the application of this provision.

⊕ 4.3.1 Infopaq International A/S v. Danske Dagblades Forening, Case CJEU C-5/08, 16 July 2009

The Infopaq case looked at what constitutes a transient copy. The court ruled that:

> An act occurring during a data capture process, which consists of storing an extract of a protected work comprising 11 words and printing out that extract, is such as to come within the concept of reproduction in part within the meaning of Article 2 of Directive 2001/29/EC of the European

Parliament and of the Council of 22 May 2001 on the harmonisation of certain aspects of copyright and related rights in the information society, if the elements thus reproduced are the expression of the intellectual creation of their author; it is for the national court to make this determination.

The act of printing out an extract of 11 words, during a data capture process such as that at issue in the main proceedings, does not fulfil the condition of being transient in nature as required by Article 5(1) of Directive 2001/29 and, therefore, that process cannot be carried out without the consent of the relevant rightholders.

In order for an act of copying to qualify as temporary or transient, all five of the conditions set out in article 5(1) of Directive 2001/29 have to be met:

1 The act is temporary
2 It is transient or incidental
3 It is an integral and essential part of a technological process
4 The sole purpose of that process is to enable a transmission in a network between third parties by an intermediary of a lawful use of a work or protected subject-matter, and
5 The act has no independent economic significance.

To qualify for the exemption as being temporary or transient would require that the copies were deleted promptly from the computer memory without the need for human intervention. This wasn't established in the Infopaq case because the content was routinely being printed out, and it would have required human intervention in order for the printout copies to be destroyed, and as such it didn't qualify as being temporary or transient.

4.3.2 Newspaper Licensing Agency v. Meltwater & PRCA

In the Meltwater case (already considered in Section 3.1 of this book), Mrs Justice Proudman rejected the temporary or transient defence, saying that the whole point of the receipt and copying of Meltwater News was to enable the end-user to receive and read it. Making the copy wasn't an essential and integral part of a technological process but was instead the end which the process was designed to achieve. As such, storage of the copy and the duration of that storage was entirely within the control of the end-user. Since the copy is the very product for which the end-user is paying Meltwater, the copy does have an independent economic significance (see paragraph 109 of the High Court judgment [2010] EWHC 3099 (Ch)).

In the subsequent Court of Appeal case, counsel for the PRCA argued that the judge had taken too narrow a view of the section.

Looking back at the Copyright Directive, recital 33 sets out what the compulsory exception relating to the making of temporary or transient copies was intended to cover:

> The exclusive right of reproduction should be subject to an exception to allow certain acts of temporary reproduction, which are transient or incidental reproductions, forming an integral and essential part of a technological process and carried out for the sole purpose of enabling either efficient transmission in a network between third parties by an intermediary, or a lawful use of a work or other subject-matter to be made. The acts of reproduction concerned should have no separate economic value on their own. To the extent that they meet these conditions, this exception should include acts which enable browsing as well as acts of caching to take place, including those which enable transmission systems to function efficiently, provided that the intermediary does not modify the information and does not interfere with the lawful use of technology, widely recognised and used by industry, to obtain data on the use of the information. A use should be considered lawful where it is authorised by the rightholder or not restricted by law.

The Court of Appeal held that the temporary or transient exception does not apply. Paragraph 35 of the Court of Appeal's 2011 judgment states:

> As is clear from a consideration of recital 33 as a whole, the reference to 'browsing' is 'to the extent that they meet these conditions'. 'They' refers to the acts of reproduction. The acts of reproduction are those occasioned by the voluntary human process of accessing that webpage. Accordingly, they fail to satisfy any of the conditions to which recital 33 refers. S.28A does not provide even a limited defence to the claims of infringement to which the business of Meltwater is likely to give rise.

In other words, the exception doesn't apply to any on-screen copy and possibly also to further copies where these are generated as a result of a voluntary human process (as opposed to being the result of a technological process).

The UK Supreme Court has granted permission (UKSC 2011/0202) to the Public Relations Consultations Association Ltd to appeal against the Court of Appeal decision in The Newspaper Licensing Agency Ltd & Others v. Meltwater Holding BV & Others [2011] EWCA Civ 890. The PRCA's appeal is on the question of whether the act of accessing a web page (and the inevitable copies made in doing so) is covered by the temporary copies exception (as set out in Article 5(1) of the Copyright Directive and s. 28A of the CDPA 1988).

4.4   Commercial purpose

The term 'commercial purpose' is not defined in the CDPA 1988. Ultimately the European Court of Justice has the final say, because the phrase appears in our legislation as a result of the Copyright Directive 2001/29/EC and the Database Directive 96/9/EC.

The test is whether the research is for a commercial purpose, not whether it is done by a commercial organization. The law cannot expect you to do more than decide what is the case on the day you ask for the copy to be made. In the wording of the exceptions for fair dealing and for library privilege there is mention of non-commercial purpose:

29 Research and private study
(1) Fair dealing with a literary, dramatic, musical or artistic work for the purposes of research for a *non-commercial purpose* (my italics) does not infringe any copyright in the work provided that it is accompanied by a sufficient acknowledgement.
(1C) Fair dealing with a literary, dramatic, musical or artistic work for the purposes of *private study* (my italics) does not infringe any copyright in the work.

The wording of the private study exception doesn't mention the purpose of the copying within the section 29 exception, but it is clear that copying for the purposes of private study must be non-commercial because tucked away in section 178 on minor definitions it makes clear that 'private study' does not include any study which is for a commercial purpose, whether directly or indirectly. It says:

'private study' does not include any study which is directly or indirectly for a commercial purpose;

38 Copying by librarians: articles in periodicals
(1) The librarian of a prescribed library may, if the prescribed conditions are complied with, make and supply a copy of an article in a periodical without infringing any copyright in the text, in any illustrations accompanying the text or in the typographical arrangement.
(2) The prescribed conditions shall include the following –
(a) that copies are supplied only to persons satisfying the librarian that they require them for the purposes of –
(i) research for a *non-commercial purpose*, or
(ii) *private study*,
and will not use them for any other purpose;

39 Copying by librarians: parts of published works

(1) The librarian of a prescribed library may, if the prescribed conditions are complied with, make and supply from a published edition a copy of part of a literary, dramatic or musical work (other than an article in a periodical) without infringing any copyright in the work, in any illustrations accompanying the work or in the typographical arrangement.

(2) The prescribed conditions shall include the following –

(a) that copies are supplied only to persons satisfying the librarian that they require them for the purposes of –

(i) research for a *non-commercial purpose*, or

(ii) *private study*,

and will not use them for any other purpose;

The case of HMSO v. Green Amps considered the meaning of 'commercial purpose'.

⊕ **HM Stationery Office v. Green Amps Ltd [2007] EWHC 2755 (Ch)**

During his holidays a student worked for Green Amps Ltd and when he departed, he left behind his username and password on Green Amps' computers, which were subsequently used at an English university by Green Amps in order to access the Ordnance Survey DIGIMAP product for their own purposes. The company down-loaded digital maps for the whole of Great Britain in three formats, namely 1:25,000 scale Colour Raster, 1:50,000 scale Raster and Land-Form Panorama, without per-mission from the claimants and without payment. The annual licence fees for a single computer terminal for these products would have exceeded £16,000.

Green Amps argued that the use was for non-commercial research purposes. However, the court held that the defence failed because the act concerned must be for the purposes of non-commercial research whereas Green Amps had used the DIGIMAP product in the process of developing a commercial product.

The judge cited Copinger,[4] which says that presumably any research which, at the time it is conducted, is contemplated or intended should be ultimately used for a purpose which has some commercial value will not be within the permitted act.

4.4.1 'Commercial' in the context of Creative Commons licensed content

The Creative Commons publication *Defining 'Non-commercial'*,[5] which was published in September 2009, considers how internet users understand the terms 'commercial use' and 'non-commercial use' when they are used in the context of content found online. Creators take a variety of factors into account when determining what constitutes non-commercial use. These factors are often considered on a case-by-case basis. Page 31 of the study lists a series of qualitative research consideration factors:

- perceived economic value of the content
- the status of the user as an individual, an amateur or professional, a for profit or not for profit organization, etc.
- whether the use makes money (and if so, whether revenues are profit or recovery of costs associated with use)
- whether the use generates promotional value for the creator or the user
- whether the use is personal or private
- whether the use is for a charitable purpose or other social or public good
- whether the use is supported by advertising or not
- whether the content is used in part or in whole
- whether the use has an impact on the market or is by a competitor.

4.5   Fair dealing

There are four different exceptions relating to fair dealing:

- fair dealing for non-commercial research
- fair dealing for private study
- fair dealing for news reporting
- fair dealing for criticism or review.

In an electronic context, fair dealing for research or private study is of limited use in a number of regards:

1 Rights owners have the exclusive right to communicate their work to the public by electronic means.
2 The exceptions would only justify the making of a single copy, and would not cover the making of multiple copies or their equivalent. So it wouldn't cover publishing to a shared resource such as an intranet, a shared drive or the world wide web.
3 Fair dealing for research doesn't currently extend to sound recordings, films or broadcasts.

Consultation on Copyright (IPO, 2011) acknowledges that the UK does not currently have a copyright exception that permits educational establishments, libraries, archives or museums to make works available for research or private study on their premises by electronic means even though such an exception is permitted by the Copyright Directive. The consultation paper says that 'The Government does not currently know the level of demand for such an exception, or its costs and benefits, but will consider the merits of introducing such an exception based on evidence gathered through this consultation.'

4.6   Library privilege – archiving and preservation

There is an exception in s. 42 of the CDPA 1988 which covers copying for preservation purposes. However, s. 42 is only available to 'prescribed libraries', and so it would only be of benefit to libraries in not-for-profit establishments such as public libraries, national libraries, parliamentary and government libraries, and the libraries of educational establishments. (The types of library which would be considered to be prescribed libraries is set out in schedule 1 of The Copyright (Librarians and Archivists) (Copying of Copyright Material) Regulations 1989: SI 1989/1212.)

Not only that, the exception for prescribed libraries is currently of limited value because:

- it doesn't cover sound recordings, films or broadcasts
- it only covers artistic works to the extent that they are illustrations accompanying a literary, dramatic or musical work
- there is a limit of ONE on the number of copies that can be made
- it doesn't permit format shifting.

The Gowers Review (2006) made two recommendations on preservation:

1 Recommendation 10a: Amend s.42 of the CDPA by 2008 to permit libraries to copy the master copy of all classes of work in permanent collection for archival purposes and to allow further copies to be made from the archived copy to mitigate against subsequent wear and tear.
2 Recommendation 10b: Enable libraries to format-shift archival copies by 2008 to ensure records do not become obsolete.

The Hargreaves Review (2011) recommends extending the archiving or preservation exception. In paragraph 5.34 of the review it says:

We have noted too that libraries are inhibited in preserving content through digitisation, that they cannot preserve all categories of works and that as a result, works continue to deteriorate. This makes no sense and it should be uncontroversial to deliver the necessary change by extending the archiving exception, including to cover fully audio visual works and sound recordings. Supporting the potential of new technologies for archiving will prevent the loss of works, and could open the way to new services based on digital use of those archives. We may well find that this public digital archive turns out to have considerable economic as well as social and cultural value, but this will not happen if our cultural institutions are prevented from securing it through digitisation.

In the December 2011 *Consultation on Copyright* the IPO set out how the government plans to take this and other amendments to the copyright exceptions forward. The government is proposing to expand the section 42 exception to enable libraries to:

* preserve sound recordings, artistic works, films and broadcasts
* make multiple copies.

And it is also planning to allow museums and galleries to benefit from this exception.

A new exception is also being proposed which would enable people to copy creative content for private, non-commercial use. This will be made future-proof by being technology-, format- and platform-neutral, permitting private copying of any type of copyright work to any type of device or medium.

4.7 Visual impairment

If a visually impaired person has lawful possession or lawful use of a copy of the whole or part of a literary, dramatic, musical or artistic work or a published edition it isn't an infringement of the copyright in the work for an accessible copy to be made for his or her personal use. This exception only applies where a copy in a suitable format isn't commercially available. The copy must clearly state that it was made under the provisions of the Act, and the source must be clearly acknowledged. However, the section does not apply if the master copy is a database or part of a database, and the making of an accessible copy would infringe copyright in the database.

The Copyright (Visually Impaired Persons) Act 2002 doesn't currently cover films, DVDs and other audio visual products. And because of the way in which the Database Directive (96/9/EC) is worded it wouldn't be possible to extend the exceptions for the benefit of visual impairment to databases without amending that Directive.

The CDPA 1988 as amended does stipulate that where there is a technical measure in place protecting the content any copy should have the same or an equally effective protection mechanism in place. In the exception on the making of multiple copies for visually impaired persons, s. 31(B)(8) says:

> If the master copy is in copy-protected electronic form, any accessible copy made of it under this section must, so far as it is reasonably practicable to do

so, incorporate the same, or equally effective, copy protection (unless the copyright owner agrees otherwise).

The existing exceptions do not benefit all groups of people who are unable to access works due to their disability – such as dyslexic people. Nor do the exceptions apply to all works; for example, they do not cover audio description of films.

The government proposes to expand the UK's exceptions that benefit people with disabilities to take greater advantage of the opportunities offered by the EU framework. It believes that the key principle underpinning these exceptions is that they should only apply to the extent that accessible copies are not available commercially, and the government does not intend to alter this approach.

The consultation paper proposes that the existing disability exceptions should be amended in order to ensure that more people are able to benefit from them. It also proposes to expand the types of work covered by the disability exceptions.

4.8   The public interest

In Fraser v. Evans [1969] 1 QB 349 the defendant had made public some papers which he was given access to, in confidence, by the Greek government. Lord Denning remarked that copyright infringement could not be held in a 'matter of public concern', and 'only making a fair comment in public interest'. So the key issue to determine is whether the release of the documents was indeed in the public interest. Section 171(3) of the CDPA 1988, entitled 'Rights and privileges under other enactments or the common law', says:

> Nothing in this part affects any rule of law preventing or restricting the enforcement of copyright on grounds of public interest or otherwise.

It is only in very rare circumstances that a defendant raises public interest grounds in order to defend themselves against an action for copyright infringement.

In Lion Laboratories v. Evans [1984] 3 WLR 539 there had been a publication of an internal memo which criticized the accuracy of breathalysers sold by the claimant. The defendant raised the public interest defence on the grounds that investigations should be made regarding the accuracy of the equipment to avoid incorrect readings when used by the police on motorists. The three members of the Court of Appeal all accepted this defence.

4.9   Educational exceptions

Sections 32–36A of the CDPA 1988 contain seven educational exceptions:

32(1)   Things done in the course of instruction or preparation for instruction
32(3)   Things done for the purposes of an examination

33   Anthologies for educational use
34   Performing, playing or showing work in course of activities of
          educational establishment
35   Recording by educational establishment of broadcasts
36   Reprographic copying by educational establishments of passages from
          published works
36A   Lending of copies by educational establishments.

Recommendation 2 of the Gowers Review says:

> Enable educational provisions to cover distance learning and interactive
> whiteboards by 2008 by amending sections 35 and 36 of the Copyright, Designs
> and Patents Act, 1988 (CDPA).

Section 35 of the CDPA 1988 currently allows the recording and showing of
broadcasts to students who are physically present at an educational establishment.
The Gowers Review (2006) proposed an expanded section which would allow
distance learning students to receive and view these recordings remotely.

An IPO consultation paper was subsequently published in 2008[6] which
considered the following issues:

1 Should the exception just apply to traditional broadcasts or be expanded to
   on-demand communications?
2 Who should have access to the recordings that are provided remotely?
3 How to ensure that material that is communicated to distance learning
   students is not communicated to others, including through secure
   environments?

Section 36 of the CDPA currently allows educational establishments to copy
passages from published works and provide hand-outs to students. The second
change to the educational exceptions which was proposed in Gowers was to enable
educational establishments to communicate such passages using interactive
whiteboards and electronically to distance learners. This proposed change raises
the following issues:

1 What limits should be placed on communication of material using interactive
   whiteboards and to distance learners? Should it be limited to secure virtual
   learning environments? Should regular e-mail be allowed?
2 How would we prevent onward communication of material to persons not
   authorized to receive it?
3 Should the exception continue to be limited to literary, dramatic and musical

works, or should teachers be able to take advantage of technologies that use a range of different works, including extracts from films, sound recordings and broadcasts?

It should be noted that sections 35 and 36 are currently of limited value because copying is not authorized under either of those sections if, or to the extent that, licences are available authorizing the copying in question. There are schemes in place from the ERA and OU (s35) and CLA (s36) which means that in practice educational establishments would normally require licences in order to record broadcasts and to copy passages from published works.

The *Consultation on Copyright* of 2011 acknowledges that there is scope to expand the education exceptions: so that they permit copying of a wider range of content types (films, sound recordings, artistic works); to enable use of those materials with digital technology (such as interactive whiteboards); and to help students access education more easily (such as within a secure distance learning environment).

While recognizing that a lot of 'on-demand' content is restricted by digital rights management, the government believes that there could be benefits to including on-demand services within the educational exceptions.

The government has considered the removal of the ability to license the educational exceptions. If they were to restrict the ability to license the exception for recording broadcasts (s35), they anticipate that this would only be to the extent that permitted 'time shifting' of broadcasts, rather than their long-term storage.

The government is also looking to widen the definition of educational establishments to include a wider range of organizations with an educational purpose in order to reflect the diversity of modern education provision.

The government doesn't set out a preferred option with regard to the educational exceptions because it doesn't have sufficient evidence as to the total impact that the various changes considered would have on rights holders, and are seeking that evidence as part of the consultation process.

4.10 Exceptions relating to computer software

The Software Directive (2009/24/EC which is a codified version of the 1991 Directive) contains a number of provisions that ensures that copyright law cannot be overridden by contract law. They include a requirement for lawful users of computer software to be able to make a back-up copy. The Directive was implemented by SI 1992/3233 – The Copyright (Computer Programs) Regulations 1992 – which inserted s. 50A into the CDPA 1988:

CDPA 1988 s50A. –

(1) It is not an infringement of copyright for a lawful user of a copy of a computer program to make any back-up copy of it which it is necessary for him

to have for the purposes of his lawful use.

(2) For the purposes of this section and sections 50B and 50C a person is a lawful user of a computer program if (whether under a licence to do any acts restricted by the copyright in the program or otherwise) he has a right to use the program.

(3) Where an act is permitted under this section, it is irrelevant whether or not there exists any term or condition in an agreement which purports to prohibit or restrict the act (such terms being, by virtue of section 296A, void).

If someone tried to contract their way out of this obligation any such provision would be considered to be void by a court. It isn't clear the extent to which the making of a back-up copy would be permitted under this section. It revolves around what is meant by the word 'necessary'. Imagine, for example, a scenario in which the original version of a computer software package becomes corrupted. Having a back-up copy means that the software user is able to quickly restore the software so that it continues to work as it should.

The other acts relating to software which cannot be overridden by a contract are decompilation (s. 50B) and observing, studying and testing of computer programs (s. 50BA).

There is also an exception in section 50C (Other acts permitted to lawful users) for a lawful user of a copy of a computer program to copy or adapt it, especially where this is necessary for the purpose of correcting errors in it. However, unlike sections 50A, 50B, and 50BA, section 50C does not specify that it cannot be overridden by a contract.

4.11   Exceptions relating to databases

It is important to distinguish between exceptions to copyright in databases and exceptions to the sui generis database right.

4.11.1 Copyright exceptions

S50D Acts permitted in relation to databases.

(1) It is not an infringement of copyright in a database for a person who has a right to use the database or any part of the database, (whether under a licence to do any of the acts restricted by the copyright in the database or otherwise) to do, in the exercise of that right, anything which is necessary for the purposes of access to and use of the contents of the database or of that part of the database.

(2) Where an act which would otherwise infringe copyright in a database is permitted under this section, it is irrelevant whether or not there exists any term or condition in any agreement which purports to prohibit or restrict the act (such terms being, by virtue of section 296B, void).

4.11.2 Database right exceptions

The Copyright and Rights in Databases Regulations 1997 (SI 1997/3032, www.legislation.gov.uk/uksi/1997/3032/contents/made) implemented the Database Directive in the UK. There are a number of exceptions to database right, the main one being a fair dealing exception. Regulation 20 of SI 1997/3032 sets out the fair dealing exception to database right (Figure 4.1).

In addition, Schedule 1 to the Database Regulations (SI 1997/3032) sets out a number of exceptions for public administration (Figure 4.2).

The exception is available so long as:

• the person extracting part of the database is a lawful user* of the database;
• that it is extracted for the purposes of illustration for teaching or research;
• that it is not for any commercial purpose;
• and that the source is indicated.

The 1997 Regulations define a 'lawful user', in relation to a database, as meaning 'any person who (whether under a licence to do any of the acts restricted by any database right in the database or otherwise) has a right to use the database'.

Figure 4.1 *Conditions for fair dealing in a database*

---

a) parliamentary and judicial proceedings
b) Royal Commissions and statutory inquiries
c) Material open to public inspection or on official register
d) Material communicated to the Crown in the course of public business
e) Public records
f) Acts done under statutory authority

Figure 4.2 *Public administration exceptions to the database right*

The database regulations contain one provision which cannot be overridden by contract. Regulation 19 of SI 1997/3032 says:

Avoidance of certain terms affecting lawful users
19. – (1) A lawful user of a database which has been made available to the public in any manner shall be entitled to extract or reutilize insubstantial parts of the contents of the database for any purpose.
(2) Where under an agreement a person has a right to use a database, or part

of a database, which has been made available to the public in any manner, any term or condition in the agreement shall be void in so far as it purports to prevent that person from extracting or reutilizing insubstantial parts of the contents of the database, or of that part of the database, for any purpose.

4.12   Abstracts of scientific and technical articles

The copyright in an original abstract lasts for the life of the author plus 70 years and is owned by the abstractor or, if created during the course of employment, by their employer (such as where the abstractor works for an online database or abstracting service). There is also the publisher's copyright in the typographical layout or arrangement, which lasts for 25 years from the year of publication.

There is a copyright exception for the copying of abstracts in s. 60 of the CDPA 1988. This is available where the abstract accompanies a scientific or technical journal article and where there is no licensing scheme in place. The wording of the exception says:

60 Abstracts of scientific or technical articles

(1) Where an article on a scientific or technical subject is published in a periodical accompanied by an abstract indicating the contents of the article, it is not an infringement of copyright in the abstract, or in the article, to copy the abstract or issue copies of it to the public.

(2) This section does not apply if or to the extent that there is a licensing scheme certified for the purposes of this section under section 143 providing for the grant of licences.

An abstracting service could potentially be protected by database right, in which case one should bear in mind that:

- copying abstracts from the database would only be possible if it was done by a lawful user;
- even a lawful user of the abstracting database would need to ensure that they were copying an insubstantial part of the contents of the database.

⊕   Financial Times v. Finsbury Data Services

Textline was a general business database. It was a content aggregator and the Textline database consisted of over nine million articles from around 600 sources, including newspapers, newswires and specialist publications. This included all of the UK broadsheets apart from the *Financial Times* (FT), for which only abstracts were provided.

In 1986 Textline found itself in a copyright infringement dispute with Financial Times over its practice of producing lengthy abstracts of FT articles.

Later that year Reuters Holdings PLC acquired Finsbury Data Services Limited, and then in 1987 the copyright dispute was settled when a full agreement was signed between the two companies which gave Reuters the right to carry abstracts from the FT and also from the *Investors Chronicle*.

By this time Financial Times was operating its own online news database – FT Profile – and in 1993 FT Profile was referred to the Monopolies and Mergers Commission. It was at that time the only historical online database in the UK that was licensed to include every up-to-date article from the FT[7].

4.13   Format shifting

Copyright law doesn't currently permit format shifting. At the moment, for example, it is illegal for an individual who has lawful possession of a work such as a music CD to make a copy for playback in the Windows Media Player. It would also be illegal for a library to use format shifting as a way of preserving content, such as copying a work that is currently held on unstable media into an accessible digital format.

The Gowers Review addressed this matter in Recommendation 10b:

'Enable libraries to format shift archival copies by 2008 to ensure records do not become obsolete'.

In 2008 the Intellectual Property Office's consultation on implementation of the Gowers recommendations on the copyright exceptions acknowledged (in paragraph 88) that there were a number of issues that would need to be addressed:

* the classes of work to which it would apply
* what is meant by personal use
* how many format shifts would be allowed
* whether it would apply to works purchased before or after the exception comes into effect; and
* its application to works where DRM tools have been applied.

Unless any potential exception allows for further format shifting beyond the initial one it is inadequate for preservation purposes. An exception needs to cater for technological obsolescence by allowing subsequent copies to be made. In addition, where a digital rights management system is present, this makes it impractical to legally circumvent the TPMs which form part of DRMs in order to benefit from the statutory exceptions.

More recently, the December 2011 *Consultation on Copyright* includes a proposal (paragraph 7.39) to create a new copyright exception that would allow people to copy creative content for private, non-commercial use. The exception that is envisaged would allow copying for uses such as format shifting and use on different devices.

4.14   Benefiting from the exceptions where there is a TPM in place

A number of user representatives have argued that the widespread use by copyright owners of technological protection measures to control access to and use of digital material has effectively rendered the copyright exceptions or permitted acts worthless. It means, for example, that disabled people using assistive technology can still be denied access to the content because of there being a TPM in place.

Article 6 of the Copyright Directive sets out obligations relating to technical measures. Article 6(4) requires member states to provide a means by which beneficiaries of exceptions or limitations can carry out the permitted acts. It says:

> Article 6(4) Notwithstanding the legal protection provided for in paragraph 1, in the absence of voluntary measures taken by rightholders, including agreements between rightholders and other parties concerned, Member States shall take appropriate measures to ensure that rightholders make available to the beneficiary of an exception or limitation provided for in national law in accordance with Article 5(2)(a), (2)(c), (2)(d), (2)(e), (3)(a), (3)(b) or (3)(e) the means of benefiting from that exception or limitation, to the extent necessary to benefit from that exception or limitation and where that beneficiary has legal access to the protected work or subject-matter concerned'.

However, Recital 53 makes clear that Article 6(4) does not apply to on-demand services where these are governed by a contract.

The requirement set out in Article 6(4) for member states to take appropriate measures to ensure that the beneficiaries of exceptions are able to exercise the means of benefiting from the exception(s) was implemented in the UK through s. 296ZE of the CDPA 1988:

> **296ZE Remedy where effective technological measures prevent permitted acts**
> Where the application of any effective technological measure to a copyright work other than a computer program prevents a person from carrying out a permitted act in relation to that work then that person or a person being a representative of a class of persons prevented from carrying out a permitted act may issue a notice of complaint to the Secretary of State.
> (3) Following receipt of a notice of complaint, the Secretary of State may give to the owner of that copyright work or an exclusive licensee such directions as appear to the Secretary of State to be requisite or expedient for the purpose of –
> (a) establishing whether any voluntary measure or agreement relevant to the copyright work the subject of the complaint subsists; or
> (b) (where it is established there is no subsisting voluntary measure or

agreement) ensuring that the owner or exclusive licensee of that copyright work makes available to the complainant the means of carrying out the permitted act the subject of the complaint to the extent necessary to so benefit from that permitted act.

The Gowers Review recommended that the procedures in place for circumventing DRM in order to allow copying for uses deemed legitimate under the copyright exceptions should be made easier, for example through a model e-mail form available on the Patent Office (now the IPO) website. Recommendation 15 of the Gowers Review (2006) said:

Make it easier for users to file notice of complaints procedures relating to Digital Rights Management tools by providing an accessible web interface on the Patent Office website by 2008.

The recommendation was never implemented and the current arrangements fail to meet the users' need for timely access to works for these reasons:

- the remedy available inspires little faith;
- the vagueness of the process serves to stifle complaints;
- even if someone were to invoke the complaints mechanism set out in section 296ZE, it is highly likely that the moment of need for the information would have long since passed by the time the Secretary of State had instructed the publisher to make the content available to the complainant;
- even if the Secretary of State receives a valid 'notice of complaint' and were to decide to issue directions to ensure that the permitted act can occur, an order made by the SoS can be ignored. If that were to happen, the onus would revert back to the user to seek redress through the courts on the grounds of there being a breach of statutory duty. Such an option would be likely to be both time-consuming and expensive to the complainant.

The government could, though, choose to name and shame errant rights owners.

4.15 Orphan works

In recent years orphan works have been high up on the copyright agenda. These are works for which the rights holder is either difficult or even impossible to identify or locate. Mass digitization initiatives have highlighted the scale of the orphan works problem. There are obvious practical difficulties for anyone needing to seek out permission to digitize content where the rights owner can't be identified or located. What is clear is that it isn't possible to fit an orphan works exception into the existing list set out in Article 5 of the Copyright Directive. The only options available would be either to amend that Directive, or else to introduce a completely new directive to cover orphan works. The Commission has opted for the second route and has published a draft directive on orphan works [COM(2011)289].

At the time of writing (July 2012), there is no legislative solution in place to cover the copying of orphan works. However, the UK government is seeking to introduce a number of measures to resolve this issue. These include:

- the introduction of a voluntary extended collective licensing scheme;
- the use of individual orphan works after a diligent search; and
- the creation of a digital copyright exchange where ownership of copyrights could be advertised and rights licensed.

On 2 July 2012 the IPO published its latest thinking (there is a link to the pdf available via the web page: www.ipo.gov.uk/types/hargreaves.htm). In *Government Policy Statement: consultation on modernising copyright* it sets out the intention to legislate to allow schemes to be introduced for the commercial and non-commercial use of 'orphan' copyright works. The government takes the view that the proposals relating to the Digital Copyright Exchange need to be developed and owned by the industry itself. For fuller details about the government's orphan works proposals see Section 8.3 of this book.

Notes and references

1   Andrew Gowers (2006) *Gowers Review of Intellectual Property*, HM Treasury, www.official-documents.gov.uk/document/other/0118404830/0118404830. pdf.

2   Ian Hargreaves (2011) *Digital Opportunity: a review of intellectual property and growth*, www.ipo.gov.uk/ipreview-finalreport.pdf.

3   Intellectual Property Office (2011) *Consultation on Copyright*, December 2011, www.ipo.gov.uk/consult-2011-copyright.pdf.

4   Copinger & Skone James on Copyright, Sweet & Maxwell.

5   *Defining 'Non-commercial': a study of how the online population understands 'non-commercial use'*, Creative Commons (CC BY 3.0), 2009, http://wiki.creativecommons.org/Defining_Noncommercial.

6   *Taking Forward the Gowers Review of Intellectual Property: proposed changes to copyright exceptions*, Intellectual Property Office, 2008.

7   Competition Commission Historical On-Line Database Services: *A Report on the Supply in the UK of Services which Provide Access to Databases Containing Archival Business and Financial Information*, www.competition-commission.org.uk/rep_pub/reports/ 1994/354historical.htm#summary.

CHAPTER 5

Licences

There are bound to be instances where copyright law appears to be too restrictive for people's needs. If anyone other than the copyright owner wishes to do any of the acts restricted by copyright with a copyright work, he or she needs either to gain ownership of the copyright or to obtain permission in the form of a licence.

Licences are governed by the law of contract, and at the time of writing (July 2012) this will normally override copyright law; although if the recommendation in the December 2011 *Consultation on Copyright* (IPO) is implemented, there will be a provision applying to every exception provided by the CDPA 1988 which would make clear that any contract term purporting to prohibit or restrict the use of an exception is unenforceable.

People take out a licence with the rights holder, or someone with the authority to act on their behalf. Usually (although not necessarily) they will pay a fee in order to be able to do more than copyright law on its own would have allowed. However, because of the way in which UK copyright law can currently be overridden by contract law, people could potentially end up paying for the privilege of being able to do less than copyright law would have allowed. In order to ensure that this doesn't happen, it would be an idea to include a clause along the lines that:

≣ This agreement is without prejudice to any acts which the licensee is permitted to carry out by the terms of the Copyright, Designs and Patents Act 1988 and nothing herein shall be construed as affecting or diminishing such permitted acts in any way whatsoever.

Copyright is a property right which, like rights in physical property, can be bought or sold, inherited or otherwise transferred, either wholly or in part. Copyright may therefore subsequently belong to someone other than the author of the protected work. An author who gets a book published, for example, may well sign over some and possibly all of their rights to the commercial publisher.

Copyright owners may choose to license others to use protected works while retaining ownership themselves. The terms of any such licence should deal with the following issues:

1 The exclusivity of the licence: is an exclusive licence to be granted to one licensee or is a non-exclusive licence to be granted to a number of licensees?

Is the copyright owner to retain rights to use the copyright work?

2 The term of the licence: is the licence intended to last forever (often described as 'perpetual'), or do the copyright owner and licensee intend it to last for a specified period of time?

3 The assignability of the licence: can the licensee transfer his or her permission to carry out the restricted acts to third parties?

4 The scope of the licence: is the licensee entitled to carry out all of the restricted acts, or does the copyright owner wish to retain some of those rights?

In the USA there is an idea currently under construction called the Library License (http://librarylicense.org). It has been designed by Jeff Goldenson of the Harvard Library Innovation laboratory (www.librarylab.law.harvard.edu), a website from the Harvard Law School. Inspired by Creative Commons, the Library License offers two options:

1 Option one grants libraries non-commercial access to copyrighted material on a defined time horizon.

2 Option two enables content producers to add a Library Licence to the terms of their publishing contracts.

Meanwhile, in Europe EBLIDA – the European Bureau of Library and Information Documentation Associations – is keen to consider the licensing of e-books in order to find solutions which would be suitable for library lending of e-books.

5.1   Contract v. copyright

In the UK, licences and contracts trump copyright law with few exceptions. When someone buys information in digital form it is likely that there will be a licence agreement which governs the use of the content. In such circumstances the licence agreement will override copyright exceptions or permitted acts, such as those relating to fair dealing. Instead, the use of the product will be governed entirely by the contractual terms and not by copyright law.

A British Library survey found that, out of 30 licences surveyed at random, the vast majority did not give provisions as generous as those that would be provided under fair dealing or library privilege in copyright law. Restrictions included limiting the extent of the material that could be copied: one licence stated that 'misuse includes . . . reproducing in any way copyright material', a clear barrier to conducting research or criticizing works.[1] There are a small number of provisions in UK law where copyright law cannot be overridden by contract law. They relate to the making of a back-up copy of a computer program, decompilation, observing, studying and testing of computer programs and a lawful user of a database being able to extract or re-utilize insubstantial parts of the contents of the database.

In *Copyright Policies and Practices 2011*[2] one of the survey respondents said: 'We have particular difficulties where copyright issues overlap with unclear subscription contracts'.

Ian Hargreaves said that the government should legislate to ensure that copyright exceptions are protected from override by copyright. The government response to the Hargreaves Review agreed that the widest possible exceptions to copyright within the existing EU framework are likely to be beneficial to the UK, subject to three important factors:

1 That the amount of harm to rights holders that would result in 'fair compensation' under EU law is minimal.
2 Adherence with EU law and international treaties.
3 That unnecessary restrictions removed by copyright exceptions are not re-imposed by other means such as contractual terms in such a way as to undermine the benefits of the exception.

Even where there are copyright exceptions established by law, administrators are often forced to prevent staff from exercising them because of restrictive contracts. Hargreaves says that the government should change the law to make it clear no exception to copyright can be overridden by contract.

Consultation on Copyright[3] says: 'The Government is, therefore, proposing to introduce a clause, applying to every exception provided by the Copyright Act, which would make clear that any contract term purporting to prohibit or restrict the use of an exception is unenforceable.'

Checklist 5.1 lists some of the key questions information professionals should ask before signing up to a licence which will enable them to provide access to digital resources.

Checklist 5.1 *Licences checklist*
* Does the licensor warrant that they have the legal right to license the content to you?
* Is this backed up with an indemnity?
* Is there a clause which ensures that the agreement doesn't affect or diminish any of the permitted acts/copyright exceptions set out in the CDPA 1988?
* What, if anything, does the licence say about the lending of content?
* Does it permit the making of copies for archival / preservation purposes?
* Does it permit the printing out of digital content, and if so, how much?
* What does the licence say about making copies in an accessible form for visually impaired persons?

5.2   Collective licensing societies

Collective licensing has advantages both for copyright owners and for users of their content. On the one hand copyright owners are able to license uses that individually they would find very burdensome to administer while on the other hand users are able to benefit from the considerable administrative savings made possible as a result of the availability of a single licence covering many copyright works.

In 2011 the Copyright Licensing Agency commissioned PriceWaterhouseCoopers (PwC) to prepare a report for them to be used in their submission to the Hargreaves Review. In it PwC say that there is an economic rationale for collective licensing societies. By entering into a collective licence covering content from a number of publishers across multiple countries it is possible to make legitimate use of a large amount of content; whereas if you didn't have a licence of that kind and had to rely on getting individual permissions the transaction costs would be likely to be prohibitive. The report[4] says that 'for the licensing of higher education institutions, the transaction costs for users and rights owners through CMOs (Collective Management Organisations) are £6.7 million. With an atomised model, we estimate that the transaction costs would be between £145 million and £720 million per year'. By 'atomised model', PwC are referring to a system in which each user would be assumed to have to contract directly with each rights owner.

Through the CDPA 1988 the UK government has encouraged the use of licensing schemes. Some of these licensing schemes have to be certified (such as the ones from the OU and the ERA), whereas others do not. Some licensing schemes are blanket schemes whereas others are transactional (such as the OU licence).

It is important for licensees to read and be aware of the contractual terms and conditions. Where they are challenged for an alleged infringement of copyright within the scope of the licence, the collecting society is required by s. 136 of the CDPA 1988 to provide the licensee with an indemnity.

The collecting societies are subject to the same wider legal framework as other companies with the same legal form. For example, the CLA, NLA, DACS and the ERA (see below for all these organizations) are all private companies and are subject to the requirements of company law. Their functions as collecting societies, however, are not currently regulated by the government. The UK is one of only three member states in the EU which doesn't regulate its collecting societies. There have been calls at both a European level and at a UK level for legislation to regulate them.

Collecting societies tend to be monopoly suppliers of the licensing products for the sectors that they cover. According to the *Consultation on Copyright* (page 40) they are an economically significant sector, collecting close to £1 billion per annum in total on behalf of their members. There have been calls from rights owners and from users for their functions to be regulated, for example with regard to:

- transparency
- distribution mechanisms
- charges for the use of works.

The *Consultation on Copyright* sought views on a proposal to publish minimum standards – for fairness, transparency and good governance – which it would like to see included in voluntary codes of conduct for collecting societies. The government also proposed that collecting societies should appoint and fund an independent and impartial person to arbitrate on disputes and review their performance against their code(s). In case the proposed voluntary system doesn't prove to be effective, the government also plans to introduce a backstop power that would allow for a statutory code to be implemented if required.

5.2.1 Copyright Licensing Agency (CLA)

CLA licences cover copying from books, magazines and journals published in the UK as well as from mandated overseas territories, apart from titles on the List of Excluded Works. Licensees may make and distribute as many copies as they require subject to the following extent limits:

- one article from a magazine, journal or other periodical
- one entire case from a published law report
- one chapter from a book
- or 5% of the publication, whichever is the greater.

The licence also covers the copying of artistic works such as photographs, illustrations and diagrams, where these are contained in the publication being copied.

Scanned images may be saved on an individual PC or in an individual password-protected area of a server but may not be stored centrally in an accessible library or intranet. The one exception to this is the pharmaceutical licence, which, according to the CLA website,[5] entitles licence holders to '. . . store digital copies in a local product or project-based searchable database, in personal or work group folders, and within a dim archive for regulatory purposes.'

There are a number of categories of works which are not covered by the CLA licence. These are:

- printed music
- maps and charts

- published tests or examination papers
- newspapers
- electronic books or journals or online publications
- internal house journals or other free publications generally not intended for public circulation.

CLA has agreements with a number of reproduction rights organizations in other countries, which means that licensees are able to photocopy titles from those territories. In addition, the agreements with some countries also cover scanning and the re-use of digital publications. The question of what a CLA licence covers does get more complicated with regard to digital content. Licensees need to be aware of the lists of specific inclusions or exclusions.

Some of the CLA licences cover the making of digital copies from free-to-view websites, where these are published by publishers who are included on the List of Participating Digital Material Publishers.

In 2011 the CLA introduced a logo consisting of a copyright tick icon, and this is a trademark of the CLA. The icon is used with the words 'What can I do with this content?' (http://whatcanidowiththiscontent.com). The logo communicates the publishers' copyright policy and terms in a clear and simple way. Clicking on the copyright tick icon brings up a series of five prompts, each of which gives fuller information about the copying that is permitted:

- print from it?
- store on intranet?
- use extracts?
- supply it externally?
- use for media monitoring?

5.2.2   Newspaper Licensing Agency (NLA)

NLA offer licences for business, education, public relations, and professional partnerships. There is also a licence for media monitoring agencies. The licences cover paper copying (photocopying, faxing and printing) and digital copying (scanning, e-mailing and hosting on an intranet site), as well as the receipt and distribution of content received from a PR or licensed media monitoring agency.

The NLA has a site (http://newspapersforschools.co.uk) which provides an online service allowing schools access to newspaper clippings in PDF format from over 140 national and regional titles, all in a single place, free of charge.

NLA has a Corporate Website Republishing Licence which gives organizations the permission required to post content from selected newspapers onto their website. Subject to the licence terms and conditions, licensees are permitted to scan an article and post it as a PDF on a corporate website; and also to republish headlines and text extracts. The licence fee is based on the number of articles posted onto the licensee's corporate website.

5.2.3 Educational Recording Agency (ERA)

The Educational Recording Agency's licensing scheme permits staff at educational establishments to record for non-commercial educational purposes the broadcast output of ERA members. It covers the use of recordings of broadcasts as teaching resources. Section 35 of the CDPA 1988 permits the ERA to license 'educational establishments' or their representative bodies. That covers:

* local educational authorities on behalf of their educational establishments, i.e. schools, media resources and teachers' centres, adult education units and off-site youth centres
* independent schools
* colleges of further education
* universities and colleges of theology and higher education
* schools of nursing and schools teaching English as a foreign language.

The ERA licensing scheme is enshrined in legislation in the form of a number of statutory instruments:

1 The Copyright (Certification of Licensing Scheme for Educational Recording of Broadcasts) (Educational Recording Agency Limited) (Amendment) Order 2011 SI 2011/159
2 The Copyright (Certification of Licensing Scheme for Educational Recording of Broadcasts) (Educational Recording Agency Limited) (Amendment) Order 2009 SI 2009/20
3 The Copyright (Certification of Licensing Scheme for Educational Recording of Broadcasts) (Educational Recording Agency Limited) (Revocation and Amendment) Order 2008 SI 2008/211
4 The Copyright (Certification of Licensing Scheme for Educational Recording of Broadcasts) (Educational Recording Agency Limited) Order 2007 SI 2007/266.

5.2.4 Design Artists Copyright Society (DACS)

DACS collects and distributes royalties to visual artists through three rights management services:

1 **Payback** Each year DACS pays Payback royalties to visual artists whose work has been reproduced in UK magazines, books or broadcast on certain UK television channels. These royalties come from a range of collective licensing

schemes, which include photocopying of books and magazines and the recording of programmes by schools, colleges and universities.

2 **Artists' Resale Right** This entitles artists to a resale royalty each time their art work is resold by a gallery, dealer or auction house for more than 1000 euros. Since 2012 the beneficiaries of deceased artists whose work is still protected by copyright have qualified for the royalty.

3 **Copyright licensing** This benefits artists and their estates where their work is reproduced for commercial purposes such as in a book, on a website, on a t-shirt or greeting card.

DACS says that it is developing new licensing solutions to meet the needs of consumers in the digital age which will enable artists to be recognized and rewarded. The problem is that people have been waiting years for DACS to provide a licence covering the use of digital images, and at the time of writing (July 2012) they were still waiting. Indeed, according to an article by Marie-Therese Gramstadt[6] the arts education community began discussions with DACS in 2003 regarding the need for a new licence to cover digital images. ARLIS (The Art Libraries Society) and ACADI (Association of Curators of Art and Design Images) have put together a wishlist for such a licence – see http://acadi.files.wordpress.com/2011/04/proposal-for-a-digital-image-database-licence.doc.

5.2.5 Copyright Tribunal

The main function of the Tribunal is to decide, where the parties cannot agree between themselves, the terms and conditions of licences offered by, or licensing schemes operated by, collective licensing bodies in the copyright and related rights area. It has the statutory task of conclusively establishing the facts of a case and of coming to a decision which is reasonable in the light of those facts. Its decisions are appealable to the High Court only on points of law. In Scotland appeals on a point of law against decisions of the Tribunal are to the Court of Session.

All the Copyright Tribunal can decide is the reasonableness of the terms in the licence. Broadly, the Tribunal's jurisdiction is such that anyone who has unreasonably been refused a licence by a collecting society or considers the terms of a licence that has been offered to them to be unreasonable may refer the matter to the Tribunal. The Tribunal also has the power to decide some matters referred to it by the Secretary of State and other matters even though collecting societies are not involved. For example, it can settle disputes over the royalties payable by publishers of television programme listings to broadcasting organizations.

The Tribunal's jurisdiction is defined in Sections 149, 205B and Schedule 6 of the Copyright, Designs and Patents Act 1988 (as amended).

5.3   Extended collective licensing

The Hargreaves Review recommended the implementation of extended collective licensing. This is where a copyright licensing body which already operates on behalf of most of the rights holders for one particular class or sector (such as printed music, books and journals, or newspapers) is given the right to represent the others in that class or category unless they come forward and object.

Ordinarily, a collective licensing society can only license content where it has been given a mandate to do so by the rights holders. But in the case of orphan works, by their very nature, it is not possible to obtain such a mandate. Extended collective licensing can thus be viewed as one possible solution to the problems posed by orphan works.

In some Scandinavian countries, a collecting society that represents a substantial proportion of rights holders is allowed to license specific uses of a work for all rights holders in a particular category, and this is what the government wants to introduce for the UK.

In *Consultation on Copyright*[7] the government set out its preferred option as being to introduce legislation that will allow collective licensing to take place on an 'opt-out' rather than an 'opt-in' basis to expedite rights clearance and reduce transaction costs. The intention is to allow collecting societies to be authorized to license the use of rights in this way provided that certain transparency and fairness conditions are met (see Section 8.3 of this book on the regulation of the collecting societies).

5.4   Creative Commons

Creative Commons Licences are trying to achieve a point in between all rights reserved and no rights reserved. The licences try to make it as easy as possible to understand what they cover, by adopting the use of four symbols:[8]

BY   **Attribution** You let others copy, distribute, display, and perform your copyrighted work – and derivative works based upon it – but only if they give credit the way you request.

NC   **Non-commercial** You let others copy, distribute, display, and perform your work – and derivative works based upon it – but for non-commercial purposes only.

ND   **No derivative works** You let others copy, distribute, display, and perform only verbatim copies of your work, not derivative works based upon it.

SA   **Share alike** You allow others to distribute derivative works only under a licence identical to the licence that governs your work.

and each licence consists of a combination of these symbols e.g. **CC BY-ND** (attribution, no derivative works). Note: A licence cannot feature both the Share

Alike and No Derivative Works options. The Share Alike requirement applies only to derivative works.

One tool that is being worked on with the World Wide Web Consortium (W3C) is RDFA – Resource Description Framework in Attributes – which could revolutionize how content gets moved around the web, because when you copy and paste information using RDFA, the copyright and licensing information is carried across as well. RDFA codifies copyright information within the HTML. It could potentially be used by anyone to express who owns this object, and what are the licensing terms; it isn't just limited to Creative Commons Licences.

Creative Commons licences are international, they are irrevocable, and above all they are enforceable – something which has been established a number of times in a variety of different jurisdictions:

- In a Belgian Case Lichodmapwa were awarded 4500 euros for infringement of a song ('Abatchouck') released under a CC BY-NC-ND licence.
- Bulgarian blogger Elenko Elenkov filed a lawsuit against the newspaper *24 Hours* for having one of his photos licensed under a CC BY-SA licence.
- In Adam Curry v. (Dutch tabloid) *Weekend* the publisher faces a fine of 1000 euros if it publishes any of Curry's pictures without permission again.
- In an Israeli case Avi Re'uveni v. Mapa Inc. the defendant was found to have violated all three licence conditions (BY-NC-ND licence) when she made a collage incorporating the photographs, sold the collages, and didn't provide attribution.

There are a number of useful resources for anyone who creates or uses CC licensed content:

⇢ Useful resource

Tynt publisher tools (www.tynt.com/publisher-tools) can be used to monitor who is copying and pasting your CC content.

⇢ Useful resource

Open Attribute (http://openattribute.com) provides a suite of tools to make it easy for anyone to copy and paste the correct attribution for any CC licensed content.

Before applying a Creative Commons Licence to a work it is important to work through Checklist 5.2.

Checklist 5.2 *Points to bear in mind when applying a CC licence to a work*
1   Make sure your work is copyrightable.

2 Make sure you own all the rights.

3 Remember that CC licences are irrevocable.

4 Think carefully about which licence is most appropriate. For example:

a. Are you willing to let other people make money from their reuse of your content?

b. Are you happy for people to be able to change and adapt your content?

5 Be specific about precisely what you are licensing (both in terms of format, e.g. text/audio/video, etc, as well as extent); e.g. is it only the text and images on the site or does it also include the style sheet and the code to run the site?

Where you use a Creative Commons licensed work, it is important to give credit for the work. Properly attributing the creator of the work is essential, and there is a simple tool called Open Attribute (http://openattribute.com) which has been designed to make attribution as easy as the click of a button.

⁕ Useful resource

Which Creative Commons Licence is right for me? Poster from Creative Commons Australia: http://creativecommons.org.au/weblog/entry/245.

5.5   Open Government Licence

On 30 September 2010 The National Archives launched the first UK Open Government Licence, making it faster and easier than ever before to freely reuse public sector information. It is a key element of the government's commitment to greater transparency. Its major features are shown in Figure 5.1 on the next page.

This licence removes the existing barriers to reusing information – it is simple, streamlined and a single set of terms and conditions provides assurance to anyone wishing to use or license government information at a glance. The licence is completely flexible and works in parallel with other internationally recognized licensing models such as Creative Commons.

The licence is applicable across the entire public sector not only in terms of geography – because its coverage includes Scotland, Wales and Northern Ireland – but also by type of public body, whether central government department, local authority or another public body that wishes to make their data more accessible to taxpayers.

The Open Government Licence replaced the Click-Use Licence and enables free reuse of a much broader range of public sector information, including Crown Copyright, databases and source codes. In addition, the licence does not require users to register or formally apply for permission to reuse data, unlike the old Click-Use Licence.

The data must have been expressly made available under the Open Government Licence.

The licence is:

- worldwide
- royalty free
- perpetual
- non-exclusive.

It lets you:

- copy, publish, distribute or transmit the information
- adapt the information
- exploit the information commercially.

What you must do:

- acknowledge the source of the information by including any attribution statement specified by the Information Provider and where possible provide a link to this licence.

What you must not do:

- use the information in any way that suggests any official status or that the Information Provider endorses your use of the information
- mislead others or misrepresent the information or its source
- use the information in a way which would breach the DPA or The Privacy and Electronic Communications (EC Directive) Regulations 2003.

The terms of the licence have been aligned to be interoperable with:

- any Creative Commons Attribution Licence which covers copyright
- Open Data Commons Attribution Licence, which covers database rights and applicable copyright.

This licence does not cover the use of:

- personal data in the information
- information that has neither been published nor disclosed under information access legislation (including the Freedom of Information Acts for the UK and Scotland) by or with the consent of the Information Provider
- departmental or public sector organization logos, crests and the Royal Arms except where they form an integral part of a document or dataset
- military insignia
- third-party rights the Information Provider is not authorized to license
- Information subject to other intellectual property rights, including patents, trade marks and design rights
- identity documents such as the British Passport.

Figure 5.1 *Key features of the Open Government Licence*

To support the UK Open Government Licence, the National Archives has developed the UK Government Licensing Framework, covering a wide spectrum of official information ranging from copyrighted images and text to data, software and source codes for both commercial and non-commercial purposes.

The Open Government Licence is available in machine-readable format on the National Archives' website: www.nationalarchives.gov.uk/doc/open-government-licence. It provides a single set of terms and conditions for anyone wishing to use or license government information and removes some of the existing barriers to reuse.

5.6   Open access

Open access is an alternative to the traditional method of publishing scholarly papers. It refers to the availability of peer-reviewed literature to the public on the internet free of charge, permitting any user to read, download, copy, distribute, print, search or link to the full texts of the articles.

This is the ideal that was set out in the landmark 2002 Budapest Open Access Initiative statement (www.soros.org/openaccess/read.shtml). In October 2003, the Berlin Declaration on Open Access to Knowledge in the Sciences and Humanities was signed by the Max Planck Society and a number of other large German and international research organizations. Signatories to the Berlin Declaration agreed to make progress by:

- encouraging their researchers or grant recipients to publish their work according to the principles of open access
- encouraging cultural institutions to support open access by providing their resources on the internet
- developing means and ways to evaluate open access contributions in order to maintain the standards of quality assurance and good scientific practice and by advocating that such publications be recognized in promotion and tenure evaluation.

Open access can be achieved in one of two ways:

1 Articles are published in open-access journals which don't levy a subscription charge to the user.
2 The articles are deposited in a subject-based or an institutional electronic repository that is accessible from remote locations without any access restrictions.

Just as with the traditional publishing market, some open-access journals are peer-reviewed. This is when the papers are submitted, reviewed, authenticated and finally published. Open-access journals are subject to thorough quality controls, and many are supported by editors who organize the refereeing process.

In December 2011 the UK government signalled in its *Innovation and Research Strategy for Growth*[9] document that it was fully behind the idea that all publicly funded research must be published in open-access journals. The strategy document says that the Research Councils will develop a UK gateway to research by 2013 which will allow ready access to research which has been funded by the Research Councils; and they will also work with their partners and users to ensure information is presented in a readily reusable form, using common formats and open standards.

5.7   Microlicensing

Technology can be used in a number of ways to help with the copyright clearance process, in terms of: managing rights and permissions data; identifying the rights owners; and providing a means at the moment of need for people to be able to pay for use of a work.

The term 'microlicensing' covers a range of different things, all of which are geared towards making it easier to comply with the terms of the licences that govern content: Figure 5.2 shows the various types of microlicensing.

Rights expression languages or standards (these define and express the legal rights in protected works in a machine readable form)

- ACAP: www.the-acap.org
- PLUS (Picture Licensing Universal System): www.useplus.com
- ONIX-PL : www.editeur.org/8/ONIX
- Creative Commons.

Registries (online databases providing information to help those wishing to identify rights holders and to clarify the rights status of protected works)

- ARROW: www.arrow-net.eu
- Book Rights Registry

Services (these provide users with a range of different ways in which they are able to use copyright protected content legitimately)

- iCopyright: http://info.icopyright.com
- Rightslink: www.rightslink.com
- OZMO: www.ozmo.com

Figure 5.2 *Types of microlicensing*

5.8   Out-of-commerce and out-of-print works

The phrase 'out of print' is something of a misnomer in a world of digital printing, where publishers can use 'print on demand' in order to print copies of works after an order has been received. 'Out-of-commerce' refers to works which are still protected by copyright but which are no longer commercially available because the authors and publishers have chosen not to publish a new edition or to sell copies through the customary channels of commerce.

The rights holders of out-of-commerce works are generally known, and so a user such as a library which wants to digitize the work will often know whom to contact in order to get the necessary permissions to use the works.

The European Commission has overseen the drafting of a Memorandum of Understanding (MoU) which relates to books and learned journals. It is focused on the mass digitization of library collections. The MoU contains a set of key principles which the publishers, authors, and collecting societies will follow when licensing libraries wishing to digitize and make available books or learned journals which are out-of-commerce:

1 It is sector-specific, providing solutions for books and learned journals.
2 It is based on voluntary licensing agreements to be negotiated in the country of first publication of the works.
3 The determination of the out-of-commerce status will be decided in the country of first publication according to criteria defined by the parties.
4 The types of use of the works will be agreed by the parties in each licensing agreement.
5 It foresees the need for solutions to situations of collective management when not all right holders are represented by a collecting society.

•❖ Useful resource

Memorandum of Understanding: key principles on the digitisation and making available of out-of-commerce works,
http://ec.europa.eu/internal_market/copyright/docs/copyright-infso/20110920-mou_en.pdf.

The Memorandum of Understanding complements the Commission's legislative proposal on orphan works COM(2011) 289 final, which provides a route by which material can be digitized if the rights holder cannot be located even after a diligent search has been carried out.

5.9   Pan-European digital licensing

The whole ethos of the EU is to create a single market for goods and services, and yet this is being hampered in the field of copyright because there isn't currently a standardized European licensing model covering copyright-protected works in the EU. As a result, territorial licensing of media content makes the creation of a Europe-wide market for services such as the streaming of content, the provision of an online music service, or an online video-on-demand service, a bureaucratic headache in terms of rights clearance because service providers would be required to deal separately with the copyrights in all 27 member states of the EU. That would be both costly and time-consuming, and would therefore be something that only big media companies would be likely to undertake.

There was a discussion paper published in July 2011, *On the Online Distribution of Audiovisual Works in the EU: opportunities and challenges towards a digital single market,* COM(2011) 427 final. Audiovisual works are particularly complex because they may contain moving and still images, speech and music, and therefore a whole bundle of different rights. A key pillar of the EU's digital agenda is the creation of a single digital market to facilitate the downloading of entertainment products (films, music, games) and streaming services across borders by simplifying the licensing of content as well as by harmonizing online payment access. The Commission will also publish a strategy on stimulating cloud computing in the European digital single market in 2012.

One important measure to unlock potential growth in this area is a proposal for a directive on collective rights management to tackle barriers to cross-border online music licensing and improve the governance, transparency and functioning of the collecting societies.[10]

5.10   Music licensing and public libraries

In 2010 the MLA issued guidelines[11] setting out the circumstances under which public libraries in the UK may need to purchase a licence for public performances of music or film. This was initiated by four library stakeholder bodies, incorporated input from the Libraries and Archives Copyright Alliance, the International Association of Music Libraries, the Society of Chief Librarians and a law firm, as well as taking into account the views of the collecting societies.

It is clear that the stakeholder bodies were unable to reach a common view with the collecting societies on one issue in particular – namely the question of whether a licence was necessary to cover the situation whereby a single library user accesses music online or offline through headphones.

Public libraries are very conscious of copyright, and also of the role of the collecting societies. They routinely make users aware of copyright law through the use of copyright notices displayed in areas of the library housing photocopiers, scanners, and computer terminals; whilst also having Acceptable Use Policies in place which cover the use of library computers.

The MLA guidance sets out a number of common activities that take place in public libraries and says whether or not they require a licence. Whilst the guidance was written following consultation with expert bodies, it doesn't constitute legal advice. They concluded that no licence fee was required where equipment is provided by the library specifically to allow users to individually listen to music or to view film media and where the user does so using headphones. However, where access to online music or film media is undertaken on a computer using speakers, this would require licences from PRS and PPL.

The guidance contains a much longer list of library users' activities, and where licences (from PPL, PRS, MPLC or Filmbank, or television licences) are required. The guidance points out that the legal definition of 'public performance' relies on relevant case law, and that they were unable to find any case law which related to the activity of one person listening to music through headphones in a library. As such they were unable to recommend that a public performance licence be purchased for that activity.

It also noted that every library-based online audio experience was a one-to-one transaction between the audio source and the user via headphones. This reflects the nature of public libraries and the need to ensure that other users aren't disturbed. As such, they pointed out that a proportionate response to the licensing of these activities is required.

⇢ Useful resource

MLA, *Public Performance Licence: an information guide: music and film activities in public libraries*, November 2011, www.iaml.info/iaml-uk-irl/resources/pub_perf_licenses.pdf.

Notes and references

1   British Library (2006) *Library Warns of 'More Restrictive' DRMs: British Library expresses concern about the impact of DRMs on access, fair dealing and digital preservation*, British Library press release 7 June, http://pressandpolicy.bl.uk/Press-Releases/Library-warns-of-more-restrictive-DRMs-British-Library-expresses-concern-about-the-impact-of-DRMs-on-access-fair-dealing-and-digital-preservation-3bc.aspx.

2   FreePint (2011) *Copyright Policies and Practices 2011*, FreePint Research Report, http://web.freepint.com/go/shop/report/1796.

3   Intellectual Property Office (2011) *Consultation on Copyright*, December 2011, www.ipo.gov.uk/consult-2011-copyright.pdf.

4   PriceWaterhouseCoopers (2011) *An Economic Analysis of Copyright, Secondary Copyright and Collective Licensing*, March 2011, www.cla.co.uk/data/corporate_material/submissions/2011_pwc_final_report.pdf.

5   www.cla.co.uk/licences/licences_available/pharmaceutical_industry/featuresbenefits.

6   Gramstadt, Marie-Therese (2010) *Changing Light: a plethora of digital tools as slides gasp their last?*, www.chart.ac.uk/chart2010/papers/gramstadt.pdf.

7   And subsequently in *Government Policy Statement: consultation on modernising*

copyright, published on 2 July 2012 (available as a pdf via a link at www.ipo.gov.uk/types/hargreaves.htm).

8   The Creative Commons logos, icons, and buttons are available at http://creativecommons.org/about/downloads.

9   Department for Business, Innovation and Skills (2011) *Innovation and Research Strategy for Growth*, December 2011, www.bis.gov.uk/assets/biscore/innovation/docs/i/11-1387-innovation-and-research-strategy-for-growth.pdf.

10   COM(2012) 372/2 on collective management of copyright and related rights and multi-territorial licensing rights in musical works for online uses in the internal market.

11   Museums, Libraries and Archives Council (2011) *Public Performance Licences: an information guide: music and film activities in public libraries*, November 2011, www.iaml.info/iaml-uk-irl/resources/pub_perf_licenses.pdf.

CHAPTER 6

The Digital Economy Act 2010

The copyright provisions in ss 3–18 of the Digital Economy Act 2010 make a series of amendments to the Communications Act 2003. They define the broad framework for dealing with infringement, but most of the operational details of the copyright regime are contained in a code of practice known as the 'Initial Obligations Code'.[1]

During the course of the 2010–2015 parliament the UK government were planning to introduce a new Communications Bill, which would make it harder for websites linking to unlawful content to prosper because it is envisaged that the Bill would require net firms, advertisers and credit card companies to cut ties with such sites. But so far there has been no sign of a green paper, and some commentators suggest that plans to overhaul broadcasting and communications policy have been pushed into the long grass. If a green paper were to emerge, though, the government would need to ensure that any new legislation complied with the provisions in the E-commerce Directive which limit the liability of some internet intermediaries.

6.1 The key players

The Communications Act 2003, as amended by the DEA, defines a number of key players, and the distinctions between them are important because they determine their responsibilities under the legislation.

6.1.1 Copyright owner

'Copyright owner' means:

- a copyright owner within the meaning of Part 1 of the Copyright, Designs and Patents Act 1988 (see s. 173[2] of that Act); or
- someone authorised by that person to act on the person's behalf (according to s. 16 of the DEA which inserts s. 124N into the Communications Act 2003).

6.1.2 Communications provider

A communications provider is defined in Section 405 of the Communications Act 2003 as 'a person who (within the meaning of section 32(4)) provides an electronic communications network or an electronic communications service'.

6.1.3   Internet service provider

'Internet service provider' means a person who provides an internet access service (Section 124N of the Communications Act 2003); and an 'internet access service' is 'an electronic communications service that – (a) is provided to a subscriber; (b) consists entirely or mainly of the provision of access to the internet; and (c) includes the allocation of an IP address or IP addresses to the subscriber to enable that access' (CA 2003 s124N).

6.1.4   Subscriber

A 'subscriber', in relation to an internet access service, means a person who:

- receives the service under an agreement between the person and the provider of the service; and
- does not receive it as a communications provider (CA 2003 s124N)

6.2   Copyright infringement reports (CIRs)

Under the copyright regime established by the Digital Economy Act 2010, copyright owners will, once the provisions are brought into force, generate and send copyright infringement reports to ISPs, which are required in turn to notify subscribers of any copyright infringement reports which detail incidents of copyright infringement in which they are alleged to have been involved.

In terms of timing, qualifying copyright owners must send the CIR to the qualifying ISP within ten working days of the required evidence having been gathered; and ISPs are required to notify subscribers within ten working days of receiving the CIR from the copyright owner. The time limit is important, because the Ofcom code is mindful of the fact that the longer the period between evidence being gathered and subscribers receiving a notification the less effective the notifications programme will be.

The notification letters provide appropriate information and advice to the subscriber, including a suitable warning that the copyright owner might take legal action in the event of repeated infringement. Paragraph 4.3 of the code sets out the minimum level of information that needs to be included in the report.

In order to benefit from this system, qualifying copyright owners must pay notification costs and qualifying costs to ISPs or Ofcom.

6.3   Copyright infringement lists

There is a three-stage notification process which is often referred to as 'three strikes'. A subscriber may be included in a copyright infringement list when they have received a third notification within the previous 12 months.

1 The first CIR would trigger the first notification.
2 The second notification would be triggered by the first CIR received on or after one month from the date of the first notification.
3 The third and final notification would be triggered by the first CIR received on or after one month from the date of the second notification.

Where a subscriber has received three CIRs within the space of 12 months, they would be added to the copyright infringement list at that point.

ISPs are required to record the number of reports made against their subscribers and provide copyright owners on request with an anonymized list – known as a copyright infringement list – which enables the copyright owner to see which of the reports it has made are linked to the same subscriber. The list provided to the copyright owner only contains details which are directly related to copyright infringement reports which have been made by the requesting owner. So, if a number of copyright infringement reports have been submitted by other copyright owners with regard to a subscriber, the list disclosed to one copyright owner only gives the details of the CIR(s) submitted by that copyright owner.

The timescale for the first warning letters to be sent out under the new code rules is the start of 2013.

6.4   Quality assurance reports

Copyright owners are required to provide Ofcom with a quality assurance report before submitting their first CIR, and from then on an annual basis, in order to ensure that the evidence-gathering processes used by a qualifying copyright owner are robust and accurate. This is important in order to be able to have trust in the whole process. Ofcom want to ensure that where allegations are made against subscribers they are based upon credible evidence, gathered in a robust manner.

Imagine, for example, someone being accused of filesharing based on their being linked to a particular IP address. What if the IP address were generated dynamically and allocated to an individual only for one particular session, and that same IP address was made available minutes later for a totally different individual to use? Add into the mix the possibility that no account was taken of the difference between British Summer Time and Greenwich Mean Time. A similar point is made by Richard Clayton in his evidence to the judicial review of the Digital Economy Act (www.openrightsgroup.org/assets/JK1RC.pdf paragraph 58):

If an inaccurate timestamp is used, even one that is just a few seconds out, then an erroneous identification may be made of the previous or next customer to use the particular IP address.

6.5   Penalties

The Digital Economy Act 2010 (s. 42) increased to £50,000 the maximum fine for offences under s. 107 (criminal liability for making or dealing with infringing articles) and s. 198 (illicit recordings).

A financial penalty of up to the maximum of £250,000 may be imposed by Ofcom in respect of any breach of the code by an ISP or copyright holder contravening their obligations under the code (Under s. 96 of the CA 2003 as amended by s. 14 of the DEA).[3] Ofcom will determine the amount that is appropriate and proportionate to the contravention to which it relates.

6.6   Appeals and costs

The ruling in the judicial review of the DEA (British Telecommunications PLC and TalkTalk Telecom Group PLC v. Secretary of State for Business, Innovation and Skills [2011] EWHC 1021) stated that ISPs cannot be made responsible for the costs incurred by Ofcom for establishing an appeals body, although it does have to pay a share in order to help the appeals system run and it also has to pay a quarter of the cost of the system of letters written to users who are identified as potentially infringing copyright. In the light of this, DCMS removed the obligation on ISPs to contribute towards the costs of Ofcom and the independent appeals body in setting up and administering the regime. This does not apply to the costs incurred by ISPs in performing their own duties under the DEA or to the appeals case fees.

The ruling was taken to the Court of Appeal (BT & Talk Talk v. Secretary of State [2012] EWCA Civ 232), who upheld the High Court decision in all but one regard, and that relates to 'case fees' (see paragraphs 106-107 in the 2012 Court of Appeal judgment). The judge said that if 'qualifying costs' are treated as 'administrative charges', then 'case fees' should also be regarded as such.

DCMS received advice from Ofcom on the potential costs of the DEA appeals system which they published in August 2011.[4] In order to minimize the risk of the system being disrupted by vexatious or non bona fide appeals they decided to introduce a £20 fee, which would be incurred by any subscriber who wanted to lodge an appeal. The £20 sum would be refundable in the event of their appeal being successful. This will be reviewed one year after the notifications have been in place in order to make sure that the fee level is still appropriate. A sharing of costs statutory instrument[5] sets out how the scheme is to be paid for. In Hansard for 23 April 2012 (Column 571W), Jeremy Hunt made clear that, in the light of the findings of the judicial review, both the wording of the statutory instrument and also of the Initial Obligations Code were in the process of being amended in order to take account of the findings regarding financial responsibility for appeal case fees.

6.7   Filesharing and the Digital Economy Act 2010

The copyright provisions in the Digital Economy Act 2010 (Sections 3-18) were passed in order to tackle illicit filesharing. As they haven't yet been brought into force, legal cases involving filesharing have had to rely on existing legislation. (Section 3.8 of this book deals with filesharing activities which have drawn upon legislation other than the DEA 2010 and covers penalties for illegal filesharing; the tactics of lawyers acting in filesharing cases; cyberlockers; and inadvertent filesharing).

At the end of April 2012 DCMS confirmed that the implementation of the copyright provisions in the DEA 2010 had been delayed once again, and that the measures wouldn't be enforced until at least 2014.

6.7.1   Unsecured Wi-Fi access

Under the Digital Economy Act 2010 it is the subscriber who will be held responsible for any infringements made using their internet account. If someone uses their wireless internet connection without permission and commits a copyright infringement, they therefore need to take steps to secure their connection and stop this from happening again. Using someone else's unsecured internet connection is known as 'piggybacking'. A 2011 study of 500 UK internet users by the PC Support Group found that 58% admitted to having used someone else's broadband connection without permission.[6]

6.7.2   Filesharing statistics

The Digital Economy Act 2010 inserted provisions into the Communications Act 2003 requiring Ofcom to monitor trends in online copyright infringement and to ascertain the effectiveness of the obligations on ISPs. Kantar Media were commissioned by Ofcom to conduct a pilot survey to establish the most effective and robust survey methodology for monitoring illegal file-sharing among consumers.[7]

Interim reports must be submitted on a three-monthly basis, with the first report covering the first full quarter after implementation (see s. 8 of the DEA 2010, which inserts s. 124F – progress reports – into the Communications Act 2003). There will also be full reports submitted annually.

In preparing for these reporting duties, Ofcom will – according to its Annual Plan 2011/12 – look to engage with stakeholders about how they can identify and capture relevant information. This includes information that relates to the development and promotion of lawful services, initiatives to raise public awareness of copyright and online infringement, and enforcement actions taken by copyright owners against alleged infringers.

6.8   Website blocking

Sections 17 and 18 of the Digital Economy Act 2010 contain reserve powers to tackle copyright-infringing websites through a court-based process in order to block access to those sites. DCMS commissioned Ofcom to report on whether or not these measures were workable. In its report[8] Ofcom concludes that the blocking of infringing websites could potentially play a role in tackling online copyright infringement, but that the approach set out in the DEA is unlikely to be effective because of the slow speed that would be expected from a full court process. This would provide site operators with the opportunity to change the location of the site long before any injunction could come into force.

Ofcom focused on four primary techniques currently available that ISPs could use within their network infrastructure to block sites.

1 **Internet Protocol (IP) address blocking**: modifying ISP network equipment to discard internet traffic destined for the blocked site. An IP address is analogous to a telephone number, as it uniquely identifies a device attached to the internet.
2 **Blocking via Domain Name System (DNS) alteration**: changing the ISP service that translates domain names, e.g. www.example.com, into IP addresses e.g. 192.0.32.10. The ISP DNS server, when blocking, tells the requesting computer or device that the site does not exist or redirects the request to an informational web page, for example one which explains why access to the site has been blocked.
3 **Uniform Resource Locator (URL) blocking**: the blocking of specific items, such as websites or addresses, e.g. www.example.com/pirate.zip.
4 **Packet Inspection**: blocking techniques which examine network traffic at a high level.

Ofcom did also consider three hybrid options: DNS blocking coupled with shallow packet inspection; DNS blocking coupled with URL blocking; and DNS blocking coupled with deep packet inspection. None of these techniques is 100% effective; each carries different costs and has a different impact on network performance and the risk of over-blocking.

In the light of the advice from Ofcom, the government decided not to bring into force ss 17 and 18 of the DEA. Indeed, at the end of June 2012, DCMS announced that the government will seek to repeal ss 17 and 18 of the DEA at an early opportunity: see www.culture.gov.uk/uk/news/media_releases/9160.aspx. However, it has expressed its intention to do more work on what other measures can be pursued in order to tackle online copyright infringement. Even though ss 17 and 18 of the DEA are not being brought into force, website blocking is still very much on the agenda. The case of Newzbin2 has demonstrated that it is perfectly possible to get websites blocked for copyright infringement without having to rely on the powers set out in the Digital Economy Act.

⊕ Twentieth Century Fox et al. v. British Telecommunications PLC [2011] EWHC 1981 (Ch)

In July 2011 the High Court instructed BT to block its customers from having access to the Newzbin2 file-sharing website. BT had argued that forcing it to ban its customers from accessing the site would usher in a new wave of online censorship. The Motion Picture Association said that Newzbin2 makes unlawful copies of television programmes and films, and receives in excess of £1m a year from its 700,000 users.

The case set a legal precedent because it was the first UK case to use Section 97A of the CDPA 1988 to get an internet service provider to block access to a website. Digital rights organizations are concerned that there is a real risk of legitimate content being blocked – that is, there is a problem of over-blocking.

On 26 October 2011 Mr Justice Arnold said that BT must block the Newzbin2 site within 14 days. BT complied with the request using a website filtering service called Cleanfeed – a technology which it had already been using in order to filter out a list of sites supplied by the Internet Watch Foundation in order to prevent its customers from viewing child sexual abuse content online.

The UK government set out an action plan to tackle counterfeiting and criminal piracy in *Prevention and Cure: the UK IP Crime Strategy 2011*.[9] This includes work on websites that are predominantly used for digital piracy and work with other states to develop international responses to these issues. Together with industry and law enforcement bodies the government has been exploring measures targeting the revenue streams of websites dedicated to infringing copyright. These include banning advertising on these sites and withdrawing payment facilities. They also want to work with search engines to investigate how to ensure that unlawful sites do not appear higher up in the search engine rankings than legitimate sources of digital content.

In February 2012 the Serious Organized Crime Agency (SOCA) took down the RnBXclusive website, which was a British music blog that posted links to unlicensed music files. This action was part of a criminal investigation in which the individuals behind the site were arrested for fraud. SOCA placed a note on the site which said 'If you have downloaded music using this website you may have committed a criminal offence which carries a maximum penalty of up to 10 years imprisonment and an unlimited fine under UK law', and it also said that 'SOCA has the capacity to monitor and investigate you, and can inform your internet service provider of these infringements'.

6.9   Practical measures to ensure compliance with the DEA 2010

Where an internet connection has been identified as being suspected of online copyright infringement, the ISP will send the subscriber a letter to inform them of this. The letter will provide advice on the steps that the subscriber might take in order to prevent their connection from being used to share copyright content illegally. Checklist 6.1 lists ways in which libraries can ensure compliance with the DEA 2010.

Checklist 6.1 *Measures for libraries to ensure compliance with the DEA 2010*
 1 Secure wi-fi networks:
   a   Use encryption such as WPA2
   b   Change the router's administrator password
   c   Change the settings to hide the network ID / SSID
   d   If possible, reduce the range that the signal is broadcast.
 2 Implement a notice and takedown system.
 3 Establish an acceptable use policy.
 4 Make sure that users have to authenticate themselves before they are given access to the internet.
 5 Prevent people from being able to install software on library machines.
 6 Educate users on the correct and incorrect use of copyright materials.
 7 Review policies for proxy servers and virtual private networks to ensure that they are consistent.
 8 Have policies in place governing the use of IT facilities and systems.
 9 Make sure everyone who uses the IT facilities actively consents to the terms and conditions.
 10 Take disciplinary action where the organization's acceptable use policy has been breached; and make sure you are consistent in the way the policy is applied.

6.9.1   Securing Wi-Fi networks

An important step that subscribers should take is to secure their wireless internet connection. This will reduce the likelihood that their connection will be used for piggybacking.

1 Make sure that you use encryption such as the Wi-Fi protected access WPA2.
2 Change the administrator password on the router. Instead of relying on the default password, change it to a stronger password which would be difficult for anyone to guess. Make use of a combination of letters and numbers, upper and lower case.
3 Hide the network ID by changing the router settings so that the SSID isn't broadcast.
4 If possible reduce the range across which the signal will broadcast.

•❖ **Useful resource**

The Digital Economy Act 2010: impact on educational institutions and public libraries, CILIP, 2012,
www.cilip.org.uk/news-media/Documents/Digital_Economy_Act_impact_
education_institutions_libraries_July2012.pdf.

6.9.2   Notice and takedown

It is good practice to have a notice and takedown policy, such as the following sample, which states clearly the action that will be taken if a complaint is received about any content on the institution's website or servers.

≡   If you are a rights owner and you believe that content on our website infringes your rights because you hadn't given permission for its use please contact us in writing either by e-mail or by post and provide us with the following information:

- your contact details, including name, organization, address and a contact telephone number
- a description of your complaint
- complete bibliographic details of the content
- the URL where you found the material
- an assertion that your complaint is accurate and is made in good faith
- confirmation that you are the rights owner or that you have been given the necessary authority to act on behalf of the rights owner.

If we are notified of a potential breach of copyright, it is our policy to remove the item promptly pending further investigation.

•❖ **Useful resource**

Korn, Naomi (2011) *Template Notice and Takedown Policy and Procedures*,
Strategic Content Alliance, March 2011,
http://sca.jiscinvolve.org/wp/files/2011/03/iDF144-SCA_
TemplateNoticeTakeDown_Mar11_v1-02.pdf.

In January 2012 the European Commission announced that it would clarify the procedures for taking down and blocking access to illegal content, after receiving complaints that the rules were unclear and that illegal content stayed online for too long.[10]

6.9.3 Acceptable use policy

Acceptable use policies are used with regard to activities undertaken on library or institutional computers. A sample acceptable use policy statement can be found in the MLA *Public Performance Licences* guide.[10] The policy statements normally cover the need for copyright compliance as one of a number of issues; typical examples of other issues covered in an acceptable use policy statement would be data protection, computer misuse, and libel.

6.9.4 User authentication

Make sure that users have to authenticate themselves before they are given unrestricted internet access, and that logs are kept as appropriate. Bear in mind the data protection and privacy implications of user logs. A user log will contain personally identifiable information and the retention of such data must therefore conform to the requirements of the Data Protection Act.

6.9.5 Manage new software installations

People who fileshare need to be able to install a BitTorrent client onto their PC. An easy way to prevent people from filesharing would therefore be to prevent them from being able to install software onto the machine.

6.9.6 Educate users on copyright

User education can play a key role in the goal of reducing copyright infringement. The Gowers [12] and Hargreaves [13] reviews both identified the role that education can play in ensuring copyright compliance. They also highlighted the need for rights owners to provide legitimate services.

The Gowers Review (p. 97) said that 'education initiatives should extend from school teaching through to industry, and to general consumer awareness, and should explain the exceptions to IP rights so that consumers understand the balance in the system'. The Hargreaves Review said that effective enforcement requires education, effective markets, an appropriate enforcement regime and a modern legal framework.

A number of submissions to the Hargreaves Review called for additional efforts to educate people, especially the young, in the importance of copyright and the way it works. The review mentioned that Ofcom had concluded that well monitored educational measures can be effective as part of a wider strategy, which also includes enforcement and readily available legitimate digital services to consumers.

On page 7 of *Copyright Enforcement in the Networked Society,*[14] a 2011 report from Ericsson, the point is made that educational and awareness-raising campaigns should be encouraged and promoted; but that such campaigns would have a realistic chance of succeeding where they were combined with consumer-friendly lawful content offerings which are made available at affordable prices and on reasonable conditions. The report also mentions that in the USA internet service providers have entered into private agreements with rights owners which include agreement to issue warnings to users where they allegedly infringe copyright repeatedly, and require such users to undergo mandatory education programs if they have received multiple warnings or else to have their internet speeds temporarily slowed down.

Libraries should undertake initiatives to educate users on copyright issues, and should take measures to raise awareness of the need to comply with copyright law. Such initiatives could include putting up copyright posters next to equipment which can be used to copy content (this would include photocopiers, scanners and computer terminals); putting together a set of FAQs on copyright; and in its acceptable use policy including as an example of unacceptable behaviour the downloading or sharing of copyright protected materials without permission or licence.

6.9.7   Review policies for proxy servers and virtual private networks

Review institutional policies for proxy servers and virtual private networks (VPNs) regularly. Proxy servers and VPNs allow users at home to appear as if they are accessing via an institutional IP address. It is important therefore to review the policies for proxy servers and VPNs to ensure that they are consistent with the institution's policies for logging activity, authenticating users, and restricting sites.

Notes and references

1   Ofcom (2012) *Online Infringement of Copyright and the Digital Economy Act 2010: notice of Ofcom's proposal to make by order a code for regulating the initital obligations*, http://stakeholders.ofcom.org.uk/consultations/infringement-notice.

2   The CDPA s173 definition of a 'copyright owner' isn't very enlightening. Section 173: '(1)Where different persons are (whether in consequence of a partial assignment or otherwise) entitled to different aspects of copyright in a work, the copyright owner for any purpose of this Part is the person who is entitled to the aspect of copyright relevant for that purpose'.

3   Any penalities will be made in line with Ofcom's statement on penalty guidelines, www.ofcom.org.uk/files/2010/06/penguid.pdf.

4   Ofcom (2011) *Digital Economy Act Copyright Infringement Appeals Process: options for reducing costs*.

5   In June 2012 Ofcom published *Online Infringement of Copyright: implementation of*

the online infringement of copyright (Initial Obligations) (Sharing of Costs) Order 2012, http://stakeholders.ofcom.org.uk/binaries/consultations/onlinecopyright/ summary/condoc.pdf.

6   PC Support Group (2011) Most British People Happy to Piggyback Online Via Unsecured Home Wifi Networks, *ISPreview,* September, www.ispreview.co.uk/story/2011/09/13/most-british-people-happy-to-piggyback-online-via-unsecured-home-wifi-networks.html.

7   Kantar Media (2010) *Illegal File-sharing Pilot Survey,* report prepared for Ofcom, 24 May.

8   Ofcom (2011) *'Site Blocking' to Reduce Online Copyright Infringement: a review of sections 17 and 18 of the Digital Economy Act,* http://stakeholders.ofcom.org.uk/binaries/internet/site-blocking.pdf.

9   Intellectual Property Office (2011) *Prevention and Cure: the UK IP Crime Strategy 2011,* www.ipo.gov.uk/ipcrimestrategy2011.pdf.

10   EU Commission Will Clarify Website Notice and Takedown Procedures, *Out-law.com,* 12 January 2012, www.out-law.com/en/articles/2012/ january-/commission-will-clarify-website-notice-and-takedown-procedures.

11   Museums, Libraries and Archives Council (2011) *Public Performance Licences: an information guide: music and film activities in public libraries,* November 2011, www.iaml.info/iaml-uk-irl/resources/pub_perf_licenses.pdf.

12   Gowers, Andrew (2006) *Gowers Review of Intellectual Property,* HM Treasury. www.official-documents.gov.uk/document/other/0118404830/0118404830. pdf.

13   Hargreaves, Ian (2011) *Digital Opportunity: a review of intellectual property and growth,* www.ipo.gov.uk/ipreview-finalreport.pdf.

14   Ericsson (2011) *Copyright Enforcement in the Networked Society: guiding principles for protecting copyright,* http://nic.suzor.net/wp-content/uploads/2011/11/ Summer-Suzor-Fair-2011-Guiding-Principles-to-Copyright-Enforcement-in-NS.pdf.

CHAPTER 7

Enforcement

7.1   Introduction

Copyright owners around the world have for some years lobbied governments on a variety of ways in which their rights can be better enforced. It is all very well having strict copyright laws in place, but if they are amongst the most broken laws on the planet, or if it is simply too costly and too time-consuming for a rights owner to take action through the courts to enforce their rights, one has to question the effectiveness of the legislative regime for protecting copyrights. It is important to ensure that intellectual property rights are properly respected. Otherwise, what incentive do the creators of the content have for generating new works?

In order for copyright to be respected widely there are a number of key components required:

1 It is partly an issue of **education and awareness** – how can consumers be expected to respect rights if they don't know what those rights are?
2 It requires **simplicity** – the copyright regime needs to be simple enough for the general public to understand rather than it being a system where you feel as though you need a lawyer on hand at all times to guide you through the copyright maze.
3 The system should be **fair and equitable**, serving the needs of users as well as rewarding creators of content.

The Hargreaves Review[1] (p. 5) says that 'effective enforcement requires education, effective markets, an appropriate enforcement regime and a modern legal framework'. Paragraph 7.17 of the *Consultation on Copyright*[2] says:

> Simplification of copyright exceptions is also proposed. The Copyright Act currently provides only 13 Sections setting out the acts restricted by copyright, compared to 66 Sections setting out the acts permitted by exceptions. Many exceptions have been implemented in ways that are complex and difficult to understand and need to be read in conjunction with additional, supporting legislation, and some may be subject to additional licences. Complex exceptions cause confusion and generate administrative costs and legal risks to those who

ought to benefit from them. The Government would like to take every opportunity to make exceptions as clear and straightforward as possible.

At the moment it feels as though you need a lawyer on hand to interpret how the law applies in particular situations, because of the complexity of copyright law.

In 2004 a European Directive (2004/48/EC) on the enforcement of intellectual property rights was passed, and according to the *Digital Agenda for Europe: annual progress report 2011*, a revision of that Directive to address online piracy is expected in the first half of 2012. There is also a Regulation (no 386/2012) on entrusting the Office for Harmonization in the Internal Market (Trade Marks and Designs) with tasks related to the enforcement of intellectual property rights, including the assembling of public and private-sector representatives as a European Observatory on Infringements of Intellectual Property Rights.

A number of countries signed the Anti-Counterfeiting Trade Agreement in 2011. ACTA seeks to improve the global enforcement of intellectual property rights through the creation of common enforcement standards and practices as well as more effective international co-operation. However, in July 2012 the European Parliament rejected ACTA, with 478 voting against and only 39 voting in favour.

Rights owners in America have also been using what are referred to as 'John Doe' suits to sue dozens, hundreds or even thousands of defendants at the same time. This type of lawsuit is a mass copyright lawsuit which list 'John Doe' as the defendant as a way of referring to anonymous people. The technique enables content owners to file a single lawsuit but to extract settlements from a large number of people.

Content owners argue that web hosts, search companies, and payment processors should assume more responsibility in protecting intellectual property rights. They have adopted a number of techniques to ensure that their rights are enforced. These include

1 The use of technology – to detect infringement; for filtering; and also for preventing access to infringing content through the use of website blocking.
2 The use of measures to cut off the sources of funding for sites that sell infringing content, by targeting card payment services and services offered by companies such as PayPal.
3 Making use of the legal system to identify infringers through the use of Norwich Pharmacal orders (see Section 7.5 below); or to seek the extradition of alleged infringers such as Richard O'Dywer (see Section 7.7).
4 Exploring the possibility that search engines be required to de-index sites containing allegedly infringing content; or else to make use of a system of traffic lights to identify which sites contain infringing content.

7.2   Protecting your content

Here are some useful measures, tips and resources for protecting your content.

Checklist 7.1 *Measures to protect your content*
If you own the copyrights in a work, then it is in your best interests to make it as clear as possible that you are indeed the copyright owner:

* Make it as easy as possible for people to be able to contact you when they want to use your work with your permission.
* Indicate intellectual property rights through the use of metadata – see, for example, the site Photometadata.org (www.photometadata.org) which promotes the use of embedded metadata.
* Use a copyright notice at the bottom of each page.
* Use licensing tools such as Creative Commons or GNU.
* Use a rights expression language such as ACAP, PLUS or ONIX-PL in order to express the legal rights in your works in a machine-readable form.

Make it harder for the wrong people to use your work:

* Use a script to disable the right mouse click facility (and therefore the ability to copy and paste).
* Use the functionality in Adobe to limit what people can do with your pdf files.
* Use software which gives images an expiration date (such as X-pire www. x-pire.de).
* Include some distinctive but redundant text in the html coding of your website to make it easy to spot where someone has copied your web pages.
* If you place some of your own images on the web, publish low resolution versions of the images rather than high resolution versions.
* Add a visible watermark (which could be your name, logo, copyright symbol etc.) embedded in the image. Doing so:
    a)   makes the photo less useful to anyone who downloads it
    b)   states that it is protected by copyright
    c)   identifies that you are the copyright owner.
* Prepare a template for a copyright infringement notice.

Monitor the web on a regular basis to see if other people have made use of your work(s). There are a number of useful tools and resources which can be used in order to do this:

➦ Useful resource

Copyscape (www.copyscape.com) can be used to search for copies of your page on the web.

➦ Useful resource

ContentGuard (www.contentguard.com) licenses the use of digital rights management systems.

➦ Useful resource

Tynt publisher tools (www.tynt.com/publisher-tools/) can be used to monitor who is copying and pasting your CC content.

➦ Useful resource

'Who stole my pictures' – this add-on for Firefox (https://addons.mozilla.org/en-US/firefox/addon/who-stole-my-pictures) enables people to reverse search with a simple right click. It looks across a number of search engines simultaneously to establish whether the pictures have been used without proper acknowledgement.

➦ Useful resource

Picscout (www.picscout.com) is a company which specializes in using its proprietary image recognition technology for finding its clients' rights-managed images being used in online commercial projects.

➦ Useful resource

Tin Eye (www.tineye.com) is a reverse image search engine. You give an image to Tin Eye to find out where it came from, how it is being used, if modified versions of the image exist, or to find higher resolution versions.

7.3   Exploiting content

Make clear what you are willing to let people do with your content; and then make it as easy as possible for people to be able to do the right thing:

1 **Attribution** – make it easy for people to be able to properly attribute you as the creator. For example, in the case of Creative Commons licensed content there is the OpenAttribute add-on: http://openattribute.com.
2 **Payment** – where you want payment in return for allowing certain uses of your work, make it as easy as possible for people to be able to pay. This could be achieved through the use of microlicensing services such as Rightslink,

where a payment option is available as part of the workflow (see Section 5.7 above for more information on microlicensing).

3 **Licensing** – make use of licences such as Creative Commons or GNU.
4 **Tracing rights owners** – make it as easy as possible for people to establish who the rights belong to. Incorporate rights information into the metadata associated with a work; support the establishment of the proposed Digital Copyright Exchange.

If you use a feature for 'article tools' on your website which enables users to print, e-mail, save, share or post your articles, consider the following:

1 Clarify where or how the content may be used.
2 Distinguish between personal use and commercial use.
3 Limit the quantity that can be printed or e-mailed.
4 Incorporate a copyright notice or links back to the publisher's site.

In 2007 YouTube launched an automated process to screen uploaded content for copyright infringement.[3] Copyright owners can specify their preferences as to what they would like to happen where a match is found between copyright-protected content and content which has been uploaded to the site. The options are to block (remove from the site), track (reports of the number of views per video are passed on to the copyright holder) or monetize their content (YouTube insert advertisements alongside the content and then the advertising revenue is shared with the rights holder).

7.4 Notice and takedown

It is good practice to have a written notice and takedown policy. This should be readily accessible on your website and should contain clear instructions on how a complaint can be made to your organization in the event of an alleged copyright infringement, and what information a complainant needs to provide you with. For example, make clear that complainants should provide you with details of the URLs where the allegedly infringing work appears. (In an American case, Wolk v. Kodak Imaging Network, Inc., 2011 WL 940056 S.D.N.Y. March 17, 2011, where Sheila Wolk sued Photobucket and its partner Kodak, the judge made clear that the complainant needed to give details of specific URLs). The notice and takedown policy should also set out what action will be taken in the event of a complaint being received about an alleged infringement of copyright.

If you receive a complaint regarding the copyright status of a piece of content on your site it is important to respond promptly to takedown notices. It is advisable to suspend access to that content with immediate effect while the grounds for the complaint are checked. This would be in accordance with the Electronic

Commerce (EC Directive) Regulations 2002 SI 2002/2013, regulations 17–19. A court would take account of factors such as whether or not takedown notices were dealt with promptly; or whether people who repeatedly infringed copyright had their access rights terminated.

In March 2009 Out-law News reported[4] that an analysis by academics of the requests that Google receives relating to the removal of content on the grounds of copyright infringement reveals that many may be unwarranted and that over half of the link removal demands came from competitor companies.

In 2009 the Publishers Association launched the **Copyright Infringement Portal** (www.copyrightinfringementportal.com) which enables publishers to issue notices requesting the removal of copyright material from infringing domains. In 2011 there were around 90,000 infringement reports sent out via the portal, relating to over 172,000 web pages. A significant amount of the infringing content – roughly two-thirds – is removed within three days of a notice being served.

7.5   Norwich Pharmacal orders

Norwich Pharmacal orders derive from a House of Lords decision in the case of Norwich Pharmacal Co v. Commissioners of Customs and Excise [1974] AC 133, which established the principle that a party to potential litigation can seek disclosure of information which is held by a third party where it could identify someone against whom a claim could be made. The device has been used on a number of occasions to identify the IP address used by a wrongdoer, such as someone who has fileshared using a BitTorrent client. The copyright owner can ask the court to grant an order against the internet service provider requiring it to disclose details of the customer to whom the IP address was allocated at the time of the infringing activity.

7.6   *Fines and prosecutions*

Copyright infringements can be dealt with either by the civil or the criminal courts. In order to be a criminal offence the court would need to establish *mens rea* or knowledge, which would therefore make the infringing activity deliberate. *Mens rea* is the Latin term for 'guilty mind' and it is one of the necessary elements of a crime. Criminal prosecutions would be limited to infringements on an industrial scale. So it would require proof of commercial activity.

The main criminal copyright offences are set out in ss 107 and 198 of the CDPA 1988:

- s107 – criminal liability for making or dealing with infringing articles, etc.
- s198 – criminal liability for making, dealing with or using illicit recordings.

There are also offences such as:

- s296ZB – devices and services designed to circumvent technological measures
- s297 – fraudulent reception of broadcasts
- s297A – unauthorised decoders
- s6 of the Fraud Act 2006 – has been used for illegal recordings in cinemas (camcording).

The maximum punishment on indictment for some criminal offences would be 10 years' imprisonment and/or a fine.

The courts have a number of remedies available for copyright infringement cases and in deciding which remedy to use they would take account of factors such as how flagrant the infringement was or what benefit the defendant gained from the infringement. Remedies include:

- injunctions – a court order prohibiting any further infringement.
- damages – for loss of royalties; the calculation is usually based on the licence fee. A copyright owner can also elect to have an account of the infringer's profit.
- delivery up (of the infringing articles) – a court order that the infringing party deliver all infringing articles into court; this might be accompanied by a destruction order.
- right to seize infringing copies – the police or trading standards can seize the infringing copies by way of a search warrant (magistrates' court).

Where an infringement constituting a criminal offence is committed by a company, the directors, managers, secretary and similar officers could also be guilty of an offence if the act was committed with their 'consent or connivance'.

> **CDPA section 110 Offence by body corporate: liability of officers**
> (1) Where an offence under section 107 committed by a body corporate is proved to have been committed with the consent or connivance of a director, manager, secretary or other similar officer of the body, or a person purporting to act in any such capacity, he as well as the body corporate is guilty of the offence and liable to be proceeded against and punished accordingly.

Critics argue that section 110 limits a directors' criminal liability for copyright infringement to actual knowledge, which means that directors who are neglectful can escape criminal liability.

7.7 Extradition
Provisions within the Extradition Act 2003 do provide the legal means for suspected

criminals to be summoned to the USA. The UK–US extradition treaty agreement allows either country to surrender a criminal suspect to the other if the crime carries a minimum punishment of a year's prison sentence. The lesson from the O'Dwyer case, already mentioned in Section 3.1.2 and summarized here, is that owners of UK websites could potentially be extradited to the USA if their sites host links to copyright infringing material, regardless of whether they have ever set foot in the USA or of whether the servers hosting the website are based in the USA.

⊕ **Government of the United States of America v. Richard O'Dwyer**

In June 2011 it was reported that a student at Sheffield Hallam University was facing the prospect of extradition to the USA to face copyright infringement charges, and could possibly spend up to five years in jail in America for a website called TVShack which provided links to film clips. Richard O'Dwyer was, at all times, resident and based in the UK. The website in question held no infringing content, merely acting as a search engine/linking site like Google, Bing, etc. (see Section 3.1.2).

In June 2010 the US Immigration and Customs Enforcement (ICE) seized and shut down the site. When that happened, Mr O'Dwyer reopened with a different domain name within one day (TVShack.cc) and carried on as before.

Mr O'Dwyer spent a night in Wandsworth Prison until his aunt paid £3000 bail money. His bail conditions required him to report weekly to a police station in Sheffield.

- On 13 January 2012 a judge at Westminster Magistrates Court agreed with US prosecutors that he should face trial in America rather than in the UK. (The ruling by District Judge Purdy is available at : www.judiciary.gov.uk/Resources/JCO/Documents/Judgments/us-v.-odwyer-ruling.pdf).
- On 13 March 2012 the Home Secretary Theresa May approved the extradition and gave Mr O'Dwyer a fortnight in which to appeal against the decision.
- On 22 March 2012 BBC News Online reported that the family of Mr O'Dwyer had confirmed that an appeal had been lodged by lawyers.[5]

7.8   Cutting off funding to sites

People involved in money transactions such as credit card companies, premium rate services (PRS), or payment service providers could potentially be targeted if they are found to play a role in the sale of counterfeit goods. Visa and MasterCard are already working with the City of London Police and IFPI (the International Federation of the Phonographic Industry) to prevent the sale of illegal content through their services.

In the past, pirated music downloads were largely paid for by consumers through the use of credit cards. However, following discussions between IFPI and the City of London Police, credit card companies have begun to identify and exclude merchants offering pirated music which means that people who are determined to offer pirated music for sale are likely to look to alternative payment methods. In July 2011 IFPI announced that PayPal will cut funding to websites which are deemed to be illegal by the music industry and the City of London Police. PayPal's acceptable use policy makes clear that it doesn't permit its services to be used in order to buy items which infringe or violate any copyright or other proprietary right.

In November 2011 PhonepayPlus, the UK's regulator of PRS services, announced that it had agreed to work proactively with IFPI (the International Federation of the Phonographic Industry) and the City of London Police in order to prevent potentially criminal activity damaging the ongoing reputation of the overall PRS market. PhonepayPlus proactively passes on details of copyright-infringing websites to service providers. Premium rate service providers who are notified of such sites could be held criminally liable under s. 328 of the Proceeds of Crime Act 2002 (POCA) if they were to subsequently make arrangements with those illicit sites and help users of those sites to pay for the pirated music.

Under POCA a person is generally guilty of an offence if they enter into or become concerned in arrangements they know or suspect facilitates (by whatever means) the acquisition, retention, use or control of criminal property by or on behalf of another person. Under the E-Commerce Regulations (SI 2002/2013) a service provider is generally not liable for any copyright-infringing material accessed by users of its service if it 'acts as a mere conduit, caches the material, or hosts the material' but in order to avoid any liability for unlawful material, the service provider must, upon gaining 'actual knowledge' act 'expeditiously' to ensure that the information is deleted from its cache or ensure that access to it is disabled.

PRS providers found guilty of a POCA offence could also face investigation under the PhonepayPlus Code of Practice which requires them to 'assess the potential risks posed' by entering into contracts for the provision, promotion, marketing and content of PRS which they help provide or facilitate 'and take and maintain reasonable continuing steps to control those risks'. PhonepayPlus can issue a range of sanctions for breaches of its Code, including handing out fines and barring companies from being involved in helping provide PRS for defined periods.

7.9   The role that search engines can play

In 2011 DCMS held meetings with copyright holders and search engines which explored how search engines might help tackle copyright infringement. The meetings were about self-regulation or private internet policing rather than legislative proposals, although a new Communications Act could formalize some of these measures.

7.9.1   Deindexing content

One measure under consideration is the manipulation of search results. They would in effect give rights holders the power to control search engine results. Similarly, in America, the SOPA (Stop Online Piracy Act) bill would require search engines to take steps to prevent pirate websites from even being found in search results.

7.9.2   Traffic lights to show illegal content

The Performing Right Society for Music believe that traffic lights have a valuable role to play as a consumer education initiative and are proposing that they would like to work with ISPs, internet security software providers, rights holders and other partners in order to deliver a solution of this kind. This would involve search engines attaching red light symbols next to sites which are categorized as being at risk of infringing copyright and green symbols next to safer sites, thereby providing a visual indication to users where a site was facilitating copyright theft. Hovering over the red tick would bring up a message to inform the internet searcher that this site links to unlicensed media.

7.10   Major legal cases

⊕ Google Books (The Authors Guild et al. v. Google Inc. in US District Court for the Southern District of New York 05-08136)

In December 2011 The Authors Guild and a number of individual authors filed a motion for a class action lawsuit alleging copyright infringement by Google relating to the Google Books project. The Google Books initiative was announced in 2004. Google entered into agreements with a number of libraries to scan out-of-print books from their collections, many of which were still in copyright. Google provided the libraries with digital copies of the works and also stored digital copies on its own servers. The contracts required the libraries to make use of technological protection measures to control access to the digital files.

Legal action against Google began in 2005. Google had neither sought nor obtained permission from the copyright owners for their copying activity, claiming that it was covered by fair use permitted by s. 107 of the US Copyright Act.[6]

A proposed settlement deal was announced in 2008 between the Authors Guild, the Association of American Publishers and Google which would have allowed Google to develop and promote a subscription service containing the library of digitized works in return for royalty payments to the copyright owners. But there were objections to the proposed settlement, which would have turned copyright law on its head:

- taking rights without first asking for permission
- operating on the basis of the principle of 'opt-out' rather than 'opt-in'
- giving Google a monopoly over the scanned works by forcing the libraries to use technological measures to restrict internet access to those digital copies, even if they are copies of works in the public domain.

In March 2011 the settlement was rejected by a federal court judge raising concerns over: Google's monopoly over the works; use of full text rather than 'snippets'; international copyright; and privacy issues. The court indicated that the Constitution delegates the role of defining the fundamental copyright principles to Congress and that courts should 'encroach only reluctantly' on Congress's prerogative.

➕ Georgia State University (Cambridge University Press et al. v. Mark P. Becker Case 1:08-cv-01425-ODE In the United States District Court for the Northern District of Georgia Atlanta Division)

Cambridge University Press, Oxford University Press and Sage Publications filed a lawsuit against Georgia State University (GSU) in 2008 asserting that GSU were engaged in the systematic, widespread and unauthorized copying and distribution of their copyrighted materials. At the heart of the complaint was GSU's practice of digitizing and electronically distributing classroom materials through its electronic course reserve system and its virtual learning environment.

A few months after the lawsuit had been filed, GSU introduced a new copyright policy which included a 'fair use checklist' setting out a number of scenarios which would weigh in favour of or against a finding of fair use. Even after the new policy had been introduced, the publishers asserted that the new policy encouraged copying well beyond what would constitute fair use.

Rather than mentioning fair use or s. 107 of the US Copyright Act, the publishing companies cited the 1976 guidelines for classroom copying,[7] which sets out a rule permitting a copy of only 10% or 1000 words of a prose work, whichever is the less. They wanted the guidelines to be imposed by the court as the maximum standard for fair use on the Georgia State campus.

The plaintiffs in their post-trial brief asked the judge to virtually eliminate fair use in academia and replace it instead with a compulsory licence. The annual cost of a blanket Annual Academic Copyright License for GSU would be US$114,000 in rights holder royalties, as well as a one-time, first year only, administrative charge of 20% of that figure.

As a state institution, Georgia State University invoked sovereign immunity, thereby making it harder for the publishers who brought the action (Cambridge University Press, Oxford University Press and SAGE Publications) to be able to seek damages.

The ruling in this case was delivered on 11 May 2012. It took into account the 'PNAM' test in section 107 of the US Copyright Act. PNAM refers to four criteria set out in that legislation – Purpose, Nature, Amount and Market Impact. The court found that only five of the ninety-nine alleged copyright infringements did actually violate the plaintiff's copyrights. Key points from Judge Evans' ruling include:

- The publishers hadn't actually proved their copyright stake in the material.
- The Guidelines for Classroom Copying should not be treated as the standard to be applied.
- The publishers had not lost significant amounts of money as a result of the alleged copyright infringements; the court said that permission fees were not a significant percentage of the plaintiff's overall revenues.
- A 10% rule should guide decisions about what constitutes fair use in an educational setting, in other words, the copying of one chapter (if the book has ten or more chapters) or 10% of a work should be considered to be 'fair use'.[8]

➕ Newspaper Licensing Agency v. Meltwater 2011 EWCA Civ 890

Meltwater provide a media monitoring service to clients. Websites are scanned for the occurrence of particular words or phrases that the client wishes to monitor, and where the word or phrase appears Meltwater sends the client a hyperlink to each relevant article, along with the opening words of the article, and an extract from the article showing the context within which the word or phrase appears.

During 2009 the Newspaper Licensing Agency proposed two new licensing schemes, one for media monitoring organizations and the other for end-users of those monitoring services. The NLA contended that end-users would need to take out an NLA licence if they wanted to make use of media monitoring services; otherwise they would be infringing copyright in the material by receiving and reading Meltwater News because by clicking on a link to the article they would be making a copy of the article within the meaning of s. 17 of the CDPA 1988, and by forwarding Meltwater News or its contents to clients they would be issuing copies to the public within the meaning of s. 18 of the CDPA 1988.

In December 2009 Meltwater Group announced that it had referred the Newspaper Licensing Agency to the Copyright Tribunal over the reasonableness of those licences. At the time of referring the dispute to the Copyright Tribunal, Jorn Lyseggen, CEO of Meltwater Group, said that 'the NLA's attempt to license our clients is essentially a tax on receiving these internet links. This fee is not only unjust and unreasonable, it is contrary to the very spirit of the internet'.

Meanwhile the Newspaper Licensing Agency launched a High Court action in order to get legal clarity on aggregator and end-user licences. David Pugh of NLA said 'The Copyright Tribunal will rule on the commercial aspects of NLA web licensing . . . But the High Court is the proper place to decide on the legality of our web licences'.

But it is worth bearing in mind first the sheer scale of the use which is being made of the content, because it would seem that a single end-user could well receive text from some 50,000 articles per annum; and secondly that the newspaper publishers have devoted very substantial resources in developing their websites and to the selection, arrangement and presentation of the material on them. Meltwater is making millions of pounds from its own activities which include 'scraping' the publishers' websites for information for its own commercial gain.

This case has already been summarized in Section 3.1 above.

⊕ Twentieth Century Fox v. British Telecommunications PLC [2011] EWHC 1981 (Ch)

In this case (known more commonly as 'Newzbin2') the court was asked by various movie studios to serve an injunction that would force BT to try to block access to the site 'Newzbin'. The website is a members-only site which aggregates a large amount of illegally copied material (film, books, music). Justice Arnold found in favour of the movie studios.

Organizations campaigning against this form of censorship asserted that blocking is pointless because it most likely won't work, will be trivial to avoid, won't stop infringement and won't bring returns for the creative industries. Blocking is also dangerous because of the significant risks of accidental 'over-blocking', the possible slowing of internet service, and because it will likely lead to the wider, everyday use of encryption and avoidance measures.

Brought by the Motion Picture Association of America, this is a landmark case because it is the first time that an ISP has been ordered to block access to such a site and it was anticipated that court orders against other ISPs would follow. The case was hailed as a victory for the creative industries. Rights holders have in effect found a cost-efficient remedy to blocking sites containing or linking to infringing content.

The court ordered BT to pay the costs of implementing the block, something it had argued it should not have to do. BT already ran a website filtering service called Cleanfeed which is updated frequently with a list of sites supplied by the Internet Watch Foundation, in order to prevent its customers from viewing child sexual abuse content online, and this filtering service is being used in order to block the Newzbin site. BT estimated that it would cost around £5,000 to adapt Cleanfeed to enable updates from other sources, such as the Motion Picture Association, and then £100 for each further domain name or numerical internet address.

⊕ The Pirate Bay

The issue of illicit filesharing is not confined to the UK. February and March 2009 saw the landmark case of 'The Pirate Bay', a website that held links to torrent files that often contained copyright protected material. Although the site did not host content itself, the case resulted in four Swedish men being found guilty of copyright offences and given prison sentences of between four months and one year and ordered to pay fines totalling the equivalent of roughly £4.1 million.

At the beginning of May 2012 the High Court ordered five of the UK's internet service providers to block their customers from having access to The Pirate Bay website; and BT blocked the site some weeks later, after having been granted more time to 'consider their position'.

A fuller summary of the case can be found in Section 3.8.1.

⊕ The Anne Muir case

In 2011, Anne Muir from Ayr became the first person in Scotland to be convicted of illegally sharing music online and was sentenced to three years probation.

A fuller summary of the case can be found in Section 3.8.1.

⊕ Oink

Alan Ellis was the first person in the UK to be prosecuted for illegal filesharing. His website Oink was hosted abroad but operated from a flat in Middlesbrough from 2004 until it was closed down in a police raid of the server premises in Amsterdam in October 2007. In that time Oink facilitated the downloading of an estimated 21 million music files and attracted over 200,000 members. The site did not actually host unlawfully copied material, but allowed active members to find other people on the web who would share files enabling users to get access to music files without considering whether the source was legitimate.

The site worked on an invitation-only basis with members paying £5.00 per friend they proposed to join. In December 2008, four former members of Oink were successfully prosecuted for copyright infringement offences at Teesside Crown Court. Three were sentenced to community service totalling 330 hours and one was fined £500. On 15 January 2009, Alan Ellis was found not guilty of conspiracy to defraud at Teesside Crown Court. Prosecutors told the jury how he had received almost US$300,000 (£200,000) in 'donations' in his PayPal account, amounting to almost £11,000 (US$18,000) a month, from people using his website; and he agreed he had about ten bank accounts with some £20,000 in savings when police raided the house he shared.

Ellis insisted that the monies were to pay for the server's rental costs (the site was hosted on a commercial server in Amsterdam) – and any surplus would eventually be used to buy a new server – and that he, unlike Oink's actual users, wasn't personally guilty of infringement, because he didn't personally host or share any infringing content. The site allowed active members to find other people on the web who were prepared to share files enabling users to get hold of free music. Users were asked to make a donation, although it was not necessary for them to do so to invite friends to join the site.

Ellis painted a picture of Oink as being a geeky student programming project that got out of control. He told the court how he created the website while studying at Teesside University and in a short period afterwards, mainly because he felt the programming skills he'd been taught were outdated and that he should endeavour to teach himself some up-to-date web-based programming to better his skills for employability. Ellis said the website was developed from a free template, which had a torrent (metadata about the location of a target file) filesharing facility included in it.

What lessons can be learned from Ellis' acquittal? Perhaps that the case should have been brought as a civil case rather than a criminal case – and, as the website was operational for three years, if it was such a threat to the copyright interests of music rights holders, why was action not taken more swiftly?

➕ HathiTrust (The Authors Guild et al. v. HathiTrust et al, Civil No. 11 CV 6351 (HB) (JLC))

The HathiTrust digital repository consists of scans of millions of complete books. It has partnerships with over 50 institutions to digitize and preserve books and other content. The HathiTrust repository was established by the University of Michigan in order to enable staff and students at the university to access orphan works. Library users are only able to view public domain works, but not copyrighted works.

The Authors Guild sued five US universities for creating online libraries consisting of millions of books scanned by Google. The Guild sought an injunction to prevent infringing reproductions, distributions and displays of works in the digital libraries. The lawsuit says that the defendants have engaged in 'the systematic, concerted, widespread, and unauthorized reproduction and distribution' of some seven million copyrighted works, a handful of which are listed in the brief. It says that the plaintiffs and Google, which has provided most of the digital scans at issue, did not seek permission to digitize those works. In February 2012 the Authors Guild and other plaintiffs asked the judge to rule on HathiTrust's fair use claim; they were aiming to get the judge to rule that the mass digitization of material was not protected by any defence recognized by copyright law. A ruling on this point was still awaited at the time of writing (July 2012).

7.11   Content identification tools

If you own rights in content and believe that those rights have been infringed, you would need to demonstrate that it was your content which had been copied. Content identification tools can assist here.

•❖ Useful resource

Attributor (www.attributor.com)

Attributor's FairShare Guardian is a web-wide monitoring and enforcement platform used by publishers to identify new sales leads and revenue-sharing opportunities, monitor licensed uses and protect against unauthorized use of their content. Attributor was promoted as being the first global content tracking and monetization platform.

- It automatically monitors usage of publisher content and stops unauthorized usage.
- Publishers program when, how and where their content is distributed online.
- Sophisticated fingerprinting algorithms, web crawlers, etc, monitor use of the content.
- It helps publishers fight piracy, monitor licensed use of content and uncover possible revenue-sharing opportunities.

•❖ Useful resource

Vobile Inc. (www.vobileinc.com)

Vobile VDNA digital fingerprinting technology is an example of a service which utilizes content identification technology: www.vobileinc.com/news_4_15_08.htm.

7.12   Copyright trolls

Copyright trolls buy up the copyright in works, and then seek to enforce those rights. They might for example troll to find an instance where a newspaper article has already been published without authorization and then seek to buy the copyright in the content with the specific intention of taking out a copyright infringement lawsuit. Such actions can lead to the trolls being paid to resolve disputes through out of court settlements, especially where the infringer is concerned at the cost of going to court. In order to sue someone through the courts for copyright infringement you would need to be the owner of the rights, or at least the exclusive licensee of the copyright. A copyright assignment is not valid unless it actually transfers copyrights. You can't simply transfer the right to sue without transferring the copyrights.

7.12.1 Righthaven

Righthaven was a prominent copyright troll whose whole business model was based around copyright enforcement actions. Righthaven sued hundreds of bloggers and websites, in Nevada, Colorado and South Carolina.

Righthaven entered into an agreement with the *Las Vegas Review Journal* and the *Denver Post* to sue third parties for alleged infringement of certain of those newspapers' works on the internet. At first Righthaven's lawsuits were fairly success- ful and the company managed to extract many small settlements out of various defendants. However, when they were forced to produce the copyright 'assignment' between itself and the newspapers it led to the dismissal of various Righthaven cases, threats of sanctions and even class actions from prior settling parties.

In Silvers v. Sony Pictures Entertainment, Inc., 402 F.3d 881 (9th Cir. 2005), the Ninth Circuit made clear that one cannot merely transfer the right to sue for a copyright infringement. Rather, to have copyright standing, you must be the owner, or at least the exclusive licensee, of an actual copyright right under section 106, whereas the newspaper assignments to Righthaven did not do this. While the agreements purported to be assignments of copyright, they made clear that the newspaper retained the right to exploit all copyrights, that Righthaven could not exploit the copyrights other than to bring infringement lawsuits, and that the newspaper even had discretion over whom to sue.

In Colorado senior US district judge John Kane said that only the 'legal owner' or the 'beneficial owner' of copyrights can sue for violations of those rights. As such Righthaven had no legal right to sue for copyright infringement on behalf of Media News Group, owner of the *Denver Post*, because the company hadn't given any of the ownership rights in the work in question to Righthaven. The judge said in his ruling that 'Media News Group had assigned to Righthaven the bare right to sue for infringement – no more, no less'. Righthaven were ordered to repay Leland Wolf the full cost of defending this action. He had posted a photograph from the *Denver Post* onto his website without permission.

In its lawsuit against the Democratic Underground a judge ordered Righthaven to pay US$5,000 for not disclosing the fact that it had a legal agreement in place whereby it would split any revenues 50/50 with Stephens Media, owner of the *Las Vegas Review Journal*. By failing to disclose its financial relationship with Stephens Media, Righthaven had violated Nevada's local rules of litigation. Instead of meeting the deadline for payment they filed a motion asking for leniency. Judge Roger Hunt did grant Righthaven additional time to comply with the sanctions, but it was clear that he was fed up with them.[9]

In March 2012 a federal judge ordered Righthaven to forfeit all of its intellectual property and other 'intangible property' in order to settle its debts. The Righthaven victims website www.righthavenvictims.com claimed that to date Righthaven had been ordered to pay US$195,497.15 in legal fees and sanctions.

7.12.2 Digital Rights Corp.

Digital Rights Corp. (DRC) claimed that it would ask everyone suspected of filesharing unauthorized copies of music to pay US$10 per infringement. The company claims to be successful in getting most ISPs to pass on such a monetary request. It's sort of a new tactic in copyright trolling: just send a bill and get the ISP to pass on the 'pay up' letters to its subscribers. The US$10 per infringement is a lot less than what copyright trolls have asked for in the past. The system is automated. DRC put together a list of IP addresses that they assume are infringing, send it to the ISP, and get the ISP to pass along the demands for cash. Two ISPs who have refused have been taken to court (but no individuals have been taken to court).

7.12.3 Shakedown schemes

In a case heard in a Virginia District Court Judge Gibney drew attention to the use of the court by the plaintiff for what was described as a shakedown scheme. This is where the plaintiff uses the court as an inexpensive way of getting access to the personal information of a large number of people in order to coerce payment out of them. In using the court they had no intention of litigating the cases, but had simply used the court and its subpoena powers in order to obtain sufficient information to shake down the John Does (mass copyright lawsuits often refer to John Doe defendants – people who are anonymous or whose identity is withheld for legal reasons). Where a John Doe threatens to litigate, the plaintiff drops that particular John Doe in order to avoid both the actual cost of litigation and also avoids the court ruling on the merits of the case.[10]

7.13   Filtering

⊕   SABAM v. Scarlett CJEU C-70/10

The Belgian collecting society Société belge des auteurs, compositeurs et éditeurs (SABAM) applied for an interim relief against the internet service provider Scarlett Extended SA. SABAM wanted Scarlett to filter all peer-to-peer traffic and block potentially unlawful peer-to-peer downloading and distribution in the country. A Belgian court ruled that Scarlett had to put in place filters to block infringement.

In 2010 the Brussels Court of Appeal asked the Court of Justice of the European Union (CJEU) to determine if delivering an injunction against the ISP forcing it to filter content suspected of copyright infringement contradicts a person's right to privacy and protection of personal data. It also asked the CJEU if a national court should balance the extent with which it orders screening to take place with the impact it would have on those fundamental rights.

The CJEU ruled in November 2011 (SABAM/Scarlett CJEU C-70/10)[11] that while the protection of intellectual property is a fundamental right under EU law, it isn't an absolute right, because it has to be balanced against other fundamental rights (such as the right to privacy and the protection of personal data, as well as the right to freedom of communication and freedom of information). It also breaches ISPs' right to conduct business; and that when a Belgian court had ordered an ISP to filter online traffic in search of copyright infringement, it hadn't struck a fair balance between the rights of a collecting society and those of an ISP.

In the SABAM/Scarlett case summarized here, the Advocate General Pedro Cruz Villalon argued that the blanket requirement that ISPs block copyright infringement is a violation of the EU's Fundamental Rights Charter. He recognized that copyright infringement wasn't obvious and can only be determined after a court ruling, whereas the filters would block sites that had not yet been determined to be infringing. The Court added that differing exceptions to copyright law across the EU would have made it difficult to distinguish what content was lawful.

The CJEU ruling in SABAM/Scarlett means that national courts cannot force ISPs to use filter systems, installed at ISPs' own expense and used for an unlimited period, to monitor all its customers' electronic communications to prevent illegal filesharing. It said that such an order would breach ISPs' rights to freely conduct business and individuals' rights to privacy, free speech and the protection of their personal data. The ruling is crucial for the future of rights and freedoms on the internet. It protects the openness of the internet. The alternative would have been a decision which would ultimately have put all European networks under permanent surveillance and filtering.

The Court's decision in the above case doesn't ban all internet blocking. The court did not and logically could not rule out the possibility that filtering and blocking systems would ever, in all circumstances, however narrowly targeted, necessary, effective and proportionate, be illegal. The decision only declares that the level of filtering and blocking that SABAM requested is disproportionate, illegal and unacceptable because it does not meet the legality test set out to enable restriction to fundamental rights, i.e. the criteria of proportionality, necessity and effectiveness. SABAM's demands were asking for measures that were too broad in terms of material and geographic scopes and also regarding the broadness of the people affected and furthermore as there is no time limitation.

The CJEU assessed EU laws on copyright, intellectual property rights enforcement, data protection, privacy and electronic communications and the free movement of information when making its ruling. It also considered rights contained in the EU's Charter of Fundamental Rights.

The EU's Copyright Directive says copyright owners can obtain a court order against intermediaries whose services are used for piracy. The E-commerce Directive says that service providers aren't liable for infringement via their services if they don't have 'actual knowledge' of the illegal activity, or if they are in possession of such knowledge, if they 'act(s) expeditiously to remove or disable access to the information'. Member states must not put ISPs under any obligation to police illegal activity on its service.

7.13.1 Terrorism

Filtering in libraries and schools was one of the recommendations in the anti-terrorist Prevent strategy.[12] Paragraph 10.108 says 'Internet filtering across the public estate is essential. We want to ensure that users in schools, libraries, colleges and Immigration Removal Centres are unable to access unlawful material'. But elsewhere in the strategy (paragraph 10.93) they refer to the need to limit access not merely to 'unlawful' but also to 'harmful' content online.

The strategy promises to 'work to tackle terrorist use of the internet for radicalisation on the internet' (p. 1), including the filtering of unlawful content by public bodies such as schools and libraries. The plans for internet filtering in libraries have come under fire for potentially creating a clandestine and unaccountable system of censorship.

The possibility of 'independent national blocking lists' is raised, though the strategy adds that 'We do not yet have a filtering product which has been rolled out comprehensively across government departments, agencies and statutory organizations and we are unable to determine the extent to which effective filtering is in place in schools and public libraries'(paragraph 10.107).

7.14   Moderation policies

User-generated content (UGC) or consumer-generated media refers to digital material which has been created by an individual or individuals and placed on websites or web services. It covers blog posts, comments on interactive websites, and material such as photographs and videos which have been uploaded to Web 2.0 services.

The High Court judgment in Karim v. NewsQuest [2009] EWHC 3205 (QB) www.bailii.org/ew/cases/EWHC/QB/2009/3205.html explains how web publishers can avoid liability for libel damages arising from third party UGC. The judgment also confirms that publishers do not need to pre-moderate or edit UGC posts on their websites in order to have a defence to a claim for libel damages. Mr Justice Eady's ruling in Karim was based on the Electronic Commerce (EC Directive) Regulations 2002, Regulation 19:

> 'Where an information society service is provided which consists of the storage of information provided by a recipient of the service, the service provider, if he otherwise would, shall not be liable for damages or for any other pecuniary remedy or for any criminal sanction as a result of that storage where:
> (a) the service provider
> (i) does not have actual knowledge of unlawful activity or information and

where a claim for damages is made, is not aware of facts or circumstances from which it would have been apparent to the service provider that the activity or information was unlawful; or

(ii) upon obtaining such knowledge or awareness, acts expeditiously to remove or to disable access to the information; and

(b) the recipient of the service was not acting under the authority or the control of the service provider.'

By his judgment, Mr Justice Eady has confirmed that web publishers who are unaware of defamatory UGC posts on their websites have a defence to a claim for libel damages if they act quickly and remove such UGC posts as soon as they are notified that a post is the subject of a complaint.

The judge held that:

1 The users of publishers' and newspapers' websites are recipients of an 'information society service';
2 UGC facilities on such websites are 'bulletin boards';
3 Web publishers have no knowledge of, or control over, UGC prior to becoming aware, or being notified, of any contentious posts;
4 Therefore, publishers have no liability if posts are removed as soon as a complaint is received.

If you become aware, or if you are notified, of defamatory or other unlawful UGC, act quickly to take it down. Failure to do so will make this defence unavailable. Do not assume that you have a defence under Reg. 19 if you are hosting an online forum on a controversial topic which has in the past repeatedly received complaints over UGC which was alleged to be defamatory. In such circumstances, you may be deemed to have had 'prior knowledge'.

Moderation of websites can take a number of different forms:

* pre-publication moderation
* technical (or automated) moderation, where it picks up particular words or phrases
* post-publication moderation.

Checklist 7.2 provides some advice on moderating a UGC site.

Checklist 7.2 *Moderation checklist*
1   Choose the right form of moderation for your site:

- pre-publication moderation
- technical (or automated) moderation where it picks up particular words or phrases
- post-publication moderation.

2 If the site is moderated, make sure that this is clear to users of the site.

3 Make it as easy as possible for people to report problems with content – for example you could use buttons to 'Report offensive content' or 'Notify operator'.

Moderation of comments or postings to a website prior to publication may appear to be the safest option. But is it a viable or practical option? And even if it is, it isn't without its own difficulties. The legal defences to the risks posed would be lost if you had moderated the content prior to publication. If, for example, the content was subsequently deemed to be libellous, your pre-publication moderation of the content means that you have assumed responsibility for it. There is also the question of who should moderate user-generated content; and whether it needs to be someone with copyright expertise. For further information see Gellis (2011).[13]

In the Sumo TV case (www.ofcom.org.uk/tv/obb/prog_cb/obb101/; Andy Milonakis clip, 6 July 2007, 23:46; and Parent/Carer and child clip, 22 July 2007, 00:34) Ofcom ruled that broadcasters are responsible for ensuring compliance of user-generated content they broadcast with the Broadcasting Code. They issued a stern warning to broadcasters over user-generated content after ruling against two clips screened by Sumo TV. The media regulator said it was concerned that some TV channels were putting too much responsibility for complying with its broadcasting code on the creators of user-generated clips rather than performing sufficient checks themselves. Ofcom ruled against two clips which had been screened by Sumo TV which had been broadcast on its Sky digital channel in July 2006 and which featured the performance of a rap containing strong language and graphic sexual references. Sumo TV were advised that any future breaches of this nature may result in further regulatory action being considered.

If you were to have insurance cover which provided for legal expenses (to cover the enforcement of intellectual property, or which covered defending yourself against an allegation of copyright infringement), the insurance company is likely to ask questions about whether a moderation policy is in place, and this will affect their willingness to provide insurance cover; and the amount of money they will want to charge for that cover.

If a reviewer of a product falsely presents himself as a consumer this could breach the Consumer Protection from Unfair Trading Regulations 2008 (SI 2008/1277).[14]

7.15 Role of internet service providers

In recent years content owners have undertaken a strategic shift away from targeting individual filesharers and are instead going after the infrastructure that supports them, of which ISPs are a key part. The objections to this strategy are:

1 Intermediaries are not responsible for their users' actions. They are not the people doing wrong.
2 Intermediaries are vulnerable to claims of liability. They will err on the side of caution and remove content if there is any legal risk.
3 Making intermediaries act on mere suggestion of wrongdoing removes due process. Intermediaries are not in a position to judge guilt.
4 Intermediaries may be able to see information, but may not be entitled to examine it or hand it over. Without a presumption of privacy, in the digital age, we risk creating a world in which little or nothing is private at all.

The first component of this decentralized approach typically involves relying on intermediaries to positively discourage users from copyright infringement by supporting public education, the distribution of information regarding the importance of respect for copyright and passing on infringement notices to ensure that end-users are aware that their actions can be monitored and that they can potentially face serious consequences for online infringement.

The second component, which has started to emerge in a number of jurisdictions worldwide, seeks to make actual enforcement more routine by requiring ISPs to impose service restrictions and/or other penalties on users repeatedly accused of online copyright infringement. ISPs have assumed responsibility as copyright enforcement agents or internet copyright cops policing customer copyright violations.

These enforcement measures, called 'graduated response' or 'three-strike' schemes, shift the burden of enforcing copyright away from judicial proceedings to the intermediaries who provide consumer internet access. By lowering economic rights holders' enforcement costs and making penalties more routine, graduated response schemes are designed to drive a fundamental shift in social norms against filesharing. There are a number of voluntary agreements between the copyright holders and ISPs which provide that notices are forwarded to internet subscribers on behalf of the rights owners. After several warnings, 'mitigation measures' commence. They include reducing internet speed and redirecting service to an educational landing page, while the 'graduated response' may result in termination of the user's internet connection and a complete loss of service.

Suing filesharers in court is no longer the main solution pursued by rights holders to combat online infringement. Instead the strategy of compelled voluntary collaboration with ISPs now seems to be a more appealing option for economic rights holders because it avoids the high costs of end-user litigation.

Several of the largest US ISPs have entered into private agreements with economic rights holders to institute a system that, while it does not explicitly require termination of alleged repeat infringers, includes issuing warnings to users and requiring users who receive multiple warnings to undergo mandatory education programs or have their internet speeds temporarily slowed.

Opponents argue that it is wrong to penalize subscribers based on allegations that haven't been tested in court. The way the system works is that the content industry monitors P2P networks for infringements and informs ISPs of the IP addresses of suspected infringers. ISPs then match the IP address to the subscriber. However, customers could receive notices of allegations without actually engaging in illegal downloading. This might occur if other people have used their connection through piggybacking or if the monitoring company makes a mistake.

The question arises as to the role the courts should play in the implementation of such a plan. Concerns are largely around the possibility of internet access being taken away on the basis of alleged infringements. Such punishments are backed by a number of governments around the world, but they are extra-judicial and do not offer the protection of a court.

7.16   EU database of IP infringers

The EU proposals for a regulation concerning customs enforcement of intellectual property rights (COM(2011) 285) would lead to the creation of a central database called COPIS (the Counterfeiting and Piracy System). The database would be a centralized information platform for customs operations regarding all IPR-infringing goods. It would contain all applications for action, decisions granting applications, decisions extending the period of validity of decisions, and suspending a decision granting the application, also including personal data; and would include the processing of sensitive data on suspected violations of IP rights by certain individuals or entities.

The European Data Protection Supervisor scrutinized the proposals and issued an Opinion[15] on the data protection implications in which he urged the Commission to identify and clarify the legal basis for the establishment of the COPIS database. He stressed that the application submitted by the rights holder should not be stored or retained by the national customs authorities and in the COPIS database beyond the date of expiry of the decision, and that any extension of the duration of the retention date should be avoided or else would have to fulfil the principles of necessity and proportionality in relation to the purpose for which it is kept.

Notes and references

1   Hargreaves, Ian (2011) *Digital Opportunity: a review of intellectual property and growth*, www.ipo.gov.uk/ipreview-finalreport.pdf.

2   Intellectual Property Office (2011) *Consultation on Copyright*, December 2011,
    www.ipo.gov.uk/consult-2011-copyright.pdf.

3   For details of YouTube's video fingerprinting facility Content ID, see
    www.youtube.com/t/contentid.

4   Notice and Takedown Process is Flawed, Says Analysis of Google Notices,
    Out-law News, 24 March 2009, www.out-law.com/page-9899.

5   Richard O'Dwyer Case: lawyers lodge extradition appeal, *BBC News Online*,
    22 March 2012, www.bbc.co.uk/news/uk-england-south-yorkshire-17472142.

6   For the Google settlement see Authors Guild v. Google Inc., 770 F. Supp.
    2d. 666 (S.D.N.Y. 2011).

7   Ad Hoc Committee on Copyright Law Revision (1976) *Agreement on
    Guidelines For Classroom Copying in Not-for-Profit Educational Institutions with
    Respect to Books and Periodicals*,
    www.unc.edu/~unclng/classroom-guidelines.htm.

8   See court ruling www.infodocket.com/wp-content/uploads/2012/05/
    GA-State-Opinion.pdf.

9   Mullin, Joe (2011) Righthaven Responds to Fine – 'a Day Late and $5,000
    Short', *PaidContent*, 3 August, http://paidcontent.org/article/419-righthaven-
    responds-to-finea-day-late-and-5000-short.

10 Courts Call Out Copyright Trolls' Coercive Business Model, *Electronic
    Frontier Foundation blog*, 5 October 2011.

11 http://curia.europa.eu/jurisp/cgi-bin/form.pl?lang=EN&Submit=
    Submit&numaff=C-70/10).

12 Home Office (2011) *New Prevent Strategy Launched*,
    www.homeoffice.gov.uk/media-centre/news/prevent-strategy.

13 Gellis, Catherine R. (2011) State of the Law Regarding Website Owner
    Liability for User-Generated Content, *The Business Lawyer* Volume 67,
    November, http://ssrn.com/abstract=2008345.

14 See also: Businesses who Commission Fake Reviews Should Be Worried
    About More Than Just Illegality, *Out-law News*, 21 June 2011.

15 Opinion of the European Data Protection Supervisor on the proposal for a
    Regulation of the European Parliament and of the Council concerning
    customs enforcement of intellectual property rights, October 2011.

CHAPTER 8

The Hargreaves Review

8.1 Overview

In November 2010 Prime Minister David Cameron commissioned Ian Hargreaves to develop proposals on how the UK's intellectual property framework can further promote entrepreneurialism, economic growth and social and commercial innovation. The review's findings were published in May 2011[1], and the government's response was published in August 2011[2] along with the UK intellectual property crime strategy[3] and the UK's international strategy for intellectual property.[4, 5]

The government broadly accepted all of the recommendations in the Hargreaves report and it also committed to no further major review of the IP system in this parliament. The recommendations were grouped under a set of ten headings:

1 Evidence
2 International priorities
3 Copyright licensing
4 Orphan works
5 Limits to copyright
6 Patent thickets and other obstructions to innovation
7 The design industry
8 Enforcement of IP rights
9 Small firm access to IP advice
10 An IP system responsive to change.

8.1.1 Evidence

The **first** recommendation was that government should ensure that development of the IP system is driven as far as possible by objective evidence. As a result, the IPO set out guidance on what constitutes open and transparent evidence, in line with professional practice.

⚹ Useful resource

Mitra-Kahn, Benjamin (2011) *Good Evidence for Policy*, Intellectual Property Office, 14 December, www.ipo.gov.uk/consult-2011-copyright-evidence.pdf.

8.1.2   International priorities

The **second** recommendation was that the UK should resolutely pursue its international interests in IP, particularly with respect to emerging economies such as China and India, based upon positions grounded in economic evidence. In addition to the UK's international strategy for intellectual property published in August 2011, on 8 December 2011 the IPO announced the appointment of the UK's first ever intellectual property attaché in China to support UK businesses (www.ipo.gov.uk/about/press/press-release/press-release-2011/press-release-20111208a.htm).

➾ Useful resource

Intellectual Property Office (2011) *The UK's International Strategy for Intellectual Property*, 3 August, www.ipo.gov.uk/ipresponse-international.pdf.

8.1.3   Copyright licensing

The **third** recommendation, on copyright licensing, said that the UK should establish a cross-sectoral digital copyright exchange and should also support moves by the European Commission to establish a framework for cross-border copyright licensing. In November 2011 Vince Cable, Secretary of State for Business, Innovation and Skills, announced[6] the appointment of Richard Hooper to lead a study on developing a Digital Copyright Exchange with a view to him reporting back before the summer Parliamentary recess 2012. This was followed up in January 2012 by a call for evidence for a feasibility study to look at whether copyright licensing is fit for purpose in the digital age.

➾ Useful resource

Digital Copyright Exchange Feasibility Study: call for evidence, www.ipo.gov.uk/types/hargreaves/hargreaves-copyright/hargreaves-copyright-dce.htm.

In March 2012 Richard Hooper published his diagnostic report on how fit for purpose copyright licensing is in the digital age. He identified a number of problems with the UK's copyright licensing processes. These include:

- the complex manner in which rights are licensed;
- the sheer complexity in terms of the number of organizations who are involved in the licensing of rights;
- the difficulties in identifying and tracking down rights owners in order to get their permission;

- as well as the difficulty and expense involved in licensing copyright where a project involves a high volume of transactions, but where these are of a low value.

➻ Useful resource

'Rights and wrongs: is copyright licensing fit for purpose for the digital age?' IPO, 2012, www.ipo.gov.uk/dce-report-phase1.pdf.

On 2 July 2012 the government published a policy statement on modernising copyright licensing, setting out its legislative intentions in this area.[7]

8.1.4 Orphan works

The **fourth** recommendation, on orphan works, said that the government should establish extended collective licensing for the mass licensing of orphan works as well as providing a clearance procedure for the use of individual works.

➻ Useful resource

Orphan Works: impact assessment, IPO, 2012.
The impact assessment documents were updated in 2012, and are available at: www.ipo.gov.uk/pro-policy/consult/consult-closed/consult-closed-2011/consult-2011-copyright.htm.

➻ Useful resource

Extended Collective Licensing: impact assessment, IPO, 2012.
The impact assessment documents were updated in 2012, and are available at: www.ipo.gov.uk/pro-policy/consult/consult-closed/consult-closed-2011/consult-2011-copyright.htm.

➻ Useful resource

Vuopala, Anna (2010) *Assessment of the Orphan Works Issue and Costs for Rights Clearance*, for the EU Commission, http://ec.europa.eu/information_society/activities/digital_libraries/doc/reports_orphan/anna_report.pdf.

➻ Useful resource

Korn, Naomi (2009) *In from the Cold: an assessment of the scope of 'Orphan Works' and its impact on the delivery of services to the public*, report for the Strategic Content Alliance and the Collections Trust, JISC, www.jisc.ac.uk/media/documents/publications/infromthecoldv1.pdf.

8.1.5   Limits to copyright

The **fifth** recommendation, on the limits of copyright, said that the government should deliver copyright exceptions at national level to realize all of the opportunities that are available within the EU framework; that the exceptions should be opened up to include areas such as format shifting and parody, as well as widening existing exceptions on non-commercial research and library archiving.

The *Consultation on Copyright*[8] makes clear that the government is proposing to widen copyright exceptions with a view to modernizing them and opening them up to the maximum degree possible within EU law. In doing so, it will be guided by the following principles:

1 Exceptions should be introduced or expanded to the maximum degree possible without undermining incentives to creators.
2 Exceptions must be compatible with EU and international law (including the Copyright Directive and the Berne 'three-step' test) and that uses permitted by the copyright exceptions should not be restricted by other means.
3 It shouldn't be possible to use contracts to override exceptions.
4 New or revised copyright laws should be clear, straightforward and avoid unnecessary regulation and bureaucracy.

↝ Useful resource

On 14 December 2011 the IPO published the Consultation on Copyright, together with impact assessments on:
- 'Introducing/widening certain copyright exceptions'
- 'Copying exception for parody'
- 'Copyright exception for private copying'
- 'Copyright exceptions for archiving and preservation'
- 'Copyright exceptions for disabled people'
- 'Use of works for public administration and reporting'
- 'Exception for use of quotations or extracts of copyright works'
- 'Extend exception for copying for research and private study'
- 'Exception for copying of works for use by text and data analytics'.
- 'Extending copyright exceptions for educational use'.

These documents are available at www.ipo.gov.uk/consult-2011-copyright.

8.1.6   Patent thickets and other obstructions to innovation

The **sixth** recommendation said that 'patent thickets' and other obstructions to innovation should be limited, and Hargreaves listed three areas relating to this:

1 To play a key role in international efforts to cut patent application backlogs.
2 To ensure patents aren't extended into sectors they don't currently cover unless there is clear evidence of benefit.
3 Working with international partners to establish a patent fee structure set by reference to innovation and growth goals as opposed to being purely set by reference to patent office running costs.

In the government response to the Hargreaves Review the IPO made a commitment to investigate the scale and prevalence of patent thickets. This included looking into the potential effects of thickets on new market entrants (such as SMEs) in technology sectors. In November 2011 the IPO published a report entitled *Patent Thickets: an overview*, which looks, among other things, at how we define patent thickets, tools which help to automatically identify them, and where they might be found.

Useful resource

Intellectual Property Office (2011) *Patent Thickets: an overview (subject to peer review)*, www.ipo.gov.uk/informatic-thickets.pdf.

8.1.7 The design industry

The **seventh** recommendation said that the IPO should conduct an evidence-based assessment of the relationship between design rights and innovation, with a view to establishing a firmer basis for evaluating policy at the UK and European level. In December 2011 the IPO published its assessment of the need to simplify the system in a paper detailing the current state of the IPO's research and its views on the need for more. The paper also records the suggestions for reform of the design IP framework that have been submitted to the Call for Evidence and survey.

Useful resource

Intellectual Property Office (2011) *Design: call for evidence*, www.ipo.gov.uk/hargreaves-designs-c4e.pdf.

Useful resource

Intellectual Property Office (2011) *IPO Assessment of the Need for Reform of the Design Intellectual Property Framework*, www.ipo.gov.uk/hargreaves-designsassessment.pdf.

8.1.8 Enforcement of IP rights

The **eighth** recommendation was about the enforcement of IP rights. Hargreaves said that the government should pursue an integrated approach based upon enforcement, education and measures to strengthen and grow legitimate markets in copyright and other IP protected fields.

8.1.9 Small firm access to IP advice

The **ninth** recommendation was that the IPO should draw up plans to improve accessibility of the IP system to smaller companies that will benefit from it and that this should involve access to lower-cost providers of integrated IP legal and commercial advice.

On 8 December 2011 the IPO announced a package of measures[9] as part of the government's Innovation and Research Strategy for Growth, outlining plans to improve accessibility of the IP system to smaller companies. These measures include:

- a new online business adviser training tool that will give advisers the skills and information they need to help businesses protect the value of their intellectual property;
- an online register of advisers to help businesses find the right advisor for them quickly and easily;
- consulting businesses, business advisers and IP specialists about how lower-cost IP legal and commercial advice can be provided;
- offering free intellectual property audits to businesses through the Technology Strategy Board;
- enhancing existing schemes such as mediation to provide a more efficient dispute resolution service that can prevent potentially costly legal cases.

8.1.10 An IP system responsive to change

The **tenth** recommendation grouped together a number of points around making the IP system responsive to change. These include giving the IPO a legal mandate to ensure that the UK's IP system promotes innovation and growth; that it should provide statutory opinions to help clarify copyright law; and that by the end of 2013 it should publish an assessment of the impact that implementation of the measures recommended in the review have had.

Of the ten recommendations contained in the Hargreaves Review, three of them were specific to copyright: (3) copyright licensing, (4) orphan works and (5) limits to copyright (of the rest, one was about patents, one was about designs, and the other five related to intellectual property rights as a whole). The remainder of this chapter will look in more detail at the three recommendations specific to copyright:

8.2 Copyright licensing

The Hargreaves Review identified a number of problems with the system for the licensing of copyright works which resulted in it being harder to start and grow businesses. Proposals to address this include: simplifying the rights clearance system through the introduction of a voluntary extended collective licensing scheme in the UK; the creation of a Digital Copyright Exchange as a marketplace where ownership of rights could be advertised and rights licensed; and publishing minimum standards – for fairness, transparency and good governance – which it would like to see included in voluntary codes of conduct for collecting societies, alongside having a backstop power that would allow for a statutory code to be implemented if the voluntary system does not prove effective.

8.2.1 Digital Copyright Exchange

The Hargreaves Review proposed that the government should bring together rights holders and other business interests to create the world's first Digital Copyright Exchange here in the UK, which it predicted could add up to £2.2 billion a year to the UK economy by 2020. The government's view is that a successful DCE is dependent on its commercial attractiveness, and that it would have to create value for both the sellers and the purchasers of rights. In its response to the Hargreaves Review, the government identified a number of steps that would need to be taken in order for it to be successful:

1 Attract a critical mass of material available and readily licensable through the exchange.
2 Be a compelling proposition to rights holders without being compulsory (bearing in mind that compulsion would be likely to contravene the Berne Convention).
3 Allow prices to be set or negotiated by the rights holder, subject to controls on unfair competition.
4 Serve as a genuine marketplace independent of sellers and purchasers.
5 Be open to access by individuals and businesses, free at the point of use, to open standards which would enable firms to easily write software to automate access and provide services which relied on the information gathered or the licences purchased.
6 Be run on a self-funding basis, with fees being charged for the licensing transactions rather than for searching the database.

In *Consultation on Copyright* the government made clear that it did not see the creation of the Digital Copyright Exchange as being primarily a legislative task, but that it needs to be developed by and owned by the industry. The DCE did not therefore form the subject of the consultation. Richard Hooper, formerly deputy chairman of Ofcom, was asked to lead a feasibility study to develop a Digital Copyright Exchange.

8.2.2   Extended collective licensing

Introducing extended collective licensing in the UK would go some way to addressing the orphan works problem. At the moment, collecting societies are only able to license the rights of people who have opted in to their repertoire. In the case of orphan works the problem is that by their very nature, there is unlikely to be anyone who will come forward and give a collecting society the mandate to represent them.

Extended collective licensing would overcome this problem by letting collecting societies that wanted to do so to apply to the government to be able to represent all rights holders within a particular sector, apart from any of them who came forward asking to opt out. It would also address the problem of high transaction costs involved in mass digitization projects, where the user has to seek multiple permissions. In its *Consultation on Copyright* the government set out its preferred option to introduce legislation that will allow collective licensing to take place on an 'opt out' rather than an 'opt in' basis in order to expedite rights clearance and reduce transaction costs.

➤ Useful resource

Intellectual Property Office (2012) *Extended Collective Licensing: impact assessment*. A revised version of the impact assessment was published in 2012, and is available at: www.ipo.gov.uk/pro-policy/consult/consult-closed/consult-closed-2011/consult-2011-copyright.htm.

8.2.3   Regulation of the collecting societies

Recommendation 3 of the Hargreaves Review deals with copyright licensing and includes the statement that 'collecting societies should be required by law to adopt codes of practice, approved by the IPO and the UK competition authorities, to ensure that they operate in a way that is consistent with the further development of efficient, open markets'.

The *Consultation on Copyright* makes clear that the government intends to publish minimum standards which must be included in a collecting society's code of conduct. These would cover:

• obligations to rights holders
• obligations to licensees
• control of the conduct of employees and agents
• information and transparency; monitoring and reporting requirements
• complaint handling

- an ombudsman
- review of the code.

The IPO will look both at how standards might be strengthened and at how to give official recognition when high standards are met. The government will also draw up proposals for a backstop power that allows a statutory code to be put in place for a collecting society that evidence shows has failed to introduce or adhere to a voluntary code incorporating minimum standards.

Meanwhile in July 2012 the EU published its own proposals for regulating the collecting societies.[10]

> **⚹ Useful resource**
>
> Intellectual Property Office (2012) *Codes of Conduct: impact assessment.* A revised version of the impact assessment was published in 2012, and is available at: www.ipo.gov.uk/pro-policy/consult/consult-closed/consult-closed-2011/consult-2011-copyright.htm.

8.3   Orphan works

Hargreaves acknowledges the problem of orphan works, namely works whose use is effectively barred because the copyright holder cannot be traced. Recommendation 4 of the Hargreaves Review said that the government should legislate to enable licensing of orphan works and that this should consist of both **extended collective licensing** for the mass licensing of orphan works, as well as a **clearance procedure for the use of individual works**. It says that a work should only be treated as an orphan if it cannot be found by searching the databases involved in the proposed Digital Copyright Exchange. In its response the government says:

> The government [are planning to] bring forward proposals for an orphan works scheme that allows for both commercial and cultural uses of orphan works, subject to satisfactory safeguards for the interests of both owners of 'orphan rights' and rights holders who could suffer from unfair competition from an orphan works scheme. These would include a **diligent search** for rights owners, licensing at market rates for commercial use and respect for the rights of 'revenant'[11] owners that come forward. The government will look to the DCE and other searchable sources of information on copyright works to deal with problems of misattribution or loss of ownership data from works.

The government considers that remuneration would need to be at market rate for the type of work and type of use in consideration (otherwise the use of orphans would undercut the market for non-orphans: see Paragraph 4.32 of the review).

➡ Useful resource

Draft Directive on Orphan Works, COM (2011) 289, European Commission, http://ec.europa.eu/internal_market/copyright/docs/orphan-works/proposal_en.pdf.

➡ Useful resource

Intellectual Property Office (2011) *Orphan Works: impact assessment*, www.ipo.gov.uk/consult-ia-bis1063.pdf.

8.4   Limits to copyright (the copyright exceptions)
8.4.1   Data analytics and text mining

Text or data mining involves the analysis of large quantities of documents in order to identify connections or patterns which help to generate new ideas or to test hypotheses. The Hargreaves Review describes text mining as 'the process of deriving information from machine-read material. It works by copying large quantities of material, extracting the data, and recombining it to identify patterns'.[12]

A survey in a report commissioned by the Publishers Research Consortium[13] found that content mining is about to accelerate, that it will expand into new areas and develop further into automated information extraction and relationship analysis. A majority of the respondents to the survey supported three common solutions for facilitating content mining:

1 More content standardization for mining-friendly formats.
2 A shared content mining platform across publishers.
3 Commonly agreed rules for the granting of mining permissions.

Mining techniques help identify the relationship between different elements or entities. In the scientific field, for example, these could be genes, proteins, chemical compounds, diseases or species; and in the business world they could be company names, people, products, or places. Examples of applications for data mining might be where it is used to accelerate the drug discovery process, or for competitive intelligence (e.g. patent analysis). In most cases, publishers will want to know the intent and purpose of the mining request:

• Can the mining results replace or compete with the original content?
• Is it for a commercial purpose?
• Is it for research?

Information retrieval systems can be used to identify the documents in a collection which match a user's enquiry. They make it possible for people to use text mining on a more manageable number of documents. The fact that the information retrieval systems are able to narrow down the set of documents to be analysed is very helpful, bearing in mind that text mining involves very computationally intensive algorithms, and they therefore help to speed up the data analysis. Users of data mining could be marketers, advertisers, business analysts or abstracting and indexing services.

The Hargreaves Review says that there should be a change in the copyright rules to enable scientific and other researchers to use modern text and data mining techniques. Hargreaves concludes that data mining is not permitted under current copyright legislation because the technology hadn't been imagined at the time that the law was formed. He also recognizes that it isn't sufficient to create a new exception to cover the activity of text mining, because it would also require a provision to ensure that a contract couldn't override a possible future copyright exception for data mining.

The copyright aspect of data mining lies in the wholesale reproduction of articles. Database right also needs to be taken into account, since researchers extract substantial parts of databases. Furthermore, there are the licences, which are often silent on the question of data mining, or where they do mention it place restrictions on the activity.

According to Richard Mollett of the Publishers Association,[14] if publishers lost the ability to manage access to allow content mining, three things would happen:

1 The platforms would collapse under the technological weight of crawler-bots.
2 There is the commercial risk. It is all very well allowing a researcher to access and copy content to mine if they are, indeed, a researcher. But what if they are not? What if their intention is to copy the work for a directly competing use?
3 Britain would be placing itself at a competitive disadvantage in the European and global marketplace if it were virtually the only country to provide such an exception.

This last point ignores the fact that some countries such as Japan and a number of the Nordic countries are already allowing content mining.

➷ Useful resource

Intellectual Property Office (2011) *Exception for Copying of Works for Use by Text and Data Analytics: impact assessment*, www.ipo.gov.uk/consult-ia-bis0312.pdf.

⚫️ Useful resource
Intellectual Property Office (2011) *Text Mining and Data Analytics in Call for Evidence Responses*, Supporting document T, www.ipo.gov.uk/ipreview-doc-t.pdf.

8.4.2   Limited private copying

Paragraph 5.30 of the Hargreaves Review says:

> The review favours a limited private copying exception which corresponds to what consumers are already doing. As rights holders are well aware of consumers' behaviour in this respect, our view is that the benefit of being able to do this is already factored into the price that rights holders are charging. A limited private copying exception which corresponds to the expectations of the buyers and sellers of copyright content, and is therefore already priced into the purchase, will by definition not entail a loss for right holders.

Similarly, recommendation 8 of the Gowers Review[15] said:

> Introduce a limited private copying exception by 2008 for format shifting for works published after the date that the law comes into effect. There should be no accompanying levies for consumers.

The government response to the Hargreaves Review published in August 2011 made clear that it was planning to introduce a limited private copying exception. This was followed up in December 2011 by the *Consultation on Copyright*, which discusses[16] a proposal to introduce a private copying exception that would permit an individual to copy creative content that they own to other devices, media and platforms.

Most European countries have a private copying exception, but they also have a system of imposing levies to recompense rights owners for the copies made under that exception. Indeed private copying levies are collected in almost all member states, with the exception of the UK, Cyprus, Ireland, Luxembourg and Malta. These levies are imposed on equipment which could be used to copy material and are designed to compensate copyright holders for 'private copying', although the rules on what devices are covered or how much should be paid vary from country to country. According to Digital Europe, the total amount of levies collected from its members rose from £500 million in 2001 to more than £2 billion in 2009.

There are people who argue that the system of copyright levies for private copying is flawed. It automatically assumes that every single one of the devices on which a levy is imposed is being used to make copies which would otherwise infringe copyright, regardless of whether this really is the case; and it collects money to distribute to the copyright owners without knowing what material has been copied using the equipment on which a levy has been imposed (such as an MP3 player, multifunction printer, blank DVD, smartphone, or photocopier).

The UK government is not intending to introduce a private copying levy, on the basis that any harm caused to copyright owners (which the levies are designed to compensate them for) as a result of a private copying exception is kept to a bare minimum.

➻ Useful resource

Intellectual Property Office (2011) *Copyright Exception for Private Copying: impact assessment*, www.ipo.gov.uk/consult-ia-bis1055.pdf.

8.4.3   Parody

The UK doesn't currently have an exception for parody, even though Article 5 (exceptions and limitations) of the Copyright Directive (2001/29/EC) would allow us to introduce one (*Article 5 (3)(a) Use for the purpose of caricature, parody or pastiche*).

Hargreaves recommends that the UK introduce an exception for parody and pastiche. The most important issues when considering parody are concerns over freedom of expression, although these were outside the Hargreaves Review's terms of reference. The *Consultation on Copyright* proposes a new fair dealing exception for parody, caricature, and pastiche, allowing people to use creative works for these purposes. The main economic beneficiaries of an exception for parody would be entertainers and comedians, the producers of comedy and entertainment shows and broadcasters. Members of the public would also benefit from the greater opportunities for freedom of expression, and introducing such an exception would be in tune with the expectation of people using new media and social networks.

➻ Useful resource

Intellectual Property Office (2011) *Copyright Exception for Parody: impact assessment*, www.ipo.gov.uk/consult-ia-bis1057.pdf.

8.4.4   Library archiving and preservation

The Hargreaves Review (p. 4) noted that the UK does not allow its great libraries to digitally archive all copyright material, with the result that much of it is rotting away. Ian Hargreaves makes the point (p. 38) that further delay to digitization means some will be lost for good. He also notes (p. 46) that the exception for archiving falls well short of current needs, and says (p. 54):

> It should be uncontroversial to deliver the necessary change by extending the archiving exception, including to cover fully audio visual works and sound recordings. Supporting the potential of new technologies for archiving will prevent the loss of works, and could open the way to new services based on digital use of those archives.

Paragraph 7.66 of the Hargreaves Review proposes that s. 42 of the CDPA be extended to make it easier to preserve a wide range of media for future generations. Changes proposed include widening the exception so that it applies to audiovisual works and sound recordings as well as literary, dramatic or musical works; that it allows for multiple copies to be made; and that it is changed to allow museums and galleries, as well as libraries and archives, to benefit from the exception.

➻ Useful resource

Intellectual Property Office (2011) *Copyright Exception for Archiving and Preservation: impact assessment*, www.ipo.gov.uk/consult-ia-bis0306.pdf.

8.4.5   Disability

There are exceptions in the current UK copyright legislation relating to the making of copies for visually impaired persons (CDPA 1988, ss 31A–E), and for subtitling of broadcasts which benefits the deaf and hard of hearing, as well as people who are physically or mentally handicapped (s. 74). The government wants to:

- widen the scope of the existing disability copyright exceptions, so that they cover all types of disability;
- broaden the scope of the existing disability copyright exceptions, so that they cover all types of copyright work (the exceptions for visually impaired persons, for example, only apply in respect of literary, dramatic, musical or artistic works but don't include films);
- prevent licensing schemes from taking precedence over exceptions for the disabled;
- and simplify the processes and procedures relating to these exceptions.

The exceptions should only apply to the extent that commercial accessible copies are not available.

➔ Useful resource

Intellectual Property Office (2011) *Copyright Exceptions for Disabled People: impact assessment*, www.ipo.gov.uk/consult-ia-bis0308.pdf.

8.4.6 Public administration and reporting

The government is proposing to amend the current copyright exception for public administration and reporting in order to permit the publication of relevant third-party documents online. This is consistent with the wider open data and transparency agenda. In line with FOI best practice, public bodies would then be able to proactively publish on their website those materials or records which would be most likely to be of public interest. Doing so would reduce the administrative burdens for both the requester and the public body with regard to material that is requested repeatedly, while at the same time providing members of the public with documents which help them to understand more about the decisions made by public bodies which affect them.

➔ Useful resource

Use of Works for Public Administration and Reporting: impact assessment, www.ipo.gov.uk/consult-ia-bis0309.pdf.

8.4.7 Quotations or extracts

The government is proposing to widen the existing exception for criticism or review to cover the use of quotations for other purposes; something which would be of particular benefit to academics and journalists, as well as people participating in online social networks. The aim is to allow copying which is fair, where the quotation of the work is only to the extent necessary and for which attribution is made so that it covers not only criticism, review, or the reporting of current events but a wider range of permitted uses such as for illustration, information, and polemic.

➔ Useful resource

Intellectual Property Office (2011) *Exception for Use of Quotations or Extracts of Copyright Works: impact assessment*, www.ipo.gov.uk/consult-ia-bis0310.pdf.

8.4.8 Research and private study

The government wants to change the scope of copyright law to allow copying of all types of copyright works for the purpose of non-commercial research or private study. Proposed changes include changing s. 29 of the CDPA on fair dealing in order to enable students and researchers to copy sound recordings, films and broadcasts as well as the other types of work that they are already allowed to copy; making the exception 'work neutral', so that it applies to every type of copyright work; and the IPO are also intending to amend the related exceptions which permit libraries to make and supply copies for the purposes of non-commercial research or private study. The consultation also considers the merits of introducing an exception which would permit educational establishments, libraries, archives or museums to make works available for research or private study on their premises by electronic means.

➨ Useful resource

Intellectual Property Office (2011) *Extend Exception for Copying for Research and Private Study: impact assessment*, www.ipo.gov.uk/consult-ia-bis0311.pdf.

8.4.9   Educational use

The government put forward a number of proposals to update and amend the copyright exceptions relating to educational uses. However, there was no indication of a preferred option at the time the 'Consultation on copyright' paper was issued in December 2011; and that was because they first needed to gather evidence of the wider impact the proposals would have on competition.

Extending Copyright Exceptions for Educational Use: impact assessment (IPO, 2011) says that the government's proposals are intended to achieve the policy objective of widening copyright exceptions for education to the extent permitted by EU law, so that copyright does not unduly restrict education and teaching, but without undermining incentives to creators. This would mean widening the current exceptions, applying them to more types of works and technologies. The aim would be to make it easier to use copyright works in education, particularly using new technology, in order to enrich and enhance the learning environment, and provide administrative and other savings to educational establishments.

➨ Useful resource

Intellectual Property Office (2011) *Extending Copyright Exceptions for Educational Use: impact assessment*, www.ipo.gov.uk/consult-ia-bis0317.pdf.

8.4.10 Other exceptions

The *Consultation on Copyright* includes proposals to implement a number of additional narrow exceptions. These would permit:

- the recording of broadcasts by social institutions (e.g. hospitals) to record broadcasts for time shifting;
- use of copyright works at narrowly defined religious or official celebrations;
- fair dealing with artistic works for the purpose of public exhibition or sale;
- and use exclusively for the demonstration or repair of equipment (e.g. electronic goods).

➔ Useful resource

Intellectual Property Office (2011) *Introducing/widening Certain Copyright Exceptions: impact assessment*, www.ipo.gov.uk/consult-ia-bis0316.pdf.

8.4.11 Override by contract

The government is planning to legislate to establish that copyright exceptions cannot be overridden by contract. The ability of contracts to override copyright is especially relevant with regard to digital content, because a significant amount of digital content is licensed to institutions through contracts which include provisions overriding the statutory exceptions.

➔ Useful resource

Intellectual Property Office (2011) *Protecting Copyright Exceptions from Override by Contract: impact assessment*, www.ipo.gov.uk/consult-ia-bis0315.pdf.

8.5   Enforcement of IPR in the digital age

The Hargreaves Review points out that IPRs cannot succeed in their core economic function of incentivizing innovation if rights are disregarded or are too expensive to enforce. It says that effective enforcement requires:

- education
- effective markets – creative businesses should make available lower-priced legal products in a form that the consumer wants
- an appropriate enforcement regime
- a modern legal framework.

8.6   Copyright opinions

It is proposed that the Intellectual Property Office be given a statutory function to publish formal opinions on UK copyright law and its application. At present the IPO doesn't have any means of clarifying copyright law where it causes misunderstanding or confusion in a way that carries formal authority.

The IPO does have a statutory tribunal function in relation to patents, trade marks and designs; and patent decisions of the IPO when acting as a tribunal are legally binding and can be appealed to the courts. And since 2005 the IPO has offered a Patent Opinions Service which enables individuals or companies to request an opinion on the validity or infringement of a patent, although the opinion is not legally binding. The service has the advantage of being low cost with a relatively quick turnaround.

The government's preferred option for a Copyright Opinions Service is to introduce a Notice service via legislation, and to introduce a duty on the courts to have regard to any notices published.

➻ Useful resource

Intellectual Property Office (2011) *Copyright Notices: impact assessment,* www.ipo.gov.uk/consult-ia-bis1056.pdf.

Notes and references

1 Hargreaves, Ian (2011) *Digital Opportunity: a review of intellectual property and growth,* www.ipo.gov.uk/ipreview-finalreport.pdf.

2 HM Government (2011) *The Government Response to the Hargreaves Review of Intellectual Property and Growth,* www.bis.gov.uk/assets/biscore/innovation/docs/g/11-1199-government-response-to-hargreaves-review.

3 Intellectual Property Office (2011) *Prevention and Cure: the UK IP crime strategy 2011.*

4 Intellectual Property Office (2011) *The UK's International Strategy for Intellectual Property.*

5 Details of progress with implementing the Hargreaves Review can be found on the IPO website at www.ipo.gov.uk/types/hargreaves.htm.

6 *Richard Hooper Appointed to Lead Digital Copyright Exchange Feasibility Study,* IPO press release, 22 November 2011, www.ipo.gov.uk/about/press/press-release/press-release-2011/press-release-20111122.htm.

7 *Government Policy Statement: consultation on modernising copyright,* HM Government, 2012: there is a link to the pdf via the web page www.ipo.gov.uk/types/hargreaves.htm.

8 Intellectual Property Office (2011) *Consultation on Copyright,* December 2011, www.ipo.gov.uk/consult-2011-copyright.pdf.

9 *New Intellectual Property Support for SMEs,* IPO press release, 8 December 2011, www.ipo.gov.uk/about/press/press-release/press-release-2011/press-release-20111208.htm.

10 COM(2012) 372/2 on collective management of copyright and related rights and multi-territorial licensing of rights in musical works for online uses in the internal market.

11 Revenant means someone who returns after a long absence.

12 Supporting document T, p. 1, in responses to *Text Mining and Data Analytics: call for evidence*.

13 Smit, Eefke (2011) *Journal Article Mining: a research study into practices, policies, plans and promises*, Publishing Research Consortium.

14 Mollett, Richard (2011) Content mining free for all would be bad for all, 9 November, Publishers Assocation blog.

15 Gowers, Andrew (2006) *Gowers Review of Intellectual Property*, HM Treasury, www.official-documents.gov.uk/document/other/0118404830/0118404830.pdf.

16 Paragraphs 7.23–7.55.

Bibliography

Books and pamphlets

All Party Internet Group (2006) *Digital Rights Management: report of an inquiry by the All Party Internet Group,*
www.apcomms.org.uk/apig/current-activities/apig-inquiry-into-digital-rights-management/DRMreport.pdf.

Bayley, Ed (2009) *The Clicks that Bind: ways users 'agree' to online terms of service,* Electronic Frontier Foundation,
https://www.eff.org/wp/clicks-bind-ways-users-agree-online-terms-service.

British Library (2008) *Analysis of 100 Contracts Offered to the British Library,*
http://pressandpolicy.bl.uk/ImageLibrary/detail.aspx?MediaDetailsID=691.

British Library (2008) *Digital is not Different – Maintaining Balance in Copyright,*
http://pressandpolicy.bl.uk/imagelibrary/downloadMedia.ashx?MediaDetailsID=634.

Bultmann, Barbara, et al. (2006) Digitized Content in the UK Research Library and Archives Sector, *Journal of Librarianship and Information Science* **38** (2), June.

Comité des Sages (2011) *The New Renaissance: report of the Comité des Sages 2011,*
http://ec.europa.eu/information_society/activities/digital_libraries/doc/refgroup/final_report_cds.pdf.

Crews, Kenneth (2008) *Study on Copyright Limitations and Exceptions for Libraries and Archives,* WIPO,
www.wipo.int/meetings/en/doc_details.jsp?doc_id=109192.

Department for Media, Culture and Sport (2009) *Consultation on The Extension of Public Lending Right to Rights Holders of Books in Non-Print Formats,*
www.dcms.gov.uk/reference_library/consultations/6283.aspx.

Department for Media, Culture and Sport (2009) *Government Response to the Consultation on The Extension of Public Lending Right to Rights Holders of Books in Non-Print Formats.*

Electronic Frontier Foundation (2010) *E-Book Buyer's Guide to E-Book Privacy,*
https://www.eff.org/deeplinks/2010/12/2010-e-book-buyers-guide-e-book-privacy.

Ericsson (2011) *Copyright Enforcement in the Networked Society: guiding principles for protecting copyright,* http://nic.suzor.net/wp-content/uploads/2011/11/

Summer-Suzor-Fair-2011-Guiding-Principles-to-Copyright-Enforcement-in-NS.pdf.

European Commission (2008) *Copyright in the Knowledge Economy*, Green paper, COM(2008) 466/3,
http://eur-lex.europa.eu/LexUriServ/LexUriServ.do?uri=COM:2008:0466:FIN:EN:PDF.

European Commission (2011) *Green Paper on the Online Distribution of Audiovisual Works in the European Union: opportunities and challenges towards a digital single market,* COM(2011) 427 final,
http://ec.europa.eu/internal_market/consultations/docs/2011/audiovisual/green_paper_COM2011_427_en.pdf.

European Commission (2011) *Memorandum of Understanding: key principles on the digitisation and making available of out-of-commerce works,*
http://ec.europa.eu/internal_market/copyright/docs/copyright-infso/20110920-mou_en.pdf.

European Parliament, Directorate General for Internal Policies (2011) *The 'Content Flat-rate': a solution to illegal file-sharing?,*
www.europarl.europa.eu/meetdocs/2009_2014/documents/cult/dv/esstudycontentflatrate/esstudycontentflatrateen.pdf.

FreePint (2011) *Copyright Policies and Practices 2011,* FreePint Research Report,
http://web.freepint.com/go/shop/report/1796.

Gowers, Andrew (2006) *Gowers Review of Intellectual Property*, HM Treasury,
www.official-ocuments.gov.uk/document/other/0118404830/0118404830.pdf.

Hales, Alma and Atwell, Bernadette (2012) *The No-nonsense Guide to Copyright in All Media*, Facet Publishing.

Handko, Christian (2010) *The Economics of Copyright and Digitisation: a report on the literature and the need for further research*, SABIP,
www.ipo.gov.uk/ipresearch-economics-201005.pdf.

Hargreaves, Ian (2011) *Digital Opportunity: a review of intellectual property and growth*,
www.ipo.gov.uk/ipreview-finalreport.pdf.

Harper, Georgia K. (2008) *Mass Digitization and Copyright Law, Policy and Practice*.

Harris, Lesley Ellen (2009) *Licensing Digital Content: a practical guide for librarians,* 2nd edn. American Library Association.

HM Government (2011) *The Government Response to the Hargreaves Review of Intellectual Property and Growth*,
www.bis.gov.uk/assets/biscore/innovation/docs/g/11-1199-government-response-to-hargreaves-review.

HM Government (2011) *Prevention and Cure: the UK IP Crime Strategy 2011*,
www.ipo.gov.uk/ipcrimestrategy2011.pdf.

Intellectual Property Office (2008) *Taking Forward the Gowers Review of Intellectual Property: proposed changes to copyright exceptions*, www.ipo.gov.uk/consult-copyrightexceptions.pdf.

Intellectual Property Office (2009) *Licensing Intellectual Property*, IP healthcheck series, www.ipo.gov.uk/licensingbooklet.pdf.

Intellectual Property Office (2011) *Intellectual Property Crime Strategy*, www.ipo.gov.uk/ipcrimestrategy2011.pdf.

Intellectual Property Office (2011) *Consultation on Copyright*, December 2011, www.ipo.gov.uk/consult-2011-copyright.pdf.

Intellectual Property Office, IP Healthcheck, https://www.ipo.gov.uk/whyuse/business/iphealthcheck.htm.

International Federation of Library Associations and Institutions, *TLIB*, www.ifla.org/files/clm/publications/tlib.pdf.

Isbell, Kimberley (2010) Who's afraid of the news aggregators, *Citizens Media Law Project,* www.citmedialaw.org/blog/2010/whos-afraid-news-aggregators.

JISC (2009) *Transfer and Use of Bibliographic Records: legal constraints on activities*, JISC Information Paper, November 2009, www.jisclegal.ac.uk/Portals/12/ccfiles/CC405%20-%20legal%20briefing.pdf.

Korn, Naomi with Oppenheim, Charles (2013) *The No-Nonsense Guide to Licensing Digital Content*, Facet Publishing, not yet published.

Licensingmodels.org, E-book model licence, www.licensingmodels.org/E-bookLicense.html.

McMillan, Gail et al. (2011) *Digital Preservation: SPEC kit 325*, Association of Research Libraries, ISBN 1-59407-869-6, www.arl.org/news/pr/spec325-25oct11.shtml.

Moeller, Erik (2009) *Wikimedia Attribution Survey Results*, for the Wikimedia Community, 6 March, http://upload.wikimedia.org/wikipedia/foundation/9/93/Attribution_Survey_Results.pdf.

Muller, Patrice et al. (2011) *Consumer Behaviour in a Digital Environment*, commissioned from the London School of Economics for the European Parliament, www.europarl.europa.eu/meetdocs/2009_2014/documents/imco/dv/consumer_behav_/consumer_behav_en.pdf.

Museums, Libraries and Archives Council (2010) *Public Performance Licences – An Information Guide: Music and film activities in public libraries,* www.iaml.info/iaml-uk-irl/resources/pub_perf_licenses.pdf.

O'Donnell, Michael (2009) *iCopyright Article Tools: maximizing revenue and minimizing piracy*, iCopyright, Inc., http://info.icopyright.com/icopyright-article-tools-maximizing-revenue-minimizing-piracy.

Ofcom (2011) *Digital Economy Act Copyright Infringement Appeals Process: options for reducing costs,* http://stakeholders.ofcom.org.uk/binaries/internet/appeals-process.pdf.

Office of the Register of Copyrights (2011) *Legal Issues in Mass Digitization: a preliminary analysis and discussion document*, United States Copyright Office.

Oppenheim, Charles (2012) *The No-Nonsense Guide to Legal Issues in Web 2.0 and Cloud Computing*, Facet Publishing.

Organization for Economic Co-operation and Development (2011) Copyright infringement. Chapter 9 in *The Role of Internet Intermediaries in Advancing Public Policy Objectives,* OECD iLibrary, ISBN 978-92-64-11563-7, http://dx.doi.org/10.1787/9789264115644-en.

Pedley, Paul (ed.) (2005) *Managing Digital Rights: a practitioner's guide*, Facet Publishing.

Pedley, Paul (2007) *Digital Copyright*, 2nd edn, Facet Publishing.

Pedley, Paul (2008) *Copyright Compliance: practical steps to stay within the law*, Facet Publishing.

Pedley, Paul (2012) *Essential Law for Information Professionals*, 3rd edn, Facet Publishing.

Poole, Nick (2010) *The Cost of Digitising Europe's Cultural Heritage: a report for the Comité des Sages of the European Commission*, the Collections Trust, November 2010, http://ec.europa.eu/information_society/activities/digital_libraries/doc/refgroup/annexes/digiti_report.pdf.

PriceWaterhouseCoopers (2011) *An Economic Analysis of Copyright, Secondary Copyright and Collective Licensing*, March 2011, www.cla.co.uk/data/corporate_material/submissions/2011_pwc_final_report.pdf.

Secker, Jane (2010) *Copyright and E-learning: a guide for practitioners,* Facet Publishing.

Smit, Eefke (2011) *Journal Article Mining: a research study into practices, policies, plans and promises*, Publishing Research Consortium, www.publishingresearch.net/documents/PRCSmitJAMreport20June2011VersionofRecord.pdf.

Stratton, Barbara (2011) *Seeking New Landscapes: a rights clearance study in the context of mass digitisation of 140 books published between 1870 and 2010*, British Library, http://pressandpolicy.bl.uk/ImageLibrary/detail.aspx?MediaDetailsID=1197.

Journals

LEH-Letter, aka *Copyright, New Media Law & E-Commerce News,* Lesley Ellen Harris (editor), ISSN 1206-8586, www.copyrightlaws.com.

The News, Copyright Circle, Graham Cornish (editor), www.copyrightcircle.co.uk.

Websites

www.out-law.com.

Blogs

At last .. the 1709 copyright blog, http://the1709blog.blogspot.co.uk.
IPKat, http://ipkitten.blogspot.com.
Laurence Kaye, http://laurencekaye.typepad.com.
Open Rights Group, www.openrightsgroup.org/blog.
Kluwer Copyright blog, http://kluwercopyrightblog.com.

Twitter Feeds

@copyrightgirl (Emily Goodhand)

Index